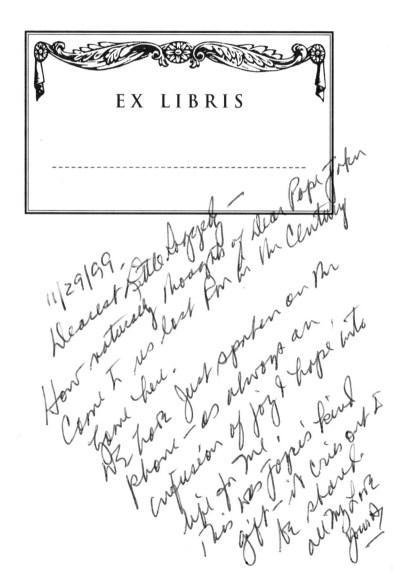

EX LIBRIS

11/29/99.
Dearest Little Aggie —
How naturally thoughts of dear Pope John
came to us last Am in the Century
here. We have Just spoken on the
phone — as always an
infusion of joy & hope into
life to me! This was Pope's kind
gift — it cries out I
be shared.
All my love
Junior

DAYS OF
DEVOTION

DAYS OF

Daily Meditations from
the Good Shepherd

Edited and introduced by
JOHN P. DONNELLY

With a Preface by
MSGR. LORIS CAPOVILLA

Translated by
DOROTHY WHITE

DEVOTION

POPE JOHN XXIII

VIKING

A GINIGER BOOK

VIKING
Published by the Penguin Group
Penguin Books USA Inc., 375 Hudson Street,
New York, New York 10014, U.S.A.
Penguin Books Ltd, 27 Wrights Lane,
London W8 5TZ, England
Penguin Books Australia Ltd, Ringwood,
Victoria, Australia
Penguin Books Canada Ltd, 10 Alcorn Avenue,
Toronto, Ontario, Canada M4V 3B2
Penguin Books (N.Z.) Ltd, 182–190 Wairau Road,
Auckland 10, New Zealand

Penguin Books Ltd, Registered Offices:
Harmondsworth, Middlesex, England

Published in 1996 by Viking Penguin,
a division of Penguin Books USA Inc.

3 5 7 9 10 8 6 4 2

Originally published in Italian under the title
Il Breviario di Papa Giovanni, 1966.

This English-language edition previously published as
Prayers and Devotions from Pope John XXIII, 1967.

Concordat Cum Originali
✠ Peter Canisius Van Lierde
Vicar General of Vatican City
3 June 1966

Grateful acknowledgment is made to the following
for permission to use excerpts from their publications:
Edizioni Paoline, Rome: *Scritti e Discorsi del Card, Angelo Roncalli,
Patriarca de Venezia*; Edizioni Cantagalli, Siena: *Scritti e Discorsi di
S. S. Giovanni XXIII*; Edizioni Storiane Letteratura, Rome: *Souvenirs
d'un Nonce, Il Cardinale Cesare Baronio* and *Mons. Giacomo Maria
Radini Tedeschi Vescovo di Bergamo,* all by Angelo Roncalli; and
Geoffrey Chapman Ltd., London: *The Journal of a Soul* and *Mission
to France.* Bible quotations are from *The Revised Standard Version of
the Bible,* copyright © 1946, 1952 by the Division of Christian
Education, National Council of Churches.

ISBN 0-670-86959-7

CIP data available

This book is printed on acid-free paper.

Printed in the United States of America
New front matter design by Virginia Norey

CONTENTS

PREFACE

This book is in answer to the requests of many people who wish to know, at least in summary form, the ascetic and pastoral teaching of a Pope who knew how to make the contemporary world listen to what he said. This is all the more necessary because several recent publications, biographies and studies of the personality and works of Pope John, must have persuaded their readers not to be content with mere chronological data or collections of anecdotes, and not blindly to accept certain prejudiced or purely subjective interpretations, but to seek out sources such as these and study them closely.

This book is an invaluable contribution to such research. It might almost be entitled: "A page a day with John XXIII", since Fr John Donnelly has very competently chosen the most significant passages to express the Pope's teaching, arranging the sequence according to the liturgical seasons as well as with regard to problems requiring the earnest co-operation of all men and arising from a consciousness of duties that cannot be ignored. In this way meditation completes the arduous work of study necessary to enable the individual and the community to encourage hopes that will not prove vain and ephemeral.

In these pages Pope John speaks familiarly to his readers, inspiring noble thoughts and arousing generous feelings in their hearts. We meet him in formal and informal dress as he speaks to men in language inspired by biblical themes which inspire and encourage not only the followers of Christ but all who long for truth and peace.

When he first faced the world as Pope on 4 November 1958, he said that in him people must not look for the "statesman, diplomat, scientist or social organizer, but for the shepherd. The new Pope, after the vicissitudes of his life, is like the son of Jacob who, meeting his brothers in distress, reveals to them the tenderness of his heart, and bursting into tears, says: 'I am Joseph, your brother' (Gen. 45.4). The new Pope. . . first of all expresses in himself the shining image of the Good Shepherd as he is described to us by the evangelist St John in the same words that were used by the Divine Saviour himself: 'I am the door of the sheep' '' (*Discorsi*, I, pp. 10-14).

Pope John's words, like his whole life, were an expression of willing and heroic obedience to the Gospel teaching, arousing admiration and assent in all peoples, without distinction of culture or religious inspiration. "The other human qualities—learning, intelligence, diplomatic tact and organizing skill—may serve as an adornment and complement of pastoral rule, but can never be substitutes for it" (*Ibid.*).

He was abundantly endowed with other gifts: he reached an uncommonly high standard of culture and initiated and completed enterprises which, even if he had never become Pope, would have given his name and service to the Church a sure place in history. But above all he was a Shepherd after Christ's own heart.

This self-sacrifice for others, according to the divine pattern, is not easily achieved; it entails such self-denial, constancy, and fervent love as to reach heroic heights. Pope John did not proclaim his plans aloud; in fact, at first he almost let it be thought that he had no personal and original programme. Above all, he was anxious to present to the world the image of the apostle as Christ had traced it in the Sermon on the Mount and in his words at the Last Supper: the servant of the servants of God.

He achieved his aim. He wanted to be, like St John the Baptist, a voice speaking to men, and he succeeded. The world, at first indifferent, ended by crowding around him; in fact, during the last days of the life of John XXIII, for the first time in the history of the world, the Roman people themselves, by their presence in St Peter's Square, composed the most beautiful encyclical letter that had ever been written on the theme of love.

Because he was recognized and welcomed as a true shepherd Pope John still lives in the veneration of all who loved and followed him, drawn by the mysterious power of the human and Christian virtues which made him great, as man and as priest.

From these pages he encourages us all to behave like brothers, learning brotherliness through reflection, prayer and Christian self-denial.

LORIS CAPOVILLA
Privy Chamberlain to the Pope's Household

Vatican City,
12 May 1966.

INTRODUCTION

Thrust on the world for a very short time, Pope John XXIII took it by storm. Almost overnight he became a symbol of what is "good" in humankind and left a mark on Catholics and non-Catholics alike, as a friend to whom particular creeds and prejudices were but a stimulus and challenge to greater friendship and love. He was a man with whom millions could feel at home—scholars and poets, saints and sinners, farmers and astronauts, the high and mighty, and simple folk.

To all but the very sceptical he was even before his entrance into eternity shining with the bright light of sanctity. To some he was "canonized" the moment he breathed his last. But whether or not the process now begun for his formal canonization ever reaches a favourable decision, in the hearts of those who heard him speak or read what he wrote, or merely watched him from a distance, Pope John will always find a place of honour and his effect is destined to be lasting.

What is a saint? As a young priest in 1907, Angelo Giuseppe Roncalli himself gave a lucid description which in retrospect might be called autobiographical:

Recent distortions have tended to spoil our conception of the saints; they have been tricked out and coloured with certain garish tints, which might perhaps be tolerated in a novel but which are out of place in the real world and in practical life.

To deny oneself at all times, to suppress within oneself and in external show all that the world would deem worthy of praise, to guard in one's own heart the flame of a most pure love for God, far surpassing the frail affections of this world, to give all and sacrifice all for the good of others, and with humility and

11

trust, in the love of God and of one's fellow men, to obey the laws laid down by Providence, and follow the way which leads chosen souls to the fulfilment of their mission—and everyone has his own mission—this is holiness, and all holiness is but this (cf. February 5).

If a man is found with such qualities, others want to find out more about him. Others, concerned about their personal perfection, will want to know what process moulded such a personality, what thoughts prompted such action, what inner conviction found such lucid and lovable external expression.

Pursuing this end, a search through his talks and writings, prayers and devotions has been made with the purpose of selecting a thoughtful passage, a prayer or an explanation of some point of spiritual doctrine for each day of the year.

This book is the result. An attempt has been made where possible to co-ordinate the meditations and prayers with particular feasts and seasons of the Church's liturgical calendar. Where this is not possible, other guidelines were followed in placing the selections, such as special devotions appointed for certain months of the year in the popular practice of the Church. Such would be the dominance of the theme of the Blessed Virgin Mary during the month of May and the recitation of her Rosary—called by Pope John the "Bible of the poor"—during October. Other selections were prompted by human customs and seasonal topics, such as the Pope's down-to-earth thoughts on vacations, sports, modest attire and responsible driving habits during the summer months.

Any attempt to co-ordinate the daily calendar with the Church's cycle of movable liturgical feasts determined by the varying date of Easter is bound to run into difficulties. This book was no exception. For the sake of the closest possible co-ordination, it was decided that selections for these changing seasons would be arranged on the basis of their incidence during the next ten years (until 1975). Thus thoughts proper to the Lenten season immediately preceding Easter are found between the dates of 7 March and 25 March, which during these years always fall within the Lenten season. After-Easter meditations post-date the latest possible occurence of Easter during this period—April 22.

Centre and key to the liturgical life of the Church are the intimately linked mysteries of the Sacrifice of the Mass and the Real Presence of Christ in the Sacrament of the Eucharist. As a result of the Second Vatican Council, a new emphasis is being laid on the "resurrectional" aspects of these mysteries—that is, an orientation towards the central fact of Christ's resurrection even more than towards his passion and death on the Cross. For this reason, ample use has been made of Pope John's references to the Mass and the Eucharist, concentrating them in the month of April which is inevitably associated with the Easter season, and during which very often the actual commemoration of the Holy Thursday institution of the Mass and the Eucharist occurs.

With but a few exceptions, selections are designed to stand on their own merits without the need of introductory explanations of the circumstances in which the various subjects came to be treated. Where such explanation was necessary it has been given briefly in a note following the date. References to all the selections are given with dates at the back of the book.

Thoughts for the more important movable feasts will be found in twenty-five appendixed selections. They could hardly be ignored because of their importance in the Church's liturgical observance, and yet they are difficult to place within the fixed calendar.

As far as possible, an attempt was made to find a selection for each of the major feasts of the fixed liturgical calendar as well. Where none suitable was available, the alternative generally was to co-ordinate the meditation with an outstanding virtue or characteristic of the particular saint's life. In other cases, seasonal motives have taken precedence over feasts in the arrangement of material.

Though the speeches, letters and other writings of Pope John from his early priesthood until his death have been examined, it was inevitable that major emphasis should be laid on his later, more matured thoughts at the time of his papacy. A close investigation will reveal, however, that much of what became the "teaching" of Pope John —and later found its way into the doctrine set forth by the Second Vatican Council he called into being—has its solid roots and incipient expression in his earlier works. It emerges as the foundation for a complex of thought which was to become known as "Johannine".

That these expressions bear such an early date in the body of his works gives staunch support to a contention growing stronger day by day: that Pope John was an extraordinary prophet of the modern world and a leader, showing that part in the world which the Church must inevitably play since it cannot become, in his words, a "museum of antiquities".

Pope John's programme and its concern for the modern world naturally enough found much of its inspiration in Pope John's predecessor under whom he served for 19 years, and from whom came much of the intellectual foundation on which the Council built. No one was more generous in acknowledging this debt than Pope John himself. In his first Christmas broadcast to the world after his election, he talked at length of the doctrinal and patoral teaching of his predecessor which, he said, "assure a place in posterity for the name of Pius XII. Even apart from any official declaration, which would be premature, the triple title of "Most excellent Doctor, Light of Holy Church, Lover of the divine law" evokes the sacred memory of this pontiff in whom our times were blessed indeed" (*Discorsi* I, p. 101).

It might be said that what Pope Pius was to the "mind" of the Church, his successor was to its "heart".

Pope John's appeal and influence went far beyond the confines of his Church, however. In an extraordinary way, he made his faith interesting to outsiders and made the papacy headline news for the eyes and ears of the secular world. Although this book has been prepared for Catholics and in the framework of their liturgical observances, and although much of what the Pope has to say on the Church, obedience and the like could be termed "intramural", certainly others will find here the recurring appeal of a universal language capable of prompting a universal response. They will find much of profit to their own spiritual lives no matter how they see God, no matter with what conviction they regard the Church of which Pope John was leader for four and a half short, breath-taking years.

It is obligatory for the editor to point out that without the valuable help of several others, he could never have compiled this book, nor would he have attempted to do so.

Among these, first acknowledgement certainly must

14

go to Monsignor Loris Capovilla, Pope John's private secretary and constant companion and the executor of his literary legacy. The book's very concept and pattern were suggested by Monsignor Capovilla, who is now Privy Chamberlain to Pope Paul VI. Without his constant help, the editor would certainly have floundered in darkness. Without his spontaneous kindness and encouragement, the work might never have come to completion at all.

Another valuable collaborator was Doctor Luciano Casimirri, director of the Press Office of the *Osservatore Romano* (Vatican City daily newspaper), who provided help "above and beyond the call of duty". The editor acknowledges deep gratitude for his considerable assistance and constant friendliness.

Don Emilio Fogliasso of Rome's Pontifical Athenæum Salesianum is an acknowledged expert on the works of Pope John. His counsel and assistance, willingly given in spite of a crowded schedule, was to the editor not only a great help, but edification as well.

Finally, recognition must be made of the "behind the scenes" assistance, so to speak, of Mr Benito Merighi and Mrs Fernanda Rutland, on whom the editor crassly imposed for much of the inglorious and difficult but necessary work of research, re-checking and proof reading. To these and all others who gave encouragement and assistance, the editor is profoundly grateful.

JOHN P. DONNELLY

Rome, 19 March 1966
Feast of St Joseph

DAYS OF
DEVOTION

JANUARY

1 JANUARY

Pope John speaks of the value of time. It is the beginning of 1962, the last complete year of his life.

NEW YEAR'S DAY

The life of every man flows on and every year, on January 1st, we all feel impelled to make good resolutions about new and sterner efforts to do our duty. These are certainly good decisions, but it is still more noble and profitable for our souls to place ourselves in the presence of God, the author of life, in order to find out how much progress we have made in the light of his law and his teachings, and to entrust ourselves to his grace. By doing this our souls draw upon that never failing youthful vigour which is the joy of God, and which continues to sustain, renew and strengthen us, and prepare us for eternal happiness.

We are all bound to examine the past, reflect upon the failures ever to be found therein, and seek a remedy; we must all try to revive our own spiritual lives, to pray better and to make progress in the essential virtues: patience, generosity, and the joyful acceptance of sacrifice. Old and young alike are called to make this salutary self-examination, and to be born again in Christ and with Christ. If they do this the good wishes of the Holy Father will be welcomed, and will bear good fruit. They will open the way to a sincere and profound understanding, and a real, lasting peace among men and nations.

We often like to compare ourselves with the noblest creatures around us. So, in so far as we can, let us imitate the angels, and on the wings of faith and prayer rise ever nearer to God. Then it will be easy for us to reconcile

17

this fleeting life with the life of eternity, and the needs of the moment with the more important needs of the spirit; so that the Lord, who sees and protects all, may be pleased with us and we, for our part, looking to heaven, may be able to say that we can trust ourselves to the grace, the power and the blessing of God.

2 JANUARY

Pope John's primary message to the world is one of peace. The famous encyclical *Pacem in terris*, written a few months before his death, is his testament to all men. It begins:

PEACE ON EARTH

Peace on earth, the profound desire of human beings in all ages, can be won and maintained only in complete harmony with the order established by God.

The progress of science and new technical inventions have shown us that a powerful order controls the creatures and the forces that make up our universe; and they also testify to the greatness of man, who discovers that order and creates the tools needed to master those forces and put them to his own use.

But, above all, scientific progress and technical inventions reveal the infinite greatness of God who has created the world and man. When he made the world he poured into it treasures of wisdom and power, as the Psalmist tells us: "O Lord, our Lord, how majestic is thy name in all the earth! . . . how manifold are thy works! In wisdom hast thou made them all" (Psalm 8. 1; 103 (104). 24). He created man in his own image and likeness, intelligent and free, setting him as lord over the universe: "Thou hast made him little less than God, and dost crown him with glory and honour. Thou hast given him dominion over the works of thy hands; thou hast put all things under his feet" (Psalm 8. 5-6).

3 JANUARY

Broadcast to the World, 23 December 1959

SOCIAL PEACE

This is founded on a general respect for the personal dignity of man. The Son of God became man, and in so doing he redeemed not merely mankind as a whole, but the individual man too: ". . . the Son of God, who loved me and gave himself for me", writes St Paul to the Galatians (Gal. 2. 20).

And if God has loved man so much it means that man belongs to him, and that the human person must be treated with the greatest respect.

This is the Church's teaching. For the solution of social problems she has always kept her eyes fixed on the human person, and has taught that material wealth and organizations—property, economics, the State—exist primarily for man's sake, not man for them. The disturbances which wreck the internal peace of nations mainly arise from this, that man has been treated almost exclusively as a tool, as merchandise, or as an obscure wheel in a mass of machinery, a mere production unit.

Only when we accept his personal dignity as our criterion for judging man and his activities, shall we find the means to placate civil strife and bridge the differences that are frequently profound between, for example, employers and workers. Above all, we shall be able to ensure for the family those conditions of life, work and assistance which will enable it better to fufil its role as a living cell of society, the first community established by God himself for the development of the human personality.

No, peace can have no solid foundations unless our hearts are filled with brotherly love, which must unite all who have the same origins and are called to the same destiny. Awareness of belonging to the same family liberates the heart from covetousness, greed, pride and the will to dominate, which are the sources of all disputes and wars; it unites all in a noble bond of generous solidarity.

4 JANUARY

INTERNATIONAL PEACE

The primary foundation of international peace is truth, for in international relations also the Christian saying holds good: "the truth will make you free" (John 8. 32).

Certain erroneous conceptions must therefore be dismissed: the myths of force and nationalism, and other inventions which have poisoned the relations between peoples. And peaceful co-existence must be based on moral principles, according to the demands of right reason and Christian doctrine.

Together with peace, and in the light of truth, there must be justice. This removes the motives for quarrels and wars, resolves disputes, assigns the ends to be sought, prescribes the duties and satisfies the just demands of all.

In its turn justice must be integrated and upheld by Christian charity. This means that our love for our neighbour, and for our own country, must not be allowed to turn in on itself, fostering a narrow egoism which is suspicious of the well-being of others, but must be enlarged and extended so as to embrace, with a spontaneous gesture of solidarity, all the peoples of the earth, and establish fruitful relations with all. Then we shall be able to speak of sharing a common life, and not merely of a co-existence which, just because it lacks this instinctive solidarity, raises barriers behind which lurk mutual suspicion, fear and terror.

5 JANUARY

UNITY AND PEACE

These conceptions continue to inspire the whole world, from its creation to its consummation in history. They express the benficent and life-giving radiance of the grace of Christ, Son of God and redeemer and saviour of mankind. . . The only condition imposed on man is that he shall have "good will", which also is a divine grace, but freely bestowed only according to man's response to it. This failure of man's free choice to answer God's call to further his merciful designs constitutes the most terrible problem of human history, and of the lives of individuals and peoples.

The law of love which the Creator impressed on man's heart was broken by the "evil will" which at once led mankind to ways of injustice and disorder. Unity was broken, and could only be restored by the intervention of God's own Son, who under obedience consented to repair the sacred links, so soon imperilled, between God and man—and he restored this unity at the cost of his blood.

This restoration still continues. Jesus founded a Church, impressing on her countenance the distinguishing mark of unity, for she was to gather together all the races of men under her immense tents, which stretch from sea to sea. Why should this unity of the Catholic

Church, constituted by divine decree for a spiritual purpose, not be directed to the re-ordering of the various races and nations in a unity necessary for the establishment of a human society based on the laws of justice and brotherhood?

Here we see the working out of the principle, so familiar to believers, that the service of God and his justice promotes also the welfare of the community of peoples and nations.

6 JANUARY

THE EPIPHANY

After the shepherds came the holy Magi kings, the great ones of the earth, who had travelled from far away to honour the divine King and Saviour of the world. Just as the shepherds rejoiced to hear the angels' good news, so the Magi too welcomed with joy the sign given them by the Lord: "We have seen his star in the east and have come to worship him".

In the wise kings' words we must admire the eagerness and earnestness with which they carried out their purpose, and the generosity of their gifts. They represent all who are endowed with worldly goods and other advantages, and use them according to the holy inspirations they receive from on high.

Considering these wonderful events from the human point of view we may think that the group of Magi kings who came to Bethlehem, representing the rich and powerful of this earth, seem more attractive to the common way of thinking, because they belong to a privileged class. It is obvious that it is more pleasant to give than to beg. And yet we know that the blessed Gospel of Jesus teaches us a sublime lesson about this. Poverty does not signify misfortune or humiliation; and the rich are bound to do many works of mercy, besides satisfying the requirements of justice. For this reason it is easy to understand why at a certain moment Jesus, the Lord of the world, chose for the whole course of his life on earth a state of poverty and want, why he proclaimed the blessedness of those who have no possessions, and those who suffer, and threatened with grave punishments the rich who are unmindful of their duties.

7 JANUARY

PEACE: A HEAVENLY GIFT

The nations are now more than ever eager for tranquillity and peace, and this longing is all the more widespread
because everyone is aware of the dangers, both latent
and obvious, which threaten the social order with the
possibility of apocalyptic calamities.

The cause of peace does not leave anyone unmoved.
But we must all strive our utmost to ensure that this
heavenly gift which Jesus called his own—"I give you
my peace"—may be the fruit of genuinely Christian
conduct, in the constant endeavour to correct ourselves
in thoughts, affections and words.

O Lord Jesus, save thy people and bless thine inheritance, and make known to this beloved portion of thy
flock the purest and most lofty truths contained in thy
Gospel, truths which are the sure guarantee of brotherliness and social progress, in every sphere and at all
times.

We shall continue to praise thee all the days of our
life, in the certainty of thy mercy and the sweetness of
thy blessings, which enter innocent hearts and raise
them to heaven. Strengthen the waverers, console the
afflicted, arouse enthusiasm for the Catholic apostolate
and enable the beatitudes of thy Gospel to bloom for
ever on this earth. Amen.

8 JANUARY

THE PEACE-MAKERS

Peaceable folks, those whom the Gospel calls blessed,
do not stand idly by; they are indeed the active builders
of peace, the people who construct it; they are the
"peace-makers" (cf. Matt. 5. 9).

In the liturgy of the Mass, in all rites and all languages,
the greeting of Christ is heard again and again: "Peace
be with you!" The celebrant, on behalf of the congregation, addresses to the Lord present on the altar this
imploring cry, sometimes repeated by the church
choristers in powerful choruses: "Grant us thy peace".
So man must first pray for this; and then he must learn
to live in peace: in the family circle and in social and
international relations.

Here we have a series of duties, grave duties familiar to us all, which presuppose our capacity to subject the exercise of our own rights to a noble discipline, and to remain on serene and respectful terms with all men, even when we are refuting an accusation or defending the sacred rights of the human person, the family and society.

This means that Christian peace is rooted in the theological virtues: faith, hope and charity. It is strengthened and extended through the loyal and willing exercise of the other virtues: prudence, justice, fortitude and temperance.

9 JANUARY

PEACE TO MEN OF GOOD WILL

We respect and honour the good will of so many pioneers and heralds of peace in this world: statesmen, experienced diplomats and writers of repute.

But human efforts to establish universal peace are still very far from the point of agreement between heaven and earth.

True peace can come from God alone; it has but one name, "the peace of Christ"; it has but one character, that impressed upon it by Christ who, as if to forestall man's counterfeit creations, said significantly: "Peace I leave with you; my peace I give to you" (John 14. 27).

Peace is first of all something interior, something spiritual, and it is founded on a loving and childlike dependence on the will of God: "O Lord, thou hast made us for thyself, and our hearts are restless till they rest in thee" (St Augustine, *Confessions*, I, 1; PL. 32, 661).

All that weakens or sunders this conformity and union of will is opposed to peace: first of all and above all there is sin. "Who has hardened himself against him, and succeeded?" (Job 9. 4). "Great peace have those who love thy law" (Psalm 118 (119). 165).

And good will itself is nothing else but the sincere intention to respect the eternal law of God, to obey his commandments and to follow in his footsteps: in a word, to be faithful to the truth. This is the glory that God expects from man.

"On earth peace among men with whom he is pleased."

THE PEACE WON BY CHRIST

The Lord came to this earth to bring peace; his birth among us was announced by the angels in their wonderful hymn about peace coming down to dwell with all men who were in friendship with God, that is, men of good will. And we know of no peace other than that which was won, bestowed and poured out by the Precious Blood of Jesus, and which, throughout the ages, he has always required of men, even if, alas! they do not always listen to the voices from heaven.

In spite of this, we must never lose heart, for the "Prince of Peace" is with us and we must entrust to him even the grave problems of the establishment and maintenance of peace; and we must pray for the immense benefits to be derived from it, for families, nations and the whole world.

This conception is indeed familiar to all Christians; it springs from the very fountain of peace, set flowing for us by our Lord Jesus Christ.

The first duty, therefore, of all who are honoured with the name of Christians, is to seek to understand the meaning of this word : the true peace demanded by all races of men, even now still crushed beneath the terrors of war.

11 JANUARY

PEACE IN THE HOME

Peace is first found and enjoyed in the family, in a man's home. To obtain this we need understanding and generosity because, even where there is mutual affection, there is always something to cause displeasure to one member or another. So patience is required, holy patience, the source of happiness; we must know how to correct our own characters, and moderate those desires which do not always conform to the divine law.

The Redeemer came to teach us to live good honest lives as individuals, in our families and in the social order of cities, nations and the whole world.

The gift of peace is immensely precious for the human family. Every priest, every bishop, and the Pope in particular, prays for this with great confidence in God. The good wishes of the Chief Shepherd and of all the other shepherds of God's Church are in this : "Peace be with you!" and this prayer rises, ever more longing, and more widely spread throughout the world. The enthusiastic and magnificent response of all believers finds its expression in a vast programme of labour and life. "But now in Christ Jesus you who were once far off have been brought near in the blood of Christ. For he is our peace . . ." (Eph. 2. 13, 14).

12 JANUARY

AN APPEAL TO ALL IN POSITIONS OF RESPONSIBILITY

It grieves us to point out—we quote from our encyclical *Mater et Magistra*—that "whereas on the one hand difficult situations are constantly increasing and the spectres of poverty and hunger begin to raise their heads, on the other hand economic resources . . . are used to create terrible instruments of ruin and death" (A.A.S., LIII (1961), p. 448).

This is an appeal to those in a position to form public opinion, and to those who have almost a monopoly of this power, to beware of the severe judgment of God, and of the verdict of history, and to proceed cautiously, with prudence and moderation. By no means rarely in modern times—we say this frankly and sadly—has the Press played its part in preparing a climate of hostility, hatred and irreconcilability.

We appeal to all those responsible for the nations, to all who hold in their hands the fate of mankind.

You also are frail and mortal men, and your fellows, first your brothers and now your subjects, look to you in their anxiety. With the authority we hold from Jesus Christ we say to you : Abolish the resort to force; regard with alarm the possibility of setting in motion a chain reaction of events, judgments and resentments that might lead to rash and irreparable actions. Great power has been given you, but to construct, not to destroy; to unite, not to divide; to give work and security to everyone, not to cause more tears to flow.

These are the various ways in which good will can and must be extended to all sections of human society. This good will lies in fortitude and self-control, patience with others, and inexhaustible charity, because charity sincerely desires the good of others, and so never loses heart.

13 JANUARY

FEAST OF THE BAPTISM OF JESUS

You also, O Jesus, were immersed in the river of Jordan, under the eyes of the crowd, although very few then were able to recognize you; and this mystery of tardy faith, or of indifference, prolonged through the centuries, is a source of grief for those who love you and have received the mission of making you known in the world.

Oh grant to the successors of your apostles and disciples and to all who call themselves after your Name and your Cross, to press on with the work of spreading the Gospel, and to bear witness to it in prayer, suffering and loving obedience to your will!

And since you, an innocent lamb, came before John in the attitude of a sinner, so draw us also to the waters of the Jordan. To the Jordan will we go to confess our sins and cleanse our souls. And as the skies open to announce the voice of your Father, expressing his pleasure in you, so, having successfully overcome our trial and lived austerely through the forty days of our Lent, may we, O Jesus, when the day of your Resurrection dawns, hear once more in our innermost hearts the same heavenly Father's voice, recognizing us as his children.

May this prayer rise, on this evening of serene religious recollection, from every house where people work, love and suffer. May the angels of heaven gather the prayers of all the souls of little children, of generous-hearted young men and women, of hard-working and self-sacrificing parents, and of all who suffer in body and mind and present their prayers to God. From him will flow down in abundance the gifts of his heavenly joys.

14 JANUARY

Address to the members of the World Congress of the Blind, 29 July 1959

THE SUPERNATURAL VISION

This is your special mission: a silent and fruitful apostolate, an apostolate by example. You know that it is not the noise we make in our lives, or the things we see, that count, but the love with which we do the will of God. In the golden words of the *Imitation of Christ:* "He is truly great who has great love. He is truly great who is humble of heart and sets no store by greatness or honours. He is truly prudent who rejects as dross all earthly things, in order to win Christ" (Bk. I, 3, 6).

Only when we are convinced of this do we enjoy the true light, that which enlightens us by opening new horizons on to eternity. There are so many people who have sight and yet do not see! There are so many who get lost chasing after the little things of this life, trifles that are of no account, and forget God, their own souls and righteousness, so that their hearts are dim with the shadows of death! The tears that Jesus shed over Jerusalem help us to understand the one thing that is needful: "Would that even today you knew the things that make for peace! But now they are hid from your eyes" (Luke 19. 42).

Have courage then, my beloved children! Your faith tells us that the most precious light, that which never sets, is your carefully cherished inheritance of truth, which sustains you in all your struggles and difficulties. Be generous in the tasks which await you; work in charity and peace, remembering that nothing done according to God's will is done in vain on this earth.

15 JANUARY

PURITY OF HEART

Purity of heart, carefully and constantly guarded, becomes the rule, and the radiance, of our whole life, and of every word and deed. This virtue is the fine flower of Christian families, where it blooms as if on its natural soil; and it has an irresistible appeal for all. Like stainless snow veiling the mire which alas! stains so much of this poor world which lies "in the power of the evil one" (I John 5. 19), it commands the respect even of unbelievers, even of those who may at times have mocked at it. . .

Purity of heart is the serene atmosphere which surrounds every earnest vocation, the soil from which must bud and flower all other good intentions.

To be sure, it is not the greatest virtue, because, if it were not accompanied by the love of God and of our neighbour, it would become but a cold exercise of natural perfection. Instead, it must be the breath of the love of God, and the indispensable condition for disinterested service to our neighbour. It is purity of heart which enables us to enjoy the incomparable happiness of long conversations with God in his holy tabernacle; it fosters enthusiasm for the apostolate and for charity; it inspires a continual serenity which is neither downcast in adversity nor extravagant in joy.

Live in the light of this virtue . . . and guard it in prayer, mortification and study.

16 JANUARY

CHARITY THE CURE FOR ALL EVILS

When we are inspired by the love of Christ we all feel united, sharing in one another's needs, sufferings and joys. And as a result of this, every man's work . . . will be more disinterested, more vigorous and more full of human sympathy because "Love is patient and kind. . . does not insist on its own way; . . . does not rejoice at wrong, but rejoices in the right. . . Love hopes all things, endures all things" (I Cor. 13. 4-7; A.A.S., LIII (1961), p. 461).

That is why the prayer for peace that rises from the cradle in Bethlehem is a prayer for kindness of heart, for true brotherliness, and a determination to seek sincere co-operation, rejecting all intrigues, and all those destructive elements which we—we repeat—call by their true names: pride, greed, hard-heartedness and selfishness.

Our appeal is all the more urgent because mutual distrust has become a reason for growing concern. Think of this, that even the sense of alarm which men feel at the sight of open violence and deliberately fostered antagonism promotes a general decay of charity, a decay which is spreading in ever wider circles. These conditions remind us of Christ's grave and solemn words, at once a warning, a prophecy and a threat: "because wickedness is multiplied, most men's love will grow cold" (Matt. 24. 12).

Man is no longer a good brother to his fellow man, a merciful and loving brother; he has become estranged, calculating, suspicious and selfish.

How necessary it is to proclaim that the only cure for this lies in the welcome we give to Jesus of Bethlehem' the Lamb of God, who came to take away the sins of the world (cf. John 1. 29), in recourse to his grace, and in the practice of the mercy he taught us!

17 JANUARY

"A SIGN THAT IS SPOKEN AGAINST"

Everywhere in the world there are some people who have heard of Jesus of Bethlehem and of the Epiphany; the twenty centuries that have passed into history have in no way impaired the truth about the heavenly child that was declared by the prophet of the Old Law, the aged Simeon. Here is the Saviour, he said, he has come to enlighten all the peoples of the earth, but he will be a point of contradiction till the end of time, a "sign that is spoken against".

And, as you know, my beloved brothers and children, the contradiction still continues. The world cannot do without Christ, but some worship him while others detest him; some love him and others oppose him. There are whole nations and continents who pour blessings on his name, and on his kingdom of truth, justice and peace; other peoples hardly get a glimpse of him through the clouds, or can but dimly see the features of his divine countenance. Even among those who glory in his name there have for long been profound misunderstandings and divisions. Everyone has seized upon one particular shred of his tattered robe.

The Church of the Apostle Peter, to whom Jesus entrusted the tangible signs of his divine right to the peaceful conquest of the world, and to whom he gave the right to rule his Church, is seen in the image of the fisherman's boat that still sails, sometimes in calm weather but often on storm-tossed waters—while from the green hills of Galilee the voice of Jesus is still heard, unweariedly reminding us: ". . . I have other sheep that are not of this fold; I must bring them also, and they will heed my voice. So there shall be one flock, one shepherd" (cf. John 10. 16).

18 JANUARY

The Catholic Church and many other Churches are now beginning the Octave of Prayer for Church Unity. At the beginning of the Octave in 1955 the Patriarch of Venice wrote to his people...

PRAYERS FOR UNITY

The Octave of Prayer for Church Unity is an observance which in recent years has become an edifying custom, with the blessing of God upon it, and welcomed as much by the faithful of the Catholic Church as by communities separated from Rome. All are animated by a sincere desire for spiritual progress, brotherly communion, and respect for the Vicar of Christ. . .

Prayer has in all ages been the liveliest and noblest expression of Christian communities who believe in the divinity of our Redeemer, and are endeavouring to establish a true Christian order on this earth, and to seek their eternal happiness in heaven. The "Octave" in fact chiefly consists in a great and solemn petition, which rises in every language and from every part of the world. This is a good reason for hope, and an encouragement to us to follow trustfully the road we have chosen.

The Church treasures the last words of Jesus, an appeal for union and peace.

And she not only treasures his last testament but, while eagerly and respectfully waiting for the work of grace to be perfected in all men's souls, continues to send out her own missionaries to preach with zeal the revealed truth entrusted to her, to recall the erring and sinners, and to speak with all men and at all times the language of truth and charity. Let us all do likewise.

19 JANUARY

GOOD RELATIONS WITH OUR NEIGHBOUR

During the thirty years in which I served the Holy See, in eastern Europe and in Paris, I came across people holding every kind of belief. I confess that sometimes my heart trembled with my eagerness to speak freely with them, not only as a priest but also as an apostle. But the circumstances of my mission permitted only the briefest reference, or unbroken silence.

Sometimes I was told: "Monsignor, I thank you for

what you have said, and for what you have allowed me to understand. . ."

The Press has credited me with witticisms which I could not have imagined, even when they were substantially in keeping with the frank simplicity of my speech. Today I will repeat some words that have long been familiar to me; they were pronounced by Cardinal Lécot, the Archbishop of Bordeaux, at the Elysée on 11 July 1893, the day he received his Cardinal's hat. He said we must all learn "to look at one another without distrust, to meet without fear, to negotiate without compromising". It is not necessary to dwell on the significance of this advice, which in any case is clear enough.

There is a moment in every man's life when he has to make ready for a departure, and at last the moment comes for him to leave his earthly home, and to give an account of his labour. May every one of us be able then to say: I have not dug furrows for division and distrust, I have not darkened immortal souls with suspicion or fear, I have been frank, loyal and trustful; I have looked those who did not share my ideals straight in the eyes and treated them with brotherly affection, in order not to impede the carrying out of God's great purpose, in his own good time—a purpose which in the end must bring about the fulfilment of the divine teaching and command of Jesus, "that we may all be one".

20 JANUARY

UNITY AMONG CATHOLICS

Unity in faith is found in our common profession of the "I believe" in God the Father Almighty and in Jesus Christ his Son, in the "I believe" in the Holy Spirit and in the Holy Catholic Church, with all that she has taught from the age of the apostles down to our own, all through the centuries: mother and mistress, ever living and ever faithful to Christ's mandate. Oh! how beautiful is the faith of our fathers!

Unity in love: *una caritas*. This is a reminder of the one heart and mind of the first pages of the Book of Acts, and of the triumph of love's miracles through the centuries; in recent times it has been taught by the bearers of greatly honoured names: St Vincent de Paul and St John Bosco.

It is love that burns in the heart and words of St Paul, eager to lead all men to Christ; it is love which governs the mutual relations of Christians and which inspires us, the Catholics, in our relations with our separated brethren, to show respect, understanding, meekness and long-suffering, in the certainty of the return, so long awaited, of all sheep to the same fold.

Obedience in unity rests upon this union, formed not by violence but by liberty, affection, and confidence, this union with St Peter who lives in his successors: a spiritual obedience, the practice of which ensures for us the dearest joys of life. The first and greatest joy of obedience is peace.

21 JANUARY

THE SCANDAL OF DISCORD

Unhappily, during the centuries the seamless robe of Christ has been torn, and it is still rent. Heresies and schisms abound, and in more recent times we see the erection of this dismal Tower of Babel—the great Babylon—a continual affront to our eyes and bitterness to our hearts, this movement called secularization, which means a gradual separation of the ordinary business of life from the whole activity of the Church.

This thought grieves every honest mind that is receptive to the grace of the Gospel, the love of Christ and of his holy Church.

Listen to what the aged Cardinal Bessarion said in the 15th century: "What excuse can we offer to God for being separated from our brothers when he himself, in order to unite us and gather us into a single fold, came down from heaven, took on our human flesh and was crucified? What will be our defence in the sight of future generations? Let us not have to suffer this shame, venerable Fathers and Brothers" (he was speaking to the Fathers of the Council of Florence), "let us not behave in such a manner, or make such poor provision for ourselves and our descendants. . . "

We are still faced with a most disheartening state of affairs, that we need not describe to you here.

Is the entire responsibility for this to be laid on the

shoulders of our separated brothers? It is partly theirs, and in great part our own.

"Those who suffer in schism", wrote Monseigneur Bénigne de Bossuet, the great French orator of the seventeenth century, "will have but a sour zeal."

It is our duty to soften this discord with our behaviour and our speech, with the example of our humility and charity—with these two virtues above all, for they overcome all resistance.

22 JANUARY

"ONE FOLD AND ONE SHEPHERD"

O Mary, why should not your Eastern children be reunited with us, in the house of our common Father who awaits them, and so restore the "one fold and one shepherd", for which Jesus asked in his last prayer, when he was about to offer himself in sacrifice for our redemption and the peace of the whole world?

We pray that the vast regions where faith in Christ, formulated in the same apostolic Creed, still groans and suffers, may find a way of peaceful return to that source of true unity of all peoples in the embrace of our common mother, in Jesus her blessed firstborn Son, and in the embrace of the other Mother we all share in common, the holy Catholic Church, to which it is our joy to belong, and which awaits the return of all.

Holy Mary, intercede for this return to unity, which will be the joy and exultation of continents and sea, of earth and heaven, in Christ Jesus your Son and our Brother, to whom in our emotion we dedicate the prayers of our lips and the throbbing of our grateful and joyful hearts, in the glorification of his blessed Mother and ours.

23 JANUARY

THE PERFECT UNION OF SOULS

"That they may all be one; even as thou, Father, art in me, and I in thee, that they also may be in us, so that the world may believe that thou hast sent me" (John 17. 21).

This is the culmination of the miracle of love, which began at Bethlehem, and of which the shepherds and the Magi kings were the first fruits: the salvation of all men, their union in faith and love, through the visible Church founded by Christ.

"That they may be one." This is the divine Redeemer's purpose, and we must do our best to further it, for it is a grave responsibility entrusted to every man's conscience. On the last day of the particular and universal judgment every individual will be asked, not whether he succeeded in restoring unity but whether he prayed, laboured and suffered for it: whether he imposed upon himself a wise and prudent discipline, patient and farseeing, and whether he gave full scope to impulses of love.

This prayer from Christ's heart must persuade us to renew and intensify our efforts, so that all Catholics may continue faithfully to love, and to manifest the Church's primary distinguishing mark, which is unity, and so that, in the vast and varied field of Christian denominations and beyond, there may be formed that unity so ardently desired by all honest and generous hearts.

O Eternal Word of the Father, Son of God and of Mary, renew once more in the secret depths of men's hearts the miracle of your birth! Re-clothe with immortality the children you have redeemed: make them aflame with charity, gather all together in the unity of your mystical Body so that your coming may bring real joy, sure peace and the true brotherhood of individuals and peoples. Amen, amen.

24 JANUARY

VARIETY OF RITUAL

Ever since his boyhood the Pope . . . has known and admired the wonderful variety which the Church, One and Holy, presents in her different rites—Latin and Oriental. And he has always felt in his heart an eager and wistful love for our separated brethren.

Now, thanks to the Lord, many misunderstandings have been smoothed out, and everywhere there is a keen longing for brotherly relations, and for the fulfilment of the wish expressed by our Saviour in his prayer to the heavenly Father at the Last Supper. We must therefore continue to strengthen the bonds of charity in order to prepare the way for increasing and ever more earnest efforts, in expectation of God's good time.

It is a long and arduous road, demanding faith and perseverance, but we must remember all that the Lord has done and still does for every one of us, and remember too that he continues to love all his redeemed, in spite of the insults and ingratitude with which they reward his kindness. So we must never give up praying and doing all we can to hasten the coming of that day for which he prayed, when "all may be one".

25 JANUARY

The Octave for Unity closes with the Feast of the great Apostle of the Gentiles

ST PAUL THE APOSTLE

The celebration of this liturgical Feast, with its magnificent passage from the Acts of the Apostles describing the interior and exterior discipline which the apostle of the Gentiles imposed upon his life and his apostolate, may well be used to illustrate the Church's constant wish that men should achieve a perfect equilibrium of soul and body.

The figure of the apostle Paul, with his bold spirit, and his body tempered and worn to the limit of physical endurance, makes a special appeal to all, but particularly to the young, who are naturally generous, impulsive, prone to enthusiasms and eager to imitate those they admire. In fact, in his Epistles St Paul is seen to be very familiar with the athletic contests of his day, drawing from them striking examples to illustrate the loftiest moral truths.

The prize offered to the athletes who run in the race suggests to him the speed and determination with which a man must run the course of virtue and self-denial in order to win the reward: "So run that you may obtain it" (I Cor. 9. 24). The athlete's rigorous self-discipline, judged necessary to win an earthly crown, serves as an example to illustrate his appeal to the faithful to be temperate and prudent if they wish to obtain the crown of eternal felicity. The art of boxing, that has no use for aimless blows, reminds him of the fortitude and fidelity with which the Christian must fight his battles: "I do not run aimlessly, I do not box as one beating the air; but I pommel my body and subdue it, lest after preaching to others I myself should be disqualified" (ibid. 9.26-27). And at the end of his life he could write to his disciple Timothy, from his Roman prison where his body was immured but whence the zeal of his apostolic spirit shone forth, even brighter than before: "I have fought the good fight, I have finished the race, I have kept the faith" (II Tim. 4. 7-8).

26 JANUARY

Pope John spoke to all the members of the Congress "*Per una nuova coscienza sportiva in Italia*", 1963, and associated the ideals of sport with the ideal of unity.

The Lord in his wisdom certainly wishes to make use of all manner of means, so that men may meet, know and love another and at some future time, by further steps known only to him, may succeed in understanding and putting into practice the command—for it is our Lord's command—"that all may be one", in one fold, under the fatherly care and leadership of one shepherd.

Today the barriers of distance have fallen, and men, drawing closer to their brother men, are learning to understand and esteem one another more, and are readier to make friends and to give mutual assistance. In this providential plan for drawing men closer together sport too has its own important role to play. In the field of free competition, in which the ever renewed youthful energies of all the countries in the world play their part, there have been increasingly frequent and friendly encounters between the nations, and these have had a good influence in fostering the growth of neigh-bourliness in charity. Athletes may contribute greatly to this, if they can bring to their international competitions not only the challenge of their skill but also the grace of a good character, the harmony between their sincere convictions and their lives, and the testimony of young people who live their Christian faith with joy and generosity.

27 JANUARY

AWARENESS OF PAST AND PRESENT TIME

The Lord has created heaven and earth, the sun to lighten us by day, and the moon by night. Even after man's first sin, followed by God's promise of redemption and grace, man's will was left free by God, in absolute liberty to choose between light and darkness, good and evil. This explains the history of the world and the course of past centuries.

So, to speak of any age as being wholly bad or wholly good does not correspond to the truth. Every epoch has had its shortcomings and its splendours. It is the ignorance and malice of men, or their goodness, which determines the squalor or the beauty of an age. And it is these qualities which determine peace or war, order or disorder, the progress or decline of the family and of the nations.

Let us then give up the habit of speaking ill of past times, even if they were unhappy, and of seeing only evil in our own times too. In the free choice made by man, who is always his own master, are to be found our individual and collective responsibilities, and every one of us has to answer for the role assigned to him by a wise Providence.

Let us not talk so much about the duties of others, but try to think more seriously about our own, and about finding in the times in which we live all that can make us good and just, beloved by God and men. Everything else can be left to Providence.

28 JANUARY

"NO ONE CAN SERVE TWO MASTERS"

The divine rule about not serving two masters means not being of two minds : not holding two contrasting opinions. When we are serving one master we may receive a clearer light of understanding than we receive when we serve another, and in that case it is easy to see which we must serve.

Christian faith teaches us to be aware of what goes on around us, but above all to look upwards, to look far away. Now when, over and above the commandments of men, we receive a grave, solemn, fundamental commandment, touching the very substance of our life, this is the one we must obey.

God has engraved his law on men's hearts; he has revealed it through Moses. It is a strict law, and sometimes it may seem a hard one. But when Jesus, the Redeemer of the world, came down to join us he explained it and made it gentler, giving it a new, fascinating and appealing character. It is the law of love, of forgiveness, of wise judgment; it is the law of forbearance, according to the various circumstances, always provided that there be no question of violating the Lord's commandment.

Therefore the true Christian, serving one master only, is on the right road and has nothing to fear. He has no anxieties. Indeed, in the same passage the Evangelist St Matthew, who heard these words as they came from the lips of Jesus, adds : "Do not be anxious about your life, what you shall eat or what you shall drink, nor about your body, what you shall put on . . ." (Matt. VI. 25). In short, we must trust to Divine Providence.

Everything is in the Lord's hands : the sun that rises and the sun that hides its radiance, the clouded days and the days that are filled with light.

29 JANUARY

In 1956, at a meeting for journalists on the Feast of St Francis de Sales, patron saint of journalists, the Patriarch of Venice spoke of the importance of the written word.

SPREADING THE TRUTH

To be a journalist means using this form of communication in the service of truth or error, good or evil, the spirit of order or the spirit of disorder. When we reflect upon this we see the grave responsibilities laid on our consciences, responsibilities for which we know that every one of us will have to render a strict account to the Supreme Judge.

In fact we have been told that we shall be judged even for every idle word. May every one of us, young journalists or veterans of the Press, examine his conscience and feel encouraged to work for what is good, for what is best.

Wielders of the pen, you are builders of the civilization which we want to protect and strengthen. This civilization of ours derives its name from Christ; this civilization, I say, was the glory of our forefathers, and it is the sacred store-house of divine energies for the future.

Labourers of the third, or sixth, or ninth hour, and those also of the eleventh hour, still new to this work, come into the vineyard of Christ, for he needs you all, the young, those in the prime of life and those who are more advanced in years. There is room for all, to work with their pens, whether by day or by night, but always in the light, always working according to the laws of justice and in the spirit of that true brotherhood which is sealed by the sacrifice and blood of Christ.

30 JANUARY

THE LORD'S COMMANDMENTS

The Lord ordered Moses to speak to the whole assembly of the children of Israel and to say to them : "I am the Lord your God . . . you shall not steal; you shall not lie; no one shall cheat his neighbour. You shall not bear false witness; you shall not take the name of the Lord your God in vain; I am the Lord" (cf. Exodus, 20. 15).

And as he gave these orders God continually repeated : "I am the Lord, I am the Lord your God". He wanted to make them understand that human life must be founded on virtue and not on the hope of some gain or advantage, or the fear lest evil should befall us—because his law is unchangeable. The Lord's commandments are mild and gentle, and they are for all. The truth is that we are not put into this world to dissipate our energies or to amuse ourselves, but to do the will of God and so deserve eternal life . . .

Body and soul must go forward together : the soul must rule the body. Whoever orders his life in this way will be a worthy, good and honest man.

This is a great lesson our Lord has taught us, and his commandments may not be set aside; if the world obeys them, all will go well with us. Otherwise all will go very, very ill, and mankind will have to suffer tears, blood and strife.

The Feast of St John Bosco: a great teacher of youth and a fine example of

GENTLENESS

"Take my yoke upon you, and learn from me; for I am gentle and lowly in heart, and you will find rest for your souls. For my yoke is easy, and my burden is light" (Matt. 11. 29-30).

The whole strength of the Christian is in these words; as you know, the yoke is borne by a pair of oxen. What an honour, what unspeakable joy, to think of our shoulders bowed, in line with the shoulders of Christ, under the selfsame yoke!

And remember: "learn from me; for I am gentle and lowly in heart"! Learn from Jesus, the Son of God, not how to create the world or launch the stars in their swift bright courses, not to rule and direct the destinies of nations—but to be gentle and lowly in heart. Oh what a mystery of the perfect life, a mystery of grace and glory!

"Nothing is harsh for the gentle", wrote St Leo the Great, "nothing is hard for the humble."

The secret of true greatness and of the miraculous success of men and saints is all in these words.

Let us pause here. St Augustine adds his own gentle counsels for us: "All who have learnt from the Lord Jesus to be gentle and lowly in heart make progress in perfection, more by praying and meditating than by reading or listening" (Epist. 112).

FEBRUARY

1 FEBRUARY

ST IGNATIUS OF ANTIOCH

Today is the Feast of St Ignatius the Martyr, Bishop of Antioch, second in line in that See after St Peter. In fact, Ignatius was appointed to Antioch by the Prince of the Apostles himself, and later on in Rome offered his life as a martyr for Christ, in the reign of the Emperor Trajan.

The thought of St Ignatius reminds us of that illustrious See. The Holy Father has been there, and treasures most dearly the wonderful memories that are linked with those of the succeeding age of St John Chrysostom, who also was Bishop of Antioch before passing to the See of Constantinople.

The invincible martyr Ignatius, before he was condemned to death, wished to explain to the faithful the meaning of the sacrifice which God required of him, and he described it in these words which in their splendid Eastern imagery are strikingly effective: "I am Christ's grain of corn. I am ground by the teeth of wild beasts, so that I may become pure and clean bread."

Certainly those were dark and blood-stained centuries. It may be that such times will come again. But we know well that the Lord's grace will strengthen all who believe in him; he will sanctify our souls and give us courage to withstand the trials of life and win merit for ourselves and for our dear ones.

41

February begins with the liturgical invocation: "*Ave Regina cælorum, salve radice, salve porta*". From the threshold of the temple we can see the blessed Mother of Jesus looking at her little Son, momentarily entrusted to the holy old man, Simeon, and held in his trembling arms. In his faint yet firm voice Simeon welcomes the Child, presenting him to the world as the light of all nations and the glory of God's faithful people.

It is always the same: for twenty centuries the vision has remained with us. The old generations pass, handing on to those who come after them our divine inheritance, the Christ. The young receive the sign from past ages and bear it onwards, shining ever more strongly and brightly on their way. The divine Child of the Feast of the Purification spoke of this again when he was a grown man, an impressive and majestic Teacher. As soon as he had sent away the adulterous woman he turned to the astonished bystanders saying: "I am the light of the world; he who follows me will not walk in darkness, but will have the light of life" (John 8. 12).

What words these are, my dear brothers and sons!

3 FEBRUARY

The struggle goes on against the Spirit of Evil, known as Beelzebub. Do not fear: by whatever name man may insult you, your innocence, your faith and your piety will yet be revealed, not only at the Last Judgment but also in this present life. Virtue is, as it were, smothered by the smoke of envy and malice, but in the end it catches fire and bursts into the flame of truth, glorifying the just man.

This is what Jesus has told us. St Jerome comments: What you know in a mystery you must show forth in all its fullness; what you have learnt in secret, tell and repeat aloud. What I have taught you in one corner of the earth, Judea, announce freely and boldly throughout the world. And do not be afraid of those who can kill the body but cannot touch the soul. Your persecutors may threaten you with death, but let not the fear of this draw you away from my faith and my commandments; do not be persuaded to do anything unworthy of you, and of me. It is the soul's hell that you must fear, not the hell of the body.

And is Providence not always with us? Two sparrows are not worth very much, and who can count the hairs on your head? But the Lord cares for the sparrows and counts the hairs of your head. Will he not also care for our souls, our life itself? So there is nothing to fear, for nothing can happen to us without our Father knowing. The Lord is the Creator of the sparrows, but to us he is even more: he is our Father. Oh what consolation there is in this doctrine!

4 FEBRUARY

Pope John was speaking to journalists when he reminded them of the grave responsibilities of their task. But in these words everyone will find motives for an earnest self-examination, and new resolutions for good relations with his fellow men.

CHRISTIAN SENSIBILITY

It is necessary for you to have a profoundly Christian delicacy of feeling, which should permeate all your actions, . . . and with grace and distinction spread that "aroma of Christ", which must characterize all we do. There must be Christian delicacy of feeling in all and with all, so that your sincerity, tempered with respect, and your clarity of ideas, mingled with ripeness of thought and expression, may be apparent to all.

Frequently, when we look through the reviews and newspapers, we are grieved to find a language that is at times cryptic, turgid or extravagant, and at other times harsh, aggressive or unnecessarily controversial. It is the mark of a habit which has crept in everywhere, sometimes even into public announcements and advertisements, the reports of sporting events or of traditional country festivals.

The Catholic journalist must beware of this habit of thinking and writing, which lacks that instinctive sense of courtesy, of good breeding, of the Christian style of writing which seeks to convince others with the persuasive power of good manners, and attract with solid arguments, and not by playing on people's feelings. This sensibility must also be shown in avoiding exaggerated praise, especially of living people, and in not attributing all merit to one particular party or organization, but in knowing how to find something uplifting in every place or situation, in order to encourage and establish fruitful contacts. It teaches us also to bear in mind the experience of all who have gone before us, not to forget what the past can teach us, and to make the most of every valid expression of the human spirit, throughout the course of our history.

Christian sensibility, as you have seen, seeks out and brings to light those universal expressions of the true, the good and the beautiful which find a voice and colour in nature, in music, and in the masterpieces of literature and art.

5 FEBRUARY

WHAT IS A SAINT ?

What does the world know of that mysterious force which stirs in the depths of so many souls who seem unsatisfied in this world because they follow another light, an ideal which never falls to attract them?

In recent times, because of a fashion that seems to me a legitimate reaction from certain traditional methods of recounting the lives of holy men (methods according to which the saints were plucked by the hair and dragged out of the society in which they lived, and even out of themselves, to be turned into demi-Gods), we have, perhaps a little too eagerly, turned to the opposite excess and concentrated too much on the study of the human element in the saint, and by so doing have to some extent failed to give enough consideration to the work of grace.

What is a saint? Recent distortions have tended to spoil our conception of the saints; they have been tricked out and coloured with certain garish tints, which might perhaps be tolerated in a novel but which are out of place in the real world and in practical life.

To deny oneself at all times, to suppress, within oneself and in external show all that the world would deem worthy of praise, to guard in one's own heart the flame of a most pure love for God, far surpassing the frail affections of this world, to give all and sacrifice all for the good of others, and with humility and trust, in the love of God and of one's fellow men, to obey the laws laid down by Providence, and follow the way which leads chosen souls to the fulfilment of their mission—and everyone has his own mission—this is holiness, and all holiness is but this.

6 FEBRUARY

FEAST OF TITUS

It is the Feast of a disciple and great friend of St Paul— and what a friend!—who survived by several years the Apostle of the Gentiles. He was a personage of primary importance in the apostolic era and in the first attempts to preach the Gospel. He lived to a great age and travelled widely through what was then known of the world, always glad to follow St Paul and to obey his precious orders, even at a distance.

The Holy Father could give you a list of the various lands visited by Titus because, during the long years of his service for the Holy See in the Near East, he was able to go wherever there still survives a memory or an echo of the teaching of St Paul and his disciples. It happened once that the Apostle had set out to journey through the Troad (the region around the Dardanelles) in the hope of meeting Bishop Titus; but he could not find him. This disappointed him very much because he had a great brotherly love for his enthusiastic collaborator. Later, as he went on through Macedonia, he found him and could exclaim: "God, who comforts the downcast, comforted us by the coming of Titus" (II Cor. 7. 6).

What can we learn from this collaboration in holy apostolic enterprise? We learn to love one another, and always to find a way of working together for the glory of God. The Lord's grace is so bountiful that at times the natural affections of the heart, and the varied circumstances of our relations with people, races and countries, may be ennobled and irradiated by the Lord's light, and by the virtues which spring from it, notably: humility, charity, gentleness, patience, prudence in speech, and the capacity to forgive.

7 FEBRUARY

THE EIGHTH COMMANDMENT

How fine this precept is, that a man must always tell

the truth to his fellow men! And how strict and terrible the commandment not to tell lies about him: "You shall not bear false witness against your neighbour" (Exodus 20. 16).

St Peter Canisius . . . explained both the negative and the positive aspects of this commandment very wisely and persuasively.

From the negative point of view: we are forbidden to bear any false and deceitful witness which might in any way, in law or outside the law, compromise the good reputation of our neighbour, after the manner of "gossip-mongers, detractors, scandal seekers, calumniators and adulators". We are forbidden to utter any falsehood or abuse about our neighbour; and this is as stern and absolute a commandment as the three which come before it: not to kill, not to fornicate, not to steal.

From the positive point of view we are told that we should speak well and courteously of our neighbour, in his defence and to his advantage, "without deceit, without invention, without malicious purpose".

8 FEBRUARY

GOD'S GIFTS

When we turn to consider the gifts God has bestowed on us in the course of the year, what a wealth of kindness and mercy he has poured out! Gifts of nature, gifts of grace, gifts of glory.

GIFTS OF NATURE. Our life prolonged, our health maintained, our preservation from so many physical and moral evils; the frequent intervention of heaven on our behalf; material prosperity, employment, a comfortable home. And we are still alive—that in itself is a great boon. . .

GIFTS OF GRACE. We are sinners and God has forgiven us, he still forgives us and is willing to go on doing so. We feel his presence as a source of constant interior peace, of Christian joy. What gifts he has showered upon us! The love of God and of our fellow men, the desire for the welfare of others, for justice and charity, for generosity to all; the spirit of forgiveness when we are offended, the enjoyment of prayer, the exercise of the angelic virtues of faith, hope and charity. And how can we speak of our close union with Jesus in the Holy Eucharist and in the Church? . . .

And there are some extraordinary graces: a wedding in our home, bringing joy to all, the birth of children, the preservation and strengthening of their innocence, and that serene happiness of family life which offers here below a foretaste of Paradise.

GIFTS OF GLORY. These are chiefly to be found in the success of our efforts to be kind and honest, our work for Holy Church, and also our endeavour to promote and maintain the civil order: "Happy the people whose God is the Lord!" (Psalm 143 (144). 15).

9 FEBRUARY

THE DIVINE POEM OF LOVE

The sacred book written by the fourth Evangelist, John, the "beloved disciple" of our Lord, offers us, particularly in chapters 6 and 17, the two fundamental themes of the divine poem of love.

In chapter 6, Jesus says that he himself, the true Son of the Heavenly Father, is the truth descended from heaven, that this truth is the true bread that will give life to the world, and that he himself, his body and blood, are this bread. We are told that we must find our nourishment in Jesus, consumed as sacrificial food, because he is necessary for our health and our life, and necessary not only to every priest and every faithful Christian, but to the whole world.

In St John's 17th chapter we feel the very heart of Jesus throbbing in his last farewell to his followers on the eve of the Passion that awaits him beyond the torrent of Kidron. That supreme prayer which speaks of the more intimate and sacred union between himself and the Father and pleads for his chosen to be united with him and with the Father, reaches the sublimest heights of charity, of that love which makes God and man one in Christ. And how moving are his last words, about the consecration of his chosen ones to the holy priesthood, which is our priesthood!

"O righteous Father, . . . I made known to them thy name, and I will make it known, that the love with which thou hast loved me may be in them, and I in them" (John 17. 26).

47

10 FEBRUARY

When every now and then, among the thorns of life, we find the Lord has set a spray of jasmine or a rose, or some other lovely flower, our hearts are filled with joy—but these little things cannot give us real peace. They are but a respite. St Gregory the Great finely says that they are like a "little breathing space"; they are indeed a breath of peace, but of an armed peace that has to be defended. . . from temptations. The enjoyment of peace is something much more perfect. It depends on the triumph of the work of God's mercy in our souls. St Augustine says: one hope, one faith, one promise: your mercy.

In Psalm 135 (136) this mercy, this "steadfast love", is referred to no fewer than twenty-six times, for his mercy endures for ever. And this is what strengthens us in the endeavour to preserve interior peace.

St Leonard of Porto Maurizio has given us precious counsel on this theme: "In my midday examination of conscience I shall look briefly into my heart, to see whether it enjoys interior peace, founded on the holy will of God, so that I may confirm this peace if it should be imperilled. My Jesus, mercy.

To preserve my peace I make four resolves:

1. To be dead to the world and to all that is not God.
2. To live in total abandonment to the will of Divine Providence.
3. To welcome suffering, interior or exterior.
4. Not to try to undertake much work, other than that pertaining to my own ministry, under obedience.

11 FEBRUARY

TO CHRIST THROUGH MARY

At Lourdes Mary is Queen, and all the churches, the holy grotto with its altar, the upper basilica, the crypt, the rosary chapel, all equally belong to her, because together they make up her domain of grace, in which she receives her devout followers and her children.

Jesus is lifted high on the cross; at his feet are Mary his Mother and John, the apostle whom he loved. Jesus says to his Mother, indicating John: "Behold your son"; then turning his dying gaze on John, he says: "Behold your Mother".

These are words one is never tired of repeating, words which describe the poetry of Lourdes, its history, its present and its future.

The truth is that, particularly in recent times, all the shrines of Mary, scattered throughout the world, have become above all centres of devotion to the Eucharist, as if the Mother of Jesus had appeared, here or there, in order to lead the faithful to the adoration and love of her blessed Son: but Lourdes is the most vast and famous of these centres.

The daily eucharistic procession in the afternoon at Lourdes is simply the re-enactment of the passing of the living Jesus through the midst of the crowds, to teach them and grant them miracles and graces of all kinds. So the visit to our Lord in these places is like a renewal of faith, adoration and love for Jesus, the true centre of Catholic liturgy as of Christian life.

12 FEBRUARY

TO REMAIN IN THE TRUTH

What wonderful lessons we find . . . in the New Testament on the beauty, the essence and the supreme wisdom of the truth, received and experienced, and of the Lord's commandment!

In the Gospel of St John we must see what Jesus says to those whom he has succeeded in converting: "If you continue in my word, you are truly my disciples, and you will know the truth, and the truth will make you free" (John 8. 30-32). But his words are terrible indeed when he leads his hearers to conclusions appalling to all those who deny the truth they have once known. "If you were Abraham's children", he says to them, "you would do what Abraham did, but now you seek to kill me, a man who has told you the truth which I heard from God... If God were your Father, you would love me, for I proceeded and came forth from God. . . You are of your father the devil, and your will is to do your father's desires."

St John says that when the wretched people heard these words they took up stones to hurl against Jesus.

"But Jesus hid himself and went out of the temple" (John 8. 39-59).

So was fulfilled what was written in the Psalm: "Love the Lord, all you his saints. The Lord preserves the faithful but abundantly requites him who acts haughtily" (Psalm 30 (31). 24).

13 FEBRUARY

TO LIVE IN THE TRUTH

We must live in the truth: here all believers come face to face with the truth, which firmly and gently rules all men.

Christ's words, in fact, confront every man with his own responsibility, that is, his acceptance or rejection of the truth; they implore us most persuasively to remain in the truth, to feed our minds on truth and to act accordingly.

My message today . . . is a solemn appeal to you all to live in the truth, thus fulfilling your fourfold obligation of thinking, honouring, telling and doing what is true.

First of all then, *to think the truth:* to have clear notions of the great divine and human realities of redemption and of the Church, of morality and of law, of philosophy and art; to have right ideas, or at least to try to form them conscientiously and with an honest intention.

To honour the truth: this is an appeal to you to be shining examples in all spheres of individual, family, professional and social life. Truth makes us free; it ennobles those who profess it openly and without considering the opinion of the world. Why then should we be afraid to honour it, and to insist on its being treated with respect?

To tell the truth: this is what every mother teaches her child: to beware of telling lies. As the years pass telling the truth becomes second nature and makes the man of honour, the perfect Christian of frank and ready speech. And this is the testimony which the God of truth requires of every one of his children.

Finally, *to do everything according to the truth:* this is the light which must irradiate our whole personality and set its mark on every act of our lives.

14 FEBRUARY

Today is the Feast of St Valentine, who has become the patron saint of couples engaged to be married. The profound Christian conception of love — and naturally also of love between those who wish to marry — is set forth by Pope John.

SUPPRESSING THE SELF

Love is all; love is at the foundation of civilization; love is the basis of all that Christ came to declare to the world.

It is the command to love which distinguishes the Christian revelation from the doctrine of all other religions. In love is found the solution of all social problems, of all political disputes. It is the keystone of the arch.

When you hear all sorts of things announced by this leader or that, but no mention of love, be on your guard, my children, beware.

Without love you may obtain temporary successes, or victories won by force, but afterwards, and very soon, all will fall to the ground. This has been proved by our experience in recent years.

Let us love the Lord. Let us love one another.

We must know how to suppress the self and how to emphasize the unity, the social nature, of man. St Thomas says that man is a *social animal*, and this is true. Our own welfare is our brothers' welfare; it is that of others, of all men.

15 FEBRUARY

In the General Audience of 25 October 1959, the first anniversary of his election, Pope John spoke of the great prayer: "Our Father". Here is a series of seven extracts, beginning today.

"OUR FATHER"

The name of God, and the worship of God, mean the exaltation of his kingdom, which means the ever greater and more effective diffusion of the Christian spirit, the spirit of convinced Christians; the effort to attain individual and collective sanctification, according to the divine will, and also our co-operation in the orderly endeavour to earn our daily bread, assured to us by the provident hand of the heavenly Father, who sanctifies the labour of men; the humility with which we implore our heavenly Father for forgiveness and forgive all who have offended us, in a spirit of all-conquering human brotherliness; and finally the expression of our trust in God's help in the anxious hours of temptation, and the eager and prudent resolve to see that we rule our thoughts and all our human activities according to the teaching, the example and the grace of Christ our Saviour and Father.

O Jesus, we implore thee, and we shall always implore thee, be pleased to grant us peace in our time; support the whole world with the power of thy mercy, so that free from all sin men may be preserved from all evil; through the merits of thy divine blood. To thee be love, honour and glory for ever and ever. Amen.

16 FEBRUARY

"THY KINGDOM COME"

When we speak of the kingdom of God we must not confuse it with political constructions based on human power, such as were frequently found in past ages and still appear here and there today, expressions of human and material domination.

We pray for the kingdom that shall come (cf. Matt. 6. 10) in the sense in which Christ conceived it, and as the liturgy sings of it in one of the Church's finest out-pourings of her official prayer: "a kingdom of truth and light", a "kingdom of holiness and grace", a "kingdom of justice, love and peace" (Preface, Feast of Christ the King).

These are beloved and mysterious expressions which make clear the choice that is set before all individuals and social communities, families, nations and the whole world.

So we are either to walk with Christ, every one of us bearing his cross, light or burdensome as it may be, or to go on without him, lost in uncertainty, danger and disorder, towards universal ruin.

17 FEBRUARY

"THY WILL BE DONE"

"Thy will be done" (Matt. 6. 10). The Lord's will is

the third shining light, set to guide and inspire all men. It points to the effort everyone must make to ensure his own salvation, because it is written:

"For this is the will of God, your sanctification" (I Thess. 4. 3).

Above the fears and griefs which move the heart of the Chief Shepherd of the Universal Church as he observes the unfaithfulness of many, too many, who yield to the temptations of the devil and become corrupted and lost, there also shines the vision to be seen from Rome, the vision in which the Vicar of Christ is able to admire the prodigies of faith, love and sacrifice which are so abundant, on a vast or humble scale, throughout the world. These miracles, sometimes wrought in blood and suffering, attest the everlasting sacrifice of Calvary, which redeems and saves all men.

18 FEBRUARY

"GIVE US THIS DAY OUR DAILY BREAD"

This is a great problem—the provision of our daily bread, and so it has its place in the programme of Christian prayer and activity.

It is the Lord who gives us our food, as the reward for every man's toil. It is he who inspires the minds of innumerable people who with awakened consciences endeavour to discover the ways and means of creating prosperity, material wealth also, so that men's bodies may be strong enough to be used to good purpose, and equal to the needs, the aspirations and the splendours of the soul.

We are certainly grieved and saddened when we see the unwillingness of many to draw light and strength from what the Church teaches us for the solution of the great problems set by economic conditions and the search for temporal well-being. When light from heaven is shut out and men's eyes are closed to the radiance of the Gospel commandments, which are the foundation of our Christian civilization, it is inevitable that the peoples should find themselves struggling in a vain endeavour even to improve economic conditions. These will never be able to provide true prosperity for human society, for this is to be sought in a wider interpretation of men's needs.

19 FEBRUARY

"FORGIVE US OUR TRESPASSES"

The great task of the Catholic Church and Christian priesthood is, besides the ministry of the word, the distribution of God's pardon to individuals and to peoples who all, more or less deliberately, ignore or scorn the sanctity of the fundamental rules of life. The Ten Commandments, completed by the evangelical precepts of social justice and charity, constitute the framework of individual and collective survival.

Sin is opposed to the Commandments and to the Gospel because it is all-destroying and poisons the whole order of existence, whether individual or collective. This explains why Jesus came, the "Lamb of God, who takes away the sin of the world" (John 1. 29). Christ came to this earth to atone for the sins of the world, and he has been immolated upon our altars, throughout the centuries, in continuation of this sacrifice.

Hardly anyone is immune to the dismal seductions of sin. The words of the Ancient Book (I John 5. 19) testify to the way in which the whole world is filled with wickedness, and unhappily bear witness to the all-pervading individual and collective disorder.

One of the Apostles said very frankly about this: "If we say we have no sin, we deceive ourselves, and the truth is not in us" (I John 1. 8). But there is forgiveness for every sin. The world still endures, and will endure, because the voice and the blood of Christ cry out for compassion and mercy.

20 FEBRUARY

"AS WE FORGIVE THEM. . ."

To this cry for pity and mercy which Christ's blood still implores with "loud cries and tears" (Hebrews 5. 7), corresponds the same divine Redeemer's appeal for mutual forgiveness between brothers, and for the true triumph—not illusory, deceitful or distorted—the true triumph of forgiveness and peace.

"Beloved," said the Evangelist St John, when he was ninety years of age, but still young in innocence and faith, John the confidant of Jesus and Mary, "let us love one another" (I John 4. 7); let us love in all sincerity. Then we shall make peace.

Every endeavour to make peace between one man and another, or one nation and another, is worthy of our heartfelt admiration. Every sincere and eager movement towards peace, from whatever quarter it may come, provided that it conceal no deceit and be inspired by pure justice and universal love, any such movement, we repeat, is worthy of our trust and respect.

All is forgiven to those who know how to forgive and are willing to do so. And everything becomes ennobled in the man who has kept, or found again, a pure and innocent soul, and expresses it in fairness, justice and brotherliness, true Christian brotherliness.

21 FEBRUARY

"DELIVER US FROM EVIL"

The divine prayer which Jesus taught us on the Mount, and which should give nobility, purpose and wisdom to every day of our lives, ends in a final trustful appeal to God Almighty, that he may save us from the Evil One: "Deliver us from evil" (Matt. 6. 13).

Human nature is subject to temptation, and it is man's surrender to this that constitutes the gravest threat and danger to his freedom and dignity.

Unhappily, "the whole world is in the power of the Evil One" (I John 5. 19). For our preservation from all these troubles we may count on the merciful assistance of God, but we must ourselves co-operate with all our will power, determined to be on our guard against evil and the spirit which inspires and prompts evil desires.

In one of the most sacred and tender moments of the Mass, immediately after the "Our Father", the Church repeats this prayer, which comes from all our hearts in this moment of time: "Deliver us, we beseech thee, O Lord, from all evils, past, present and to come, and by the intercession of the blessed and glorious... Mother of God, ... thy Apostles Peter and Paul and Andrew, and all the Saints", who have watched over the Church during so many centuries, "mercifully grant peace in our days, that through the bounteous help of thy mercy we may be always free from sin and secure from all disturbance", through the merits of Jesus Christ our Saviour.

22 FEBRUARY

FEAST OF ST PETER'S CHAIR AT ANTIOCH

The Apostolic Chair of St Peter: what a wonderful expression of the unity of the great human family, of whose members the Church is composed! From Jerusalem or Antioch, or Rome, the light is seen to beat most fully upon this Chair, its rays reflected from the words addressed by Jesus, as St Matthew tells us, to Peter himself, in one of the most beautiful and touching passages in the New Testament; "on this rock I will build my Church. . . I will give you the keys of the kingdom of heaven" (Matt. 16. 18-19).

What is the meaning of these keys, entrusted personally to Simon, son of John, to "Peter", if not the sign that the universal government of the Church had been given into his hands? From Jerusalem to Antioch, and then to the heart of the Roman Empire, the way now lay open to the Apostle, to preach throughout the world under the inspiration of the Holy Spirit. To him the Lord entrusted his sheep and his lambs: "Feed my lambs, feed my sheep" (John 21. 15-17).

He was then to be the prince and shepherd of all, to lead his flock in the name of Christ himself. And this primacy was to be claimed by all Peter's successors, and acknowledged, in the care of souls, by his brother bishops all over he world. From this Chair are for ever consecrated the bishops of the universal Church, One, Holy, Catholic and Apostolic.

From Christ to Peter, and from Peter to every shepherd of the Christian flock, the power of the keys, bestowed from heaven upon the person of the Roman Pontiff, is handed on, through the bishops and the whole Christian community, for the government and sanctification of mankind redeemed by Christ's blood.

23 FEBRUARY

We sometimes chance to hear trembling voices raised in accents of exaggerated alarm, murmuring prophecies which disturb the imagination of feeble minds.

St Matthew, the first of the Evangelists, tells us that one evening, after a tiring day, Jesus went alone to a hill top to pray. The boat with the disciples in it remained on the lake and was blown about by the winds. At nightfall Jesus alighted on the waves and called out to the disciples: "Take heart, it is I; have no fear". "Lord, if it is you," said Peter, "bid me come to you on the water." And Jesus said to him "Come". So Peter got out of the boat and tried to get nearer to his divine Master. But the violence of the wind alarmed him, and when he felt he was sinking he cried out, "Lord, save me!" At once Jesus stretched out his hand and caught hold of him, saying: "O man of little faith, why did you doubt?" And when they were all together in the boat again, the wind ceased (cf. Matt. 14. 22-23).

When Jesus speaks to us his words suffice to save us and to give us the victory over fear.

This is one of the most beautiful episodes of the New Testament. It is encouraging, and of good augury.

24 FEBRUARY

Do not be like those people who think they are inaugurating a new era: as if before they came along there had been nothing but emptiness or chaos. Before we came there were our parents, and they were the latest link of a long and sacred chain. The generations which went before us left such wonderful proofs of their noble victories in the cause of truth and goodness that we fear we may never equal them in merit and glory.

It would be a meritorious thing for us all frankly to admit that we should still be very wretched indeed, and hardly out of the phase of barbarism, if the civilization of past centuries had not seen to our baptism.

The fashion of the day tends to change ideas and intentions with every change of season. Do not follow this fashion. We have our obligations to God, to society

and to our own consciences. We accepted these obligations in precious moments of intimate and sacred
solemnity: let us therefore not yield to the blandish-
ments of our own convenience and advantage.

May the sign of the Cross, impressed upon your soul,
shine on your foreheads . . . as the mark of fortitude and
sincerity, and in this sign may it be less difficult for you
all to stand firm and act courageously.

25 FEBRUARY

PRAYER

The Apostle Paul wrote his letter to the Ephesians from
Rome where he was held a prisoner, bound with chains
to a Roman soldier who guarded him. In fact, at the
close of this letter he drew his imagery from the equip-
ment of a soldier when he wanted to teach the Christians
what weapons they needed to defend themselves, and
to attack their spiritual enemies. And we are not surprised that at the end of his list he attaches special
importance to prayer as the most affective weapon of
all. Listen to his words: "Pray at all times in the Spirit,
with all prayer and supplication. To that end keep alert
with all perseverance, making supplication for all the
saints. . ." (Eph. 6. 18).

In times of distress the world-wide prayer to God
Almighty,Creator of the world, to his Son Christ Jesus
who became Man for the salvation of mankind, and to
the Holy Spirit, Lord and Giver of life, have received
miraculous answers from heaven and upon this earth,
answers which inspired the happiest and most glorious
epochs in the story of mankind and in that of the individual nations. We must open our hearts, emptying
them of the malice with which at times the spirit of error
and evil seeks to contaminate them, and when we have
purified them in this way we must be of good courage,
sure of possessing the things of heaven, which will bring
us also an abundance of the good things of this earth.

Let us continue to pray. . . as St Paul begs us to do,
at the end of his moving message. Let us pray together
and for one another, and for all the creatures of God,
scattered over the earth, who make up the Church
and the human family, which also is entirely his creation.

RIGHT-MINDEDNESS

We must be "without a stain": this means that our life must be blameless and our personal conduct worthy of the admiring gaze of the Lord's angels, of the emulation of the faithful, and of the respect of all unbelievers who come into contact with us. Any other sort of praise, of our personal qualities or talents, of our skill or worldly success, is but vanity and deceit.

We must also be just and honest in our thoughts. The habit of thinking ill of everything and everyone is tiresome to ourselves and to all around us. We must behave modestly with all, but keep our gaze open and alert to see what is happening to ourselves and to those who live with us. We must make a habit of self-knowledge, so that we may have compassion on our fellow men and sweeten everything around us, turning it to good, inspired in our fervour by others' example.

Above all, we must be on our guard against imprudent speech: we are not to speak evil about others, not to insult or injure our neighbour. . .

Knowing how to control ourselves in this matter in a great effort to seek perfection does not dispense us from severely judging the dishonesty of the world, or from being for ever on our guard. We must not allow ourselves to be deceived, and, above all, we must not admit of any compromise with the world, for the sake of financial profit for ourselves or material advantage, especially if, and this would be even more wicked and reprehensible, these advantages were won at the expense of innocent souls.

27 FEBRUARY

"YOU ARE CHRIST'S"

The moral sense, directed towards total and willing obedience to the commandments of God, is an indispensable condition for the peaceful and constructive progress of the nations; wherever this has become dulled, souls are enfeebled and the whole social community suffers thereby. So in defending our precious moral inheritance, founded on God's law, which is written on men's hearts and solemnly sanctioned by the divine commandments, the Church not only carries out her mission to save souls but at the same time ensures for the nations the defence of their temporal well-being.

The moral sense is needed to safeguard the family, which is intended to prepare souls for the difficulties of life by educating their consciences; it is needed by the young, on whom we base our trustful hopes for the future, and it is needed by society, which requires men who are in sympathy with the needs of social life, conceived on a large and comprehensive scale, and men who are always ready to serve the common cause.

The centre of all thoughts and aims must be the human person, created in the image and likeness of God, and redeemed by the Precious Blood of Christ. The human person must be the focal point for all the activities around it, those of the family, the school, political and economic sciences, art and literature, the Press and the provision of entertainment.

All must converge on this centre, in order to preserve the dignity of the human being, ennoble his faculties, and train his judgment, so that his complete personality may develop in harmony with God's plan for our salvation: "All things are yours; . . . and you are Christ's, and Christ is God's" (cf. I Cor. 3. 22-23).

28 FEBRUARY

THE SAVING TRUTH

The truth makes us free, as the apostle St John tells us. And yet nothing on earth is more ill-treated than truth.

The Holy Father does not wish to hurt anyone's feelings, and so he will not enumerate the different ways in which truth is being betrayed. He merely points out what is happening every day in the way of inventions and falsehoods, and in attempts to interpret the intentions of others, boldly attributing to them quite incongruous thoughts and propositions. All this is contrary to the truth.

But we hold fast to the Lord's truth, for this will remain inviolable for ever. "The faithfulness of the Lord endures for ever" (Psalm 116 (117). 2).

The child's mother teaches him to have a horror of falsehood; as the years go by the grown man clearly perceives that truth is always our salvation, that compromise with the truth must at all times be rejected, and that in social relations a man's honour is judged by his fidelity, at all times, to the truth.

MARCH

1 MARCH

The month of March is dedicated to the saint who was, after Our Lady, dearest to Pope John. . . .

ST JOSEPH

At the beginning of St Joseph's life of glory there is a historical reality, incomparable in its grandeur but steeped in a light of heart-warming humility: the Holy Family of Nazareth.

St Joseph may indeed be called the silent saint. What we know of him is not derived from his sayings or teachings, but from what the Gospel tells us about him, from what the angel of the Lord, on more than one occasion, told him to do.

We see him—and these memories of the infancy and early years of Jesus stir our hearts profoundly—at Nazareth, at Bethlehem, in Egypt and back again at Nazareth: always ready to obey the divine commands, always faithful to the supreme obligations of his particular mission, and to the duties of his daily work.

After two thousand years this wonderful example of the Holy Family is still as bright as ever. It has inspired the profound changes that have taken place in all that has to do with the labour of men and women. Think of the condition of the workers before Christianity, of the horrors of slavery and of the sufferings of the poor in bitter servitude! And yet Christ did not impart to us this lesson from one of the famous teaching centres which flourished in the great cities; he did not surround himself with splendour. He chose a poor family as the first class-room for his teaching mission; he himself undertook manual labour. Throughout the centuries Christian families have found profound joy in meditating upon this.

2 MARCH

THE SERENITY OF ST JOSEPH

The high-minded and lovable serenity that shines out upon us from the foster-father of Jesus is an invitation to us to draw closer to him . . . with holy confidence, in order to learn to apply to ourselves and to our own lives the lessons he imparts with such discretion.

St Joseph speaks very little, but he lives intensely, and never seeks to evade any responsibility placed upon him by the will of God. He sets us an appealing example of obedience to the divine commands, of serenity at all times, and of perfect trust in God, attained through a life of superhuman faith and charity, and above all through that great means: prayer.

It is moving to recall the few episodes in which he figures, revealed to us through the scanty references in the Gospel. St Joseph is silent while he is being severely tested, and, as he is a just man, he refrains from judging and does not seek to anticipate God's wishes; when, through the ministry of angels, the Lord speaks to him, he listens and obeys in silence. He has the honour of bestowing on Jesus the name that is blessed throughout all ages. He is the stalwart protector of the Virgin Mary in the poverty of Bethlehem. In the middle of the night he takes Jesus and sets out with Mary, to face the unknown future. When the right moment comes, and the angels tell him to return to his own land, he is ready to do so, and to resume once more the life of a humble artisan in the house at Nazareth.

The angel's words, which make him known to us, lend themselves perfectly to those applications to the religious life which have been suggested through the centuries. The man of faith does not tremble with fear, does not act rashly, and does not alarm his fellows.

3 MARCH

A MOST POWERFUL INTERCESSOR

We firmly believe that God speaks in the conscience of

every man, and is present in all that happens to all men; we believe in his love.

This confidence is rooted in the unfailing help we receive from Jesus, the Founder of the Church, who walks serenely on the storm-tossed waves of the sea: "Take heart, it is I; have no fear" (Matt. 14. 27).

When these mysterious words were first uttered, the apostles and disciples, we know, were but a meagre band; and yet Jesus called out to them unfalteringly: "Have no fear, have no fear!"

Thinking of this, the man of faith learns humility, the foundation of all solid constructive work; he preserves a healthy sense of proportion and a Christian indifference to the world's judgments—and he becomes more and more convinced that we are instruments, and no more, docile and ever ready instruments and co-workers with God, who in his mercy associates his creatures with his purposes of immortal splendour, which reflect upon this earth a radiance of grace and peace.

In order to preserve this fidelity of humble collaborators in the divine plan for our humble lives, we need first of all the protection of the Virgin Mary and then also the protection of St Joseph, a most powerful intercessor: "A faithful friend is a strong defence" (Exodus 6. 14).

To this faithful friend, who protected Jesus during the days of his mortal life, and now from heaven watches over his Mystical Body... we commend in confident prayer the present and future cares of the government of the Church.

4 MARCH

THE HOLY FAMILY

Every family that is founded upon an industrious life, mutual respect and the fear of God, is the strength and support of villages, cities and nations; it is the nucleus and basis of all virtue, a bulwark against all danger of corruption, and a reserve of wholesome and ever renewed energy to be used for the well-being of individuals and of society.

We kneel in reverence before the hidden glory of the Family of Jesus, before its treasures of purity, humility and self-sacrifice, before the trials and sufferings which this family accepted and endured; and in the light of Nazareth our thoughts go out especially to those families with numerous children which, because of their fidelity to God's law, frequently have to suffer penalties and privations, families living in obscurity, or held in scant esteem; and we think also of those families which, because they lack means, or work, or health, live in a state of continual and harassing anxiety. For all these suffering children, and for those in a more secure and tranquil condition, whom we beg to aid the others with Christian solicitude, our fervent prayers rise to Jesus, Mary and Joseph, in order that all may receive the fullness of heavenly grace, and the consolations of this world also.

5 MARCH

HUMILITY, RESERVE, SILENCE

Humility, reserve and silence were the characteristics of the husband of Mary, the foster-father of Jesus: his spirit was constantly in attendance on God, in order to hear his voice and immediately obey his supreme commands.

Certainly the great patriarch's thoughts did not dwell on the immense privilege he had been granted, that of guarding the incomparable treasures entrusted to him by God: his mind was fully engaged in the perfect accomplishment of his task as a faithful executor of the wishes of Almighty God. This is the light of Nazareth; this is the wonderful example set for the life of the great family of Christ, perpetuated through the ages. Whenever we try to draw nearer to all that is noblest, purest and infinitely lovely in our religion, we begin by contemplating the Holy Trinity, and then immediately afterwards we find Jesus, Mary and Joseph. . . How precious are the offerings we make, and the prayers we say, to Jesus, his Mother, and the protector of both: " . . . I give you my heart and my soul"; ". . . help me in my last hour"; "may I die at peace with you!"

The life of the Christian may be described as an active sharing in the life of the Church, by means of the Sacraments, beginning with the most holy Eucharist. It must also be constantly nourished with the fervour of prayer. . . and the Christian must beg for the intercession, first of all of God's most Holy Mother, and then of St Joseph and the other heavenly advocates.

6 MARCH

PRAYER TO ST JOSEPH

O glorious St Joseph, who concealed your royal and incomparable dignity of protector of Jesus and of the Virgin Mary under the humble appearance of an artisan, and supported them by your daily toil, protect with your loving power the children whom we especially entrust to you.

You know our difficulties and our sufferings, because you also experienced them, with Jesus and his Mother. Do not let these children be so overburdened by their anxiety as to forget the end to which God has called them; let not the seeds of infidelity take root in their immortal souls. Remind all who work in the fields, factories, mines and laboratories, that they are not alone in their labour, their joys or their sufferings, because Jesus is by their side, with Mary, his Mother and ours, supporting them, wiping the sweat from their brows, and setting a value on their toil.

Teach them to use their labour, as you did, as a supreme means of attaining holiness.

7 MARCH

The Feast of St Thomas Aquinas, Patron of Schools

THE TEACHER'S MISSION

The figure of our teacher, which we all cherish in our hearts among the dearest memories of our childhood, speaks to us of his supreme office as a teacher of souls, by word and by example, and by patient and persevering efforts amid many difficulties and at the cost of much self-sacrifice.

The profound words in which St John Chrysostom describes this supreme mission are very familiar to you: "What can be greater than the work of educating souls, and training the character of adolescents? I have no doubt that the most excellent of all painters, sculptors and artists is the man who is expert in the art of modelling the souls of the young" (Hom. 59-60 *in cap.* Matt. 18; PG 58, 584). This art is neither learnt from books nor acquired by experience, but is attained through the grace of God, through prayer, and through the long apprenticeship of a life that has been profoundly Christian ever since the first fruitful years of study and school.

The greatness of this teaching mission can be judged also by the responsibilities attached to it: to the teacher are entrusted the very destinies of human society, in order that he may form the men of the future, instilling into their hearts, still young and receptive, doctrines and impressions which will rule their whole lives.

Meanwhile every one of us must strive continually to strengthen his own faith, by a sure understanding of Catholic doctrine. . . and every one should be exemplary in the conscientious performance of his duty, generous in the social apostolate, and in working for the good of the human society to which he belongs.

8 MARCH

LENT

The old problem of the connection between faith and works, which goes back to apostolic times, is coming more and more to the fore in our own day. The answer is: not faith alone, or good works alone, but the perfect association of faith with works. And it is in his power of strong and enlightened faith, and according to his greater or less fervour in good works, that the worth of the perfect Christian may be seen, and he may be distinguished from the weaker men, the indolent, the ineffective and the unhappy. . .

From the Old Testament we all receive the command to "fight", each for his own salvation. What strong words these are! They teach us that it is our duty to fight until death against the temptations of the world, in order to win salvation for our own souls, and for the souls of all most dear to us in this life.

The New Testament gives us the words of Jesus, among the last he uttered before his sacrifice: "I have said this to you, that in me you may have peace. In the world you have tribulation; but be of good cheer, I have overcome the world" (John 16. 33).

The period of Lent stretches out before us as the most propitious time for an attempt at a spiritual renewal that may correspond to what I have been explaining to you. We must look into our own souls, count our failings, seek out the most suitable and effective ways of doing our several duties and then, having in this way refreshed our souls, go on our way more happily and more eagerly and more full of confidence.

9 MARCH

GOD'S LAW

God's holy law is set before us. We all learnt it when we were children: ten points, ten commandments. A great deal is said today about civilization, and peace, and about the tasks and triumphs of the Church. But, as we all know well, these tasks and these triumphs are all contained in the affirmation and observance of the Ten Commandments. The worship and love of God, who created us and sent his own Son to redeem us; perfect obedience in refraining from doing what he has forbidden us to do, for example, from telling lies, which has in all ages been considered a grave sin even in this world. Instead, we must always bear witness to the truth, and raise our souls to higher things by purifying our desires. St Paul warns us that we must turn away from all base impulses, and from the innumerable passions of life.

It is our strict duty to listen to these commands. Sometimes the Lord speaks to us in solitude, in the silence of our soul.

Remember—he says—the holy faith in which you were born and reared is not a fairy tale, or an invention. It goes back very many centuries, and Jesus confirmed it with his doctrine of charity and love, of forgiveness and self-denial, so that we may all dedicate ourselves to Christ's own work, which is the truest and noblest civilization.

10 MARCH

"IF YOU ARE THE SON OF GOD. . ."

". . . if you are the Son of God, command this stone to become bread." The world around us is just stone, nothing else. It may be transformed into something precious if water, that is, the grace of Our Lord, penetrates and softens it, turning it into a source of blessings.

". . . and he set him on the pinnacle of the temple, and said to him: 'If you are the Son of God, throw yourself down from here, because the angels of the Lord will come to your aid and will not let you be hurt.' And Jesus answered him: 'You shall not tempt the Lord your God.'" Is this not the story of many of us? How many of us run the risk of coming to terms with this lord, this prince of the world, who afterwards shows himself in his true colours: Satan, the enemy of God, who has vowed eternal hatred to God, and can do no less, because of his rebellious and perverted nature.

He took him up a high mountain and showed him all the kingdoms of the world and their glory, and said to him: "I will give all this to you, if you will bow down and worship me". Then Jesus answered: "Begone, Satan! for it is written: You shall worship the Lord your God and him only shall you serve." How magnificent is the Lord's stern rejection of this vile and wretched suggestion—the fruit of utter ignorance—from the author of all evil!

But Satan is always repeating to men, at every moment: "See, how alluring are the desires of this life, the passions that, once aroused, are never satisfied, the desire for honours, glory and self-assertion! You see, all is for you, all that you see before you: the fields, the heights, the resources of the earth, if you will fall down and worship me." Our reply must be as prompt as the Lord's: "Begone! do not tempt me!" Only in this way can the Christian be worthy of Christ.

11 MARCH

SUFFERING

Many of us are inclined to think of all the physical sufferings of this world as evils, absolute evils. We have forgotten that pain is the legacy we have inherited from Adam; we have forgotten that the only real evil is sin, which offends the Lord, and that we must look to the Cross of Jesus as the Apostles, martyrs, saints, teachers and witnesses looked to it. For in the Cross we find strength and salvation, and in the love of Christ there is no life without suffering.

Thanks be to God, not all souls turn rebellious under the burden of pain. There are some infirm people who understand the meaning of suffering and are aware of the opportunities they have been given to contribute to the salvation of the world—and so they accept their life of pain as Jesus Christ accepted his, as most holy Mary accepted hers on the Feast of her Purification, and as her chaste and faithful husband St Joseph accepted his.

What more useful counsel can we give than this: never let your gaze turn away from the Cross of Jesus, which the liturgy invites you to contemplate?

Look at this Cross, my beloved children, when you have to suffer. If those who are in pain make this their rule of life they will never feel alone; in Paradise they will see the rich fruits of their spiritual efforts, in Paradise where there are no more tears, or pain or separations, and no more possibility of offending God.

12 MARCH
Feast of Pope Gregory 1

THE CONSTANT PRESENCE OF JESUS

The Gospel of St John . . . describes the appearance of the risen Lord to the Apostles on the shores of the Lake of Tiberias. . .

St Gregory observes that on this occasion also, Peter, the Prince of the Apostles, was busy fishing, and wonders why he was still engaged in this work after the Lord had told him to leave all and follow him. Another Apostle, St Matthew, whose profession was that of handling money in an office connected with banking, or money changing, or tax collecting, had given up his job at once. And St Gregory answers his own question: It is one thing to procure your daily food by fishing, and another to be busied in earning and accumulating money, for this latter occupation might impede the growth of a true conversion. St Peter was awaiting the special mandate the Lord was to entrust to him; St Matthew was already intent on gathering together the teachings of the divine Master, and preparing to write his life, as he did later on in his Gospel.

St Gregory next observes the different way in which

the Lord now spoke to his Apostles, when he met them by the Lake of Tiberias. A year before they had all, including Peter, been fishing, but a storm had arisen and Jesus had walked upon the waves to encourage them and to make their fishing miraculously successful. Now, after his Resurrection, he stayed on the shore. There is a lesson for us in all this. In fact, the Lord is always present, in moments when we are most sorely tried, and during the storms of life. He encourages us, strengthens us, and supports us so that we may always win our battles against evil. But when all is calm he is still with us.

13 MARCH

THE LENTEN SPIRIT

". . . We entreat you not to accept the grace of God in vain. For he says: At the acceptable time I have listened to you, and helped you on the day of salvation" (II Cor. 6. 1-2).

This entreaty is particularly precious and timely during the forty days of Lent. Every one of us, looking into his conscience, must find out how far his own life is ruled by faith, in what way and to what extent he indulges in acts and words contrary to the Christian law, and in what measure he practises the virtues, particularly those of patience and self-denial. And although our fond Mother the Church has softened the former severity of the laws about fasting, no one can consider himself dispensed from making voluntary compensating sacrifices for the good of his soul.

After we have made this necessary spiritual examination during the sacred period of Lent, we must also remember to cultivate and maintain a great respect for the priesthood, which represents the very substance of the Christian life, with all the wealth of grace which, through the Catholic priests, is administered and distributed by means of the Sacraments, and the word of God preached to all men. . .

Moreover, we are all asked to be united, and to love one another; we must not let our mutual relations get entangled in pettiness or malice, but cultivate the good seed of the Gospel so as to give new vigour to the religious life of all peoples, according to our Saviour's precepts, and we must also try to strengthen social relations in a Christian order.

14 MARCH

TRUE REPENTANCE

First of all we wish to encourage you to make proper use of this period of Lent by attending to the grave duties of religious instruction, and by giving its due importance to true and effective repentance, according to every man's vocation and condition.

By studying and meditating the eternal virtues which God has revealed to man, thus ennobling his mind and unfolding before his eyes the infinite horizons of his purpose of salvation and love—only by doing this and in the light of this truth can man discover himself, find out his own difficult and unavoidable obligations, and have recourse to the noble practice of penitence, understood as the love of the Cross. It is by this sign that we recognize the sincere and determined Christian. Only through austerity of life, which puts into practice the rules of poverty and renunciation taught by our Lord Jesus Christ, can the domestic and social order receive a decisive impulse towards renewal in the truth, in the liberty of the children of God, and in the truest and profoundest justice, which is capable of denying itself in order to give to the poor and the disinherited.

In this way, through the institution of Lent, the Church does not impose upon us, her children, a mere regime of exterior practices, but a serious effort of love and generosity, for the sake of our fellow men.

This is the meaning of Lent, this is the practice of true penitence, and this is what the Lord expects from us all in the "acceptable time" of grace and forgiveness.

15 MARCH

LENT

In Christian families the ancient and robust traditions of ecclesiastical discipline find alert and willing souls, whom we gather around us in a spiritual embrace, so that our hearts may rise together in prayer to the divine Redeemer.

O Lord Jesus, you who at the beginning of your public life withdrew into the desert, we beg you to teach all men that recollection of mind which is the beginning of conversion and salvation.

Leaving your home at Nazareth and your sweet Mother, you wished to experience solitude, weariness and hunger. To the tempter who proposed to you the trial of miracles, you replied with the strength of eternal wisdom, in itself a miracle of heavenly grace.

It is Lent.

O Lord, do not let us turn to "broken cisterns", that can hold no water (Jer. 2. 13). or imitate the unfaithful steward or the foolish virgins; do not let us be so blinded by the enjoyment of the good things of earth that our hearts become insensible to the cry of the poor, of the sick, of orphan children and of those innumerable brothers of ours who still lack the necessary minimum to eat, to clothe their nakedness and to gather their family together under one roof.

16 MARCH

UNSELFISHNESS

St Gregory warns us "not to desire what belongs to others".

We understand this to mean that we must not covet other people's possessions, and must not let ourselves be tormented by envy, jealousy, or the immoderate love of wealth.

It is a profound consolation for a Christian to be able to say to the Lord: I am here in the state in which you chose to place me. Even if I am poor I intend to remain faithful to your holy law, and to the Gospel which teaches me humility, purity, the devotion to duty and self-sacrifice. And how meritorious it is to add: Here I am, O Lord; if I possess anything of value in this world I am ready to obey the commandment of charity!

The accumulation of vast wealth while so many are languishing in misery (and we have seen in recent statistics what an immense number of human beings in some continents are dying of hunger) is a grave transgression of God's law, with the consequence also that the greedy, avaricious man is never at ease in his mind: he is in fact a most unhappy creature.

What radiance, instead, what overflowing joy, when we practise kindness, and show a cheerful unselfish spirit, appealing to all our brother men to do the same! This is the foundation of perfect harmony and peace in this world.

17 MARCH

FEAST OF THE GREAT APOSTLE OF IRELAND

Fifteen hundred years ago St Patrick, the good and faithful servant, was, after an unwearied and fruitful ministry, called into the joy of his Master (Matt. 25. 21): his labours had transformed a heathen people into a fervent Christian community, from which there soon flowered innumerable vocations to the apostolate and to lives of consecrated virginity, while centres of learning and civilization sprang up all around, and there began a wonderful irradiation of faith which repaid a hundred-fold to Europe and the world all that this blessed land had received from Christian evangelization. It was Patrick who had worked this profound transformation.

God enabled him to do what few Christian heroes were able to accomplish, even with gigantic efforts: to see the transfiguration, within the life span of one generation, of the land which had once welcomed him as a young slave, and to which he had returned in the fullness of his apostolic fervour, with the mandate and authority conferred on him by the Supreme Pastor of the Church.

And from his death until our own day, see how his labours have continued to bear fruit! How many saints have followed in the furrow he traced, triumphantly extending the frontiers of Christendom: Columba and Columban, Aidan and Catald, Virgil and Gall, who preached the Gospel through the length and breadth of Great Britain and Europe! How many priests and missionaries, whose names are written in heaven (cf. Luke 10. 20) left, and still leave, their beloved fatherland to continue so praiseworthy a mission! How many struggles and sufferings, hardships and persecutions, overcome with serene courage, have ensured for their ministry the stability of God's own work!

The memory of this saint still inspires a fervour of

ever renewed holy resolves and enterprises: his tender and intense piety impels us to live in the light of the Blessed Trinity, guarding for ever the precious gifts of grace and of the spiritual life.

18 MARCH

FIDELITY

A humble family consisting of father, mother and son once lived in captivity in Assyria. The head of the family, Tobias, was well known for his many works of mercy in his neighbour's service, and for his fidelity to God and to God's law. The family endured trials of various kinds and then there suddenly fell upon Tobias another calamity, the grave misfortune of blindness. At times he found no understanding or support even among those most dear to him. Nevertheless, as he prayed incessantly and his thoughts were always with the Lord, he never lost heart, and remained calm and constant, an upright and virtuous man.

The day came when his young son had to make a journey to a far country; at once there appeared a mysterious travelling companion who protected his young charge from grave dangers and led him safely back to his father's house.

The little family were not slow to show their gratitude to this unexpected and generous helper for his extraordinary kindness. Father and son decided to offer him half the sum they had been able to recover as repayment of an old loan. But their guest gently declined their offer and departed, leaving behind him a supremely noble memory, asking them to bless the Lord: "I discover then the truth to you, and I will not hide the secret from you. When thou didst pray with tears, and didst bury the dead, and didst leave thy dinner, and hide the dead by day in thy house, and bury them by night, I offered thy prayer to the Lord. And because thou wast acceptable to God, it was necessary that temptation should prove thee. And now the Lord hath sent me to heal thee. . . I am the angel Raphael, one of the seven, who stand before the Lord. . . Bless ye God, and publish all his wonderful works" (Tobias 12. 11-15. 20).

It seemed as if the messenger of the Almighty had wished to praise the loftiest qualities that can grace a human being; charity, peace, repentance, industry, and an unbreakable fidelity to God and to men, the sure source of all well-being.

Feast of the Universal Protector of the Church

THE LIFE OF ST JOSEPH

When we reflect upon it we see that this is what St Joseph and his devoted followers have to do: to remain faithful to the Lord Jesus, and never to lose heart when confronted with the apparent success of the enemy of all good, or when they see the sudden eclipse of so many men who also are the objects of divine love—the eclipse, we mean, of right judgment, of good conscience, of generous activity. . .

Temptations are strong, and dangers grave. So it was yesterday, so it is today, and so it will always be. Lust is threefold: the lust for money, for this, above all, wields a terrible power over men; the lust to dominate others, which is irrepressible, and the lust for the pleasures of this life which make us weak and tolerant of evil.

It is no use just talking about it. Whoever wishes to save himself, find shelter in his Father's house, and preserve the precious gifts of nature and grace which God has bestowed upon him, has only to model his soul according to the eternal doctrine of the Gospel and the Church, thus following the beloved example of St Joseph's humble life.

To learn to obey, to learn to keep silence, to speak, when need arises, with moderation and courtesy—this is what St Joseph teaches us. Think of him—setting out at once for Bethlehem, in obedience to the divine command; seeking a lodging for Our Lady, guarding the stable. A week after the birth of Jesus he presided over the Hebrew rite that marked the newborn male children as belonging to the chosen race. And we see him receiving with due honour the Magi Kings, those splendid ambassadors from the East; then on the road to Egypt, and once more back home in Nazareth, always obeying in silence.

He was there to show Jesus to the world, and to hide him when need arose, to protect and nourish him, and then to follow him at a distance and remain in the shadows of the Lord's mysteries, shadows which were every now and then lit with a heavenly radiance by the light touch of a passing angel.

20 MARCH

THE LAW OF SACRIFICE

It is only natural that when we behave in a proper manner towards the Lord and towards our fellows we come up against hardships and sacrifices. The good Christian knows that without the cross and tribulations, without spiritual struggles, it is difficult to fight the enemy of light, who is indefatigable, astute and full of wiles. Unhappily, the law of sacrifice which is intimately and profoundly linked with the sufferings of Christ, is not well understood by frail humanity.

Nevertheless, life must be accepted as a duty to be performed, not as a pleasure to be procured and enjoyed.

It is around the tree of the Cross of Christ that the noblest and loftiest Christian witness must flourish; it is at the foot of his Cross that we must endeavour to work together with Christ for the triumph of justice and peace, which means the true well-being of society.

The holy religion which we profess is not a superficial exercise of gestures, rites and external observances, some of which may be superstitious; it is the knowledge and profound understanding of a divine and practical doctrine which illuminates the civilization of which we boast, illuminates and directs it. It is above all the affirmation of justice and charity understood and lived in every man's soul, and in the society in which he moves.

21 MARCH

ST BENEDICT

St Benedict of Norcia, the great patriarch of the monks of the West, taught the whole world not only the way to heaven but also the art of cultivating the land and making it fertile. I still remember with emotion what my father, in my native village, used to tell me and my little brothers, when I was still a child: "My children, you see these beautiful hills and the rich and fertile plains—it was the sons of St Benedict who came here first, from beyond the mountains, and it was they who taught our forefathers, a thousand years ago, to cultivate these plains and make them fertile.''

The centuries pass, but all that is good remains, to teach and encourage us. The world looks to the future with confidence. The mystery of this future lies largely, and today more than ever before, with the sons of the countryside, numerous, healthy, peace-loving and industrious.

Let us enter this great church together; let us seek in the light of the high God who has created heaven and earth, and in the presence of the mortal remains of St Benedict, the promises of this heavenly grace and of this rewarding toil which now, after the great tribulation, will be the joy of hearts and families, the inexhaustible source of prosperity for the whole world.

22 MARCH

THE SPIRIT OF SACRIFICE

Do you remember how at the beginning of his Passion, Our Lord, having loved his own, and wishing to cherish them to the end (cf. John 13. 1), gave them a proof of his immense love. Before he instituted the Eucharist and began his painful sufferings in the Garden of Gethsemane, he performed an act of extreme humility: kneeling down, he, the Son of God, and King of glory, washed the feet of his apostles. . .

Some days before this occurred, when he was on his way up to Jerusalem to begin the Passion, he had solemnly declared: "The Son of Man came not to be served, but to serve" (Matt. 20. 28). And what a service! . . . "to give his life as a ransom for many", to ransom us all, for we were all slaves of sin.

Of course it is not merely a question of the actual washing of feet, or of any other particular service, but above all a question of the spiritual energies which every Christian must spend for his neighbour, in a spirit of humility and love. . .

This service finds its ultimate motive in the supreme and universal obligation to serve God: for this we were created by the Father, redeemed by Jesus and sanctified by the Spirit. "My food", said Jesus, "is to do the will of him who sent me" (John 4. 34), and so he taught us how to say, in the Our Father: Thy will be done, on earth as it is in heaven.

If sometimes, in the Christian's life, the service of God is very arduous, what joy there is for us in the knowledge that most holy Mary has gone this way before us, Mary who with her prompt and generous "Behold, I am the handmaid of the Lord, let it be to me according to your word", gave us the Word Incarnate.

23 MARCH

THE WAR AGAINST SATAN

"Undoubtedly", Satan seems to murmur in our ear, "undoubtedly the Christian law is magnificent, a most powerful law, in fact divine—but does anyone obey it?" No man can give the answer.

St Augustine proclaims emphatically: "In the name of Jesus our Saviour, trample upon the lion and the dragon: the lion that quivers and roars with rage, the dragon that cleverly ensnares us with his flattery."

Everyone, in his own place and with perfect confidence in God, must obey the Gospel precepts: everyone, clergy, laity, parents, teachers, officers of the State. It is in Christ that every one of us must find his strength and his glory. The man who understands this bears Christ within himself and does the work of Christ when he cares for his fellow men.

The devil is to be feared above all, but unhappily there are men who through ignorance or perfidy or for self-interest labour in his service, hostile to Christ and to Holy Church.

The battle is waged against the wiles of these malicious creatures who wander about the world corrupting the incautious, the simple and humble. Ours is the fight "against the principalities, against the powers, against the world rulers of this present darkness", as St Paul in his own day pointed out, in his letter to the Ephesians (6. 12).

It is a bitter struggle and requires from us firmness of resolve, and weapons which are made not of iron but of persuasion, perseverance and apostolic self-sacrifice, and with these weapons we are sure of final victory—because this is the victory which overcomes the world. . . our faith.

FEAST OF ST GABRIEL THE ARCHANGEL

Today the Gospel reminds us of that great event which binds the Old Testament to the New, and so brings about the fulfilment of the centuries of history which preceded the coming of Christ, and of the centuries that have followed, down to our own. . .

One of the most glorious angelic spirits, Gabriel, announces the divine birth; heaven and earth meet in an ecstasy of love; the Son of God descends from on high and in the womb of a pure Virgin becomes the Son of Man.

A sign of consent from Mary, the humble maiden of Nazareth, and the mystery is accomplished. From the first cry of the infant Jesus in Bethlehem till his last gasp on Golgotha, the miracle is worked: the fountains of salvation are unsealed, the redemption of mankind is accomplished. . . peace is assured to men of good will. And with peace comes grace, every boon of heaven and earth; the gates are opened to that eternity of bliss so ardently desired by every living soul here below.

This is the poem of Christianity, the poem of the redemption of mankind. . . But the first notes of this divine music were brought from heaven by the Archangel Gabriel, who sang them when he greeted Mary: Hail Mary, full of grace—words which were to be the fairest and sweetest greeting ever repeated by Christian generations. In fact, they contain the whole mystery of the glory of the Mother of Jesus who became, as her dying Son declared, our own blessed Mother too.

25 MARCH

Feast of the Annunciation

THE WORD MADE FLESH

The great historical event of the Incarnation, which opens the New Testament and is the starting-point of Christian history, well deserves to be celebrated by the pealing of bells throughout the whole world, three times every day; and it is very natural that churches and chapels . . . should be consecrated to the memory of the first Joyful Mystery, which has become for us a fountain of meditation and good resolutions.

In fact we are all pilgrims on this earth, and the prayer on our lips, in spite of its many and varied versions, is common to us all; we are all going home! This is the goal of our daily march, the longing of our hearts. The heavens open above us and the divine messenger reminds us of the miracle by which God became man, and man the brother of God's Son.

The mystery of the Incarnation sanctifies the thirty years Jesus spent with Mary and Joseph in the seclusion of Nazareth.

And just as the Incarnation provides the new starting-point for man's pilgrimage to his heavenly fatherland, and to his elevation to the dignity of a co-heir of heaven, so from every hidden life there rises the canticle praising the dignity and greatness of the human family, and the sacredness of duty, and its nobility.

26 MARCH

THE MYSTICAL BODY

From the contemplation of the physical and social body our thoughts now rise to the Mystical Body, the Church of Jesus Christ. It is the duty of every one of us to be a living and working member of this Body, united to the Supreme Head who is Christ, in whom "speaking the truth in love, we are to grow up in every way" (Eph. 4. 15).

So we are not strangers to one another, and certainly we are not hostile, as unhappily an erroneous doctrine would have us believe, a doctrine which seeks to sow an unjust hatred between class and class. Instead, every one of us, in the place assigned to him by God, is called to help and serve his fellows with charity, patience and gentleness, following the example of our Saviour Jesus, the Lamb sacrificed for our salvation. This thought of the precious union of all in mutual collaboration gives us now the motive for our fatherly appeal for charity, which alone can inspire your labours, soften the inevitable sorrows of life, and make them a means of attaining eternal life.

We beg you to be faithful to the Lord's law, and to be constantly obedient to his holy will, in your family duties and in your work, for your work also is a precious brotherly service in the love of God.

And finally we beg you always to be apostles of goodness, cheerfulness and good will, in your own house and with your companions at work, in the grace and joy of the Risen Christ.

27 MARCH

PARABLE OF THE UNFRUITFUL TREE

This is the parable of the fig tree, recorded by St Luke, in the 13th Chapter of his Gospel: "A man had a fig tree planted in his vineyard; and he came seeking fruit on it. . ."

The end of the parable is sad: the lord of the vineyard wanted to cut the tree down, but his vine-dresser begged him to give it one more chance, one more season. . .

The Gospel story, in its stark simplicity, is rich in wisdom and in counsel for us all.

In family life the mother is asked to be patient with her children and to study their characters closely in order to succeed in training them in the right way. In the same way, the Lord is patient with us and studies our souls, seeking to win us with long-suffering and mercy. If, in spite of all this, we obstinately resolve to go against the will of Providence, we become like unfruitful trees, whose fate is sealed.

This lesson is followed by another in the same Gospel: the story of the infirm woman who begs the Lord for mercy.

Life has its seasons which follow one another and pass on beyond recall. In youth we are strong and impetuous; in later life the years lay their burdens upon us. These are the difficulties of life, which teach us a great lesson: the Lord wants us to understand that, in spite of bodily infirmities and frailties, the spirit must remain lively and alert in order to be found worthy of eternal life.

28 MARCH

OUR FATHER

The prayer "Our Father", which Jesus taught us to say, sums up the whole Gospel. In the first invocation we pray to our Father in heaven: amid the conflicting judgments and prejudices, the uncertainties and sorrows of men, the reactions of individuals and peoples, we turn to the supreme Giver of all strength and all light. We pray first of all that God's holy name may be respected, blessed and honoured. Unhappily, there are many Christians who dishonour their baptism by using certain expressions of impatience and anger! . . .

Then we pray that our Lord's kingdom may come. It is a reign of peace, not of violence or tyranny. It is not a revolt against the fundamental laws of the human spirit; it is a reign of love, forgiveness and justice, a justice loftier than that of this world, because our own justice has recourse to armed power, when this seems necessary in self-defence. The kingdom of God has no use for arms and their terrifying power.

We come to the third petition: that God's will may be done in us all, while every one of us co-operates in God's work with all his strength, and with a keen sense of personal responsibility.

When we do this the Lord never fails to come to our help; he arouses us from dangerous torpor and strengthens us so that we may never wish to impose our will on others, but may always work for the final triumph of brotherhood and peace.

Therefore the duty of every Christian is to "seek first of all the kingdom of God" (Matt. 6. 33).

Everything else will be given to us in superabundance in a life that is honoured, civilized, tranquil and law abiding. Those who are unfamiliar with the Gospel find the truth hard to admit; indeed, they laugh it to scorn, and pity the faithful Christian. We must disillusion them and show them that the highest dignity and the richest and truest rewards are won by fidelity to the teaching of the Gospel.

29 MARCH

DISCRETION IN SOCIAL RELATIONS

Charity! This is the Lord's will, the Lord's commandment, as St John the Evangelist, the apostle of love, has taught us.

This charity gently impels you to be united among yourselves, in faith and works, in convictions and ideals, in your work and in your apostolate.

Be united; help faithful and convinced Catholics to remain united among themselves, to have faith in the social teaching of the Church and in her legislation, the carefully sifted grain of centuries of experience, which they must know and fully understand. Help them to be more and more imbued with the Christian way of thinking, judging and deciding, to resist all temptation towards singularity, resentment, or self-interest, and not to let themselves be deceived by the mirage of a misunderstood liberty which becomes intolerant of all order and discipline.

. . . The respect we owe to whoever has not yet reached complete Christian and Catholic maturity, and remains on the threshold of the temple, does not authorize us to make compromising and dangerous concessions, or renunciations which betray our sacred heritage of truth and justice: the Gospel.

The gravest danger, and one to which some of our children are exposed, is truly this: the danger of impatient revolt against a common discipline, an impatience which degenerates into tolerance or indifference when confronted with the errors and dangerous attitudes encountered in the various spheres of public life today, in politics as well as in the world of entertainment, in literature as well as in the practice of religion.

30 MARCH

RESPECT FOR HUMAN LIFE

Living means moving about, meeting one another; it means courageously partaking in the joyful and good things of this life.

But unhappily these meetings with one another do not always end in tranquillity or happiness; not all encounters are pleasant ones: frequently they are terrible and fatal.

It is true that never before have men enjoyed such perfection of swift and effective means of travelling along the ways of the ground, the sea and the sky. But it is also painfully true that frequently the traveller's tale ends in a tragedy of death and mourning,

. . . The inventions of science and technical skill therefore confront mankind with an unexpected problem, to add to the great and tremendous problem of the restlessness of human beings in our own day, a problem which seems difficult to solve and full of menace.

The guardian of the heavenly doctrine, taught by Christ to men, rejoices at every advance in science and technical skill. But at the same time he is neither surprised nor dismayed by the phosphorescent display of power which conceals a menace and a disillusion. The sense of his responsibility leads him to assert and proclaim aloud that the duties of our life become more onerous and binding in proportion to man's increasing capacity and power to do and to dare.

What our blessed Jesus preached was a doctrine for the whole of life, in its integrity, inspired by the noblest and most precious conception of the value of human life.

31 MARCH

THE HIDDEN LIFE OF ST JOSEPH

The gentle and lovable figure of St Joseph, the divinely chosen husband of Mary, is particularly dear to the hearts of all who are most sensitive to the appeal of Christian asceticism, and to its characteristic expression in religious piety, modest and reserved in tone, but because of this all the more attractive and delightful.

In the life of Holy Church Jesus, the Word of God made Man, immediately became the unique object of supreme worship, because he was the splendour of the substance of the Father, which was reflected in the glory of the saints. Mary his Mother has after him been the most revered, ever since the early centuries of our era, when we see her treated with the greatest reverence in the imagery of the catacombs and basilicas, as Holy Mary, Mother of God. Joseph, on the other hand, apart from a few scattered references to him in the writings of the Fathers, remained for many centuries in characteristic silence and seclusion, as if he were but an ornamental figure in the picture of our Saviour's life. It was a long time before the figure of St Joseph became familiar not only to the eyes but to the hearts of the faithful, and was honoured with a special outpouring of prayer and trustful love. These were the fervent joys reserved for the piety of our own times, and how widely spread and how impressive is the modern devotion to St Joseph!

APRIL

1 APRIL

In April falls Easter, and frequently also Holy Thursday, the day when we commemorate the institution of the Eucharist. Let us in the words of Pope John dedicate this month to the Eucharist.

THE SACRAMENT OF THE ALTAR

The Sacrament of the Altar is, in the very act of consecration, called the "Mystery of Faith", that is, the living substance of the whole Catholic creed. From it, in fact, shines out the Sun of Justice, Jesus, the only Mediator between God and men, the victim here offered in a bloodless rite for the reconciliation of heaven and earth. It contains the everlasting memorial of his immolation on Calvary for our salvation. In it he is present as Head of the Mystical Body, and source of the sacraments which give fertility and beauty to the spiritual garden of the Church.

Foreseeing the triumph which would be his, through the ignominy of the Cross, Jesus said one day: "I, when I am lifted up from the earth, will draw all men to myself" (John 12. 32). These words may fittingly be used of the Eucharistic Bread, because of the wealth of heavenly treasures which it contains. For indeed the Sacrament of the Altar too has a mysterious power of attraction.

The twenty centuries of progress . . .have in no way diminished the significance of Christ's words: "Truly, truly, I say to you, unless you eat the flesh of the Son of man and drink his blood, you have no life in you. . . This is the bread which came down from heaven . . . he who eats this bread will live for ever" (John 6. 54, 58).

So, overcoming by the power of our faith and the
fervour of our acclamations the confused outcry of our
enemies, who will always be with us, and considering
the countless hosts of martyrs and saints who drew from
the Eucharist the secret and strength of their greatness,
let us all pray to Jesus: "Lord, give us this bread always",
for you are indeed the "bread of life" (John 6. 34, 35).

2 APRIL

OUR DAILY BREAD

We wish to emphasize the threefold quality of that
"daily bread" for which the children of the Church must
pray, and which they must expect, with longing and with
confidence, from our heavenly Father's provident hand.

First of all, it must be "our" bread, that is, requested
in the name of all of us. "The Lord", St John Chrysostom tells us, "has in the Our Father taught us to pray
to God for our brothers too. He wants us to address to
God prayers which concern not only our own interests
but those of our neighbours also. In this way he wishes
to put an end to divisions among us, and to repress greed"
(*In Matth.*, c. VI, *Homil.* XIX, PG 57, 278).

It must, moreover, be a "substantial" bread, which
means food necessary for our nourishment. And, since
man is made up of body and immortal soul, the bread
we are to beg from God must be not only our "temporal"
bread but, as St Thomas, the Master of the Eucharistic
Doctrine, wisely observes, above all the "spiritual"
bread, that is, God himself, truth to contemplate and
goodness to love—and we must also receive the "sacramental" Bread, the Body of our Saviour, pledge and
foretaste of eternal life (cf. *Comm. in Matth.*, c. VI).

The third and last characteristic of our daily bread is
no less important: it must be "one" bread, that is, the
symbol and source of unity. St John Chrysostom continues: "In fact, as that body is united to Christ, so we
also are joined together by this Bread" (*In Epist. I ad
Cor. Homil.* XXIV, 2; PG 61, 200).

3 APRIL

DEVOTION TO THE EUCHARIST

True devotion to the Eucharist teaches us to be loyal,

upright and obedient to the moral law, even at the cost of personal sacrifice for the common good.

Indeed we do not hesitate to assert that rulers and peoples are doomed to remain at the mercy of natural egoisms and divisions, if they do not make their laws conform to those principles of justice and Christian love of which the Sacrament of the Altar is the true and inexhaustible source. So we must not see in the Eucharist only the reward of the faithful communicant, but, in the words of the Angelic Doctor, "the common spiritual good of the whole Church, for the whole Church is substantially present there" (*Sum. Theol.* 3, q. 65, a. 3, *ad* 1).

O living Bread, that came down from heaven to give life to the world! O loving shepherd of our souls, from your throne of glory whence, a "hidden God", you pour out your grace on families and peoples. . . we commend to you particularly the sick, the unhappy, the poor and all who beg for food and employment, imploring for all and every one the assistance of your providence; we commend to you the families, so that they may be fruitful centres of Christian life . . . May the abundance of your grace be poured out over all.

4 APRIL

THE HOLY MASS

The Mass is the adorable sacrifice in which the Son of God himself is at the same time victim, priest, and the divine majesty to whom the sacrifice is offered: the same sacrifice of the Cross for ever mysteriously re-enacted without the shedding of blood. This is the immolation of the Just Man—remotely prefigured in Abel—who comes to absorb into himself the sacrifices of all persecuted souls, especially of those who suffer as a result of their endeavours to do the Lord's own work.

What treasures there are in the Holy Mass! But how often it is neglected or ignored! Many who pass by seem unaware of this wonderful source of light, grace and holiness. And yet it is the Mass which most closely binds man to his Lord, to the One who created and redeemed him.

However, thanks be to God, there are many who can still appreciate the infinite treasures of the Eucharist. At the foot of the altar the humble and the great of this world still gather in their crowds. Souls are as it were captivated by this sacrament of perfect unity with their Saviour, which bestows such infinite graces. Holy communion gives us a resolution and a courage which no human assistance or skill can offer. It provides us with those exceptional powers which we need to do our duties, to preserve patience and to continue the struggle against evil, not in warfare, to be sure, but in a constant effort of resistance, spreading abroad the spirit of holiness and extending the social apostolate.

5 APRIL

THE TABERNACLE

Jesus is there, the prisoner of love. Whether the tabernacle be poor or precious, Jesus is always there. The good parishioner of Ars who was surprised by his saintly Curé as he stood gazing silently at the dwelling place of Jesus, his lips not even moving in prayer, replied very simply: "I look at him, and I think he looks at me; and this feeds my soul, gives me strength". So there may be prayer, or even contemplation, in the mere gaze of the eyes.

And we must never forget the visits to the Blessed Sacrament. Modern forms of piety, even when most devout, seem to have less time to spare for this act of homage to Jesus, this keeping him company for a while. Even pious souls are sometimes heard to say: "We live so intensely that we have no time to linger talking with the Lord".

How our soul rejoices when we return to the fervent invocations of St Alphonsus de' Liguori, uttered on his visits to the Blessed Sacrament! The horizons seem to lift around us. About these conversations between God and the soul there exists a whole literature, abundant, modern, attractive and enjoyable. Let us turn to it for our consolation, for the hidden delight of days that sometimes seem lukewarm in fervour and full of uncertainties.

6 APRIL

GOD WITH US

This is the great reality of Christian history: Jesus, the sacred host, the Bread of life, in the midst of his Church.

This is that brightest star which enables us to look forward with great confidence to the future kingdom of Christ. And as we bless and adore Jesus in the most holy Eucharist we wish to raise our hearts in trustful prayer to Mary, his sweet Mother, and our Mother too.

So let us turn to her as our own dear Mother. It is she who bore and presented to the world Jesus, our Redeemer and Saviour. It is she who leads innocent souls, and penitent souls, to Jesus. It was at her request at the wedding in Cana that our Saviour worked his first great miracle, to the joy and delight of all believers.

In her sanctuary of Lourdes, and in so many other sanctuaries all over the world, she continues her motherly and pious task of leading to her Divine Son's arms all who pray to her, for the safety, peace and joy of the holy Universal Church. Is this not the literal accomplishment of our fervent resolve: "to Jesus through Mary"?

Let us then understand one another, beloved children, as we worship Jesus in the holy Eucharist: God with us! God with us!

The Sacrament of Jesus remains with us as our divine inheritance, for our salvation and for the joy of the Catholic and Apostolic Church.

When we pray before the Blessed Sacrament may the Mother of Jesus, who is our Mother too, continually be remembered, as our intercessor and protectress, the joy and gladness of our hearts. Amen.

7 APRIL

THE CHALICE

The most mysterious and sacred part of the Eucharistic liturgy revolves around the chalice which holds the precious Blood of Jesus. He is our Saviour, and we share, mystically, in his Body, Holy Church.

Christian life is sacrifice. Through self-sacrifice inspired by love we share in that which was the final purpose of the earthly life of Jesus, who became our Brother, sacrificed himself and died for us, in order to ensure for us through this human life our joy and glory in eternity.

The chalice upon the altar, and the venerable rites which link the bread and wine together, consecrated in a single sacrament, mark the climax, the sublimity of the union between God and man, and the perfection of the Christian faith.

It is from the altar, from this sacred height, that we must consider earthly things, judge them and make use of them.

Even the gravest questions, which sometimes tear human society asunder, must find here the principles for a just solution.

Honourably to profess the holy religion in which we have been reared means above all loving God, and to love God is to love justice.

St Leo the Great spoke of this far back in the fifth century when he urged Christians to recognize the greatness of their dignity: "Acknowledge, O Christian soul, the dignity of your wisdom, and think to what rewards you are called, by the help of these doctrines" (*Sermo XLV*, cap. 7).

The practice of goodness which springs from a Christian's familiarity with Holy Communion makes the image of his Creator shine in him so brightly that he succeeds in expressing in his own countenance the characteristic look of Jesus.

8 APRIL

SACRAMENT OF LOVE

When the Christians of the first centuries met around the Table of the Eucharist they prayed with hearts full of love and longing: "To you, O Lord, be glory for ever! As this bread we have broken together was once scattered in ears of corn on the hills, and became one when it was harvested, so let your Church be gathered from the ends of the earth into your kingdom. For yours is the glory, and the power, through Jesus Christ, for ever."

The doctrine of the Mystical Body has cast gleams of shining light on this question of the union of Christians with Christ, and for their union with each other. It has resulted in an amazing understanding of the union of the masses of the faithful, through the power of the Body and Blood of Christ, drawn together to scale the heights of Christian perfection.

In the light of this teaching we find the truest conception of human, Christian and Catholic brotherhood, inspired and renewed by the holy Eucharist.

O Sacrament of love: may you always remain inviolate at the summit of Catholic doctrine and devotion! Open our minds to soaring flights of thought, and our hearts to the impulses of charity. Lead us on to the fulfilment of the supreme ideals of justice and social peace. Amen. Amen.

9 APRIL

PRAYER TO JESUS IN THE BLESSED SACRAMENT

O Jesus, divine Food of the soul, this immense concourse turns to you. It wishes to give to its human and Christian vocation a new, vigorous power of interior virtue, and to be ready for sacrifice, of which you were such a wonderful pattern in word and in example.

You are our elder Brother; you have trodden our path before us, O Christ Jesus, the path of every one of us; you have forgiven all our sins; you inspire us each and all to give a nobler, more convinced and more active example of Christian life.

O Jesus, our true Bread, and the only substantial Food for our souls, gather all the peoples around your table. Your altar is divine reality on earth, the pledge of heavenly favour, the assurance of a just understanding among peoples, and of peaceful rivalry in the true progress of civilization.

Nourished by you and with you, O Jesus, men will be strong in faith, joyful in hope, and active in the many varied expressions of charity.

Our wills will know how to overcome the snares of evil, the temptations of selfishness, the listlessness of sloth. And the eyes of men who love and fear the Lord will behold the vision of the land of the living, of which the wayfaring Church militant is the image, enabling the whole earth to hear the first sweet and mysterious voices of the City of God.

O Jesus, feed us and guard us, and grant that we may see the good things in the land of the living! Amen.

10 APRIL

PRAYER IN HONOUR OF THE EUCHARISTIC KING

O Jesus, King of all peoples and all ages, accept the acts

of adoration and praise which we, your brothers by adoption, humbly offer you.

You are the "living Bread which comes down from heaven and gives life to the world" (John 6. 33), Supreme Priest and Victim. On the Cross you offered yourself to the Eternal Father as a bloody sacrifice of expiation, for the redemption of the human race, and now you offer yourself daily upon our altars by the hands of your ministers, in order to establish in every heart your "reign of truth and life, of holiness and grace, of justice, love and peace" (Preface of the Mass of Christ the King).

O King of glory, may your kingdom come! Reign from your "throne of grace" (Hebrews 4. 14), in the hearts of children, so that they may guard untainted the white lily of baptismal innocence. Reign in the hearts of the young, that they may grow up healthy and pure, obedient to the commands of those who represent you in their families and schools and in the Church. Reign in our homes, so that parents and children may live in peace in obedience to your holy law. Reign in our land, so that all citizens, in the harmonious order of the various social groups, may feel themselves children of the same heavenly Father, called to co-operate for the common good of this world, happy to belong to the one Mystical Body, of which your Sacrament is at once the symbol and the everlasting source.

Finally, reign, O King of kings and "Lord of lords", (Deut. 10. 17) over all the nations of the earth, and enlighten all their rulers in order that, inspired by your example, they may make "plans for welfare and not for evil" (Jer. 29. 11).

O Jesus, present in the Sacrament of the Altar, teach all the nations to serve you with willing hearts, knowing that "to serve God is to reign". May your Sacrament, O Jesus, be light to the mind, strength to the will, joy to the heart. May it be the support of the weak, the comfort of the suffering, the wayfaring bread of salvation for the dying, and for all the "pledge of future glory". Amen.

11 APRIL

Feast of Pope St Leo I

"THE MYSTERIOUS POETRY OF LIFE"

We know well that even the purest joys are never without thorns: in fact, everyone has his own cross to bear. This truth is well expressed by Pope St Leo the Great: "The Church too has her thorns and her crosses, as Jesus, of whom she is the Mystical Body, had his."

Whoever believes he has found happiness in dedicating himself solely to the pleasurable but fleeting things of this world, without reflecting on all the other things which are essential and eternal, is playing a game that can last but a little time.

The Pope too has his crosses, his great cross, certainly not an enviable one. Since Divine Providence decreed what is now known to all, His Holiness has often thought of people whom he loved and revered in the past, and who now perhaps look down on him with pity and sympathy for the very heavy burden which the Lord had placed upon him.

But, when we reflect upon it, this is the mysterious poetry of life, and gives us the opportunity to welcome our various situations and duties and inevitable trials with a smile of supernatural understanding and serenity.

12 APRIL

THE EUCHARIST AND THE CHURCH

The Holy Eucharist is at the heart of Catholic theology and liturgy: its light streams out in every direction, its grace touches all hearts. Whereas the other Sacraments have an immediate effect on the individual, the Holy Eucharist, while it too works in the intimacy of every man's soul, at the same time permeates the whole social body of the Church and the world. One may say even more: its divine institution is pre-ordained to express and to inspire the whole mass of believers in Christ.

Read the sixth chapter of St John: the announcement, the doctrine, the exaltation of the Sacrament. Compare this passage with his first chapter, the so-called Prologue to his Gospel: "In the beginning was the Word. . ." and you will find in a few words, whole and entire, the three-fold poem of the Incarnation, the Redemption and the Blessed Sacrament.

"Conceived by the Holy Ghost, born of the Virgin Mary"—and for what purpose? "For us men and for our salvation." It is understandable that at the sound of these words the throng of faithful should kneel in adoration of the most sacred and venerable of all mysteries: the divine united with the human, the human in Jesus and through Jesus united with the divine: the Son of God and Son of Mary becoming the first of the brethren that make up the new family of which he is Head: the new family of believers, the new covenant, the Holy Catholic and Apostolic Church to which we belong.

13 APRIL

THE IMMENSITY OF DIVINE LOVE

Man is saved and forgiven, the world is redeemed.

This redemptive incarnation and this sacrifice once offered were not enough to celebrate for ever more the reconciliation between God and his new children, and the reconciliation of men among themselves in a community as vast as the world itself, tranquil, industrious and reassured of its supreme destinies.

Certainly it would have sufficed—but for the immensity of divine love it was not enough. The Redemption was to remain always with us, for the salvation of all peoples, who were to form one single people, the Church, the Church of the Apostles, the Church of centuries of evangelical witness, the Church, even in the midst of opposition, persecution and blood, always engaged in furthering and extending her conquests—a Church Militant until the end of time. And in the Church Militant of yesterday, today and tomorrow, as in the Church of the first Apostles, Jesus was to be present, the living Jesus, in soul and body, as he was in Bethlehem, and Nazareth, in Palestine and on Golgotna—always the same Jesus, the Divine Word, the Son of Mary in the act of giving himself as a sacrifice for every man, and for the whole human family.

It is from this primary truth that there emerges in splendour the theological doctrine of the Blessed Sacrament, the perpetual miracle of divine wisdom and infinite love.

14 APRIL

In 1920 the priest Don Angelo Giuseppe Roncalli gave an address to the National Eucharistic Congress of Bergamo, where he was then a professor in the Seminary. The three extracts which follow illustrate his thoughts on the theme of "The Eucharist and Our Lady".

ORGANIZATION IS NOT ALL

Allow me to speak about what I know, gentlemen. Let me speak of my own Bergamo, which is giving you such a festive welcome, and of the people to whose faith and piety you are pleased to render homage. Meanwhile, they are preparing for you—I can already assure you of this—a spectacle of such magnificence that it will remain unforgettably in your memory.

Generally speaking, those who judge us from a distance assert that in this region religion has been kept alive and active by the power of the social economic organizations.

I know I shall offend no one when I hasten to say that the truth is exactly the opposite. Whereas nearly everywhere else in Italy the organizations have been and remain a means of leading back the misled working classes to Christ, through successful plans for material welfare, in Bergamo instead the vast and powerful organization was, and still is, but a spontaneous expression of the religious piety of the masses, an integral application of Christian principles to the various relations of public life.

Bergamo is supreme among all the dioceses of Italy for the unconquerable faith of her children and for the universal fervour of their piety which, in devotion to the Blessed Sacrament and to Our Lady, finds here more than anywhere else its loftiest and most wonderful expression.

What is being done now began, not yesterday but centuries ago.

15 APRIL

The reader will remember that Pope John was a military chaplain during the First World War.

''NO ONE IS AN ATHEIST IN THE TRENCHES''

The war has barely ended and our eyes are still haunted by its terrible and bloody sights. It seemed as if it might destroy even the last surviving fragments of the faith and piety of our forefathers. Blessed be the Lord! this did not come to pass. War has always been, and still is, a very grave evil; and whoever is familiar with the mind of Christ and his Gospel, and has the spirit of human and Christian brotherhood, can never sufficiently detest it. Yet, in the midst of the squalor and suffering seen and experienced by so many of us, we have the right to linger over the more consoling aspects which have lightened our pessimism.

Oh! the long nights spent watching by the pallets of our beloved and valiant soldiers, to hear their confessions and prepare them to receive, at dawn, the Bread of the strong! Oh! the beautiful hymns to Mary sung before the roughly improvised altars!

How often have we bent down to hear, in the last gasps of our young brothers, the anguished breathing of our motherland in her suffering and agony! It is impossible to describe what the heart of a priest feels in those moments. Frequently . . . I had to fall on my knees and cry like a child, alone in my room—no longer able to control the emotion aroused by the sight of the simple and holy death of so many poor sons of our own people. . . They died with the Sacrament of Jesus on their heart and the name of Mary on their lips—without cursing their hard fate, content to offer their youth in sacrifice to God for their brothers.

16 APRIL

THE EUCHARIST AND OUR LADY

The economic situation is the terrible problem of this turbulent age of ours: the question of food and of the elementary comforts of life is full of a painful uncertainty which distresses us; we hear the clamour of the crowds, unsatisfied and sometimes, alas! insatiable.

It is the sacred duty of every one of us to contribute, at the cost of renunciation and sacrifices, to a just solution that shall conform to the supreme requirements of Catholic doctrine, and be founded upon the Gospel and the instructions of the Church, which are so clear and authoritative.

But we shall labour in vain to fill stomachs with material bread, and satisfy immoderate greed, if we do not succeed in feeding souls with the Bread of life, true, substantial, divine; we must feed them on Christ, for whom they hunger, and through whom alone we can continue our ascent to the Lord's mountain. We shall strive in vain to procure from economic science and from new legislation the means of social assistance and co-operation, if we turn the eyes of our people away from the kind and motherly smile of Mary, who opens wide her arms to gather all her children into one family, in which angry hearts are soothed by the holy touch of love and Christian peace.

Ah! let us all do our best, so that no one may ever remove or tear away from the hearts of the people what God in Catholic doctrine and in the history of our land has so wonderfully joined together: the Eucharist and Our Lady.

17 APRIL

THE EUCHARISTIC BREAD

The thought that "we are all one in Christ" is for us a motive of joy and hope. Indeed, what means is more effective, valid and sure for gathering all the faithful closely around Christ, the Head of the Mystical Body, than the exaltation of the Sacrament of the Holy Eucharist? The Word of God, who with the Father and the Holy Spirit feeds the angels in heaven, feeds men on earth in a mysterious manner under the sacramental species of bread and wine, but not in the same way as the common food which we take every day; the Bread of eternal life feeds us in just the opposite way, miraculously:

"I am the food of grown men; grow to manhood and you shall feed on me. You will not change me into yourself as you do with your body's food; on the contrary, you will be changed into me" (St Augustine, *Confessions* VII, 10).

The Church, offering herself united with Christ, Priest and Victim, to God the Father in the Eucharistic Sacrifice, is also paying her eternal tribute of adoration and praise, which is of infinite value; and the faithful, on their part, receive through the Eucharistic Sacrifice the power of the virtues, radiant with glorious light in the divine Saviour who is full of grace and truth, "and from his fullness have we all received" (John 1. 16). And all who are familiar with these heavenly mysteries shine with faith, hope, mercy, justice, peace, innocence, modesty, honesty of life, and the love of heavenly things, above all of charity, the peak and perfection of virtue.

18 APRIL

THE ADORABLE SACRIFICE

The Mass is the adorable sacrifice in which God himself is at the same time Victim, Priest and the divine Majesty to whom the sacrifice is offered; not merely the symbol of the sacrifice of the Cross but the sacrifice itself, mysteriously renewed and re-enacted for ever, without the shedding of blood.

It is an infinite sacrifice, the efficacy of which is restricted only by our own lack of fervour and devotion.

All light in this world streams from the Sacrifice of the Mass. There is no alleviation of the pains of Purgatory that is not distilled like balm from the overflowing chalice of the Eucharist; there is no increase of heavenly glory but through this Sacrifice. Moreover, and this is a much graver thing: no newcomer can enter heaven except through the Sacrifice ever present in the Mass.

It is impossible to find or imagine a closer bond between Man and God.

19 APRIL

HOLY COMMUNION

Think of this: "The bread of God is that which comes down from heaven, and gives life to the world" (John 6. 33). And when his disciples begged him always to give them this bread Jesus added: "I am the bread of life, he who comes to me shall not hunger, and he who believes in me shall never thirst. . ." And he chided them for murmuring among themselves because he had told them that he was the bread which came down from heaven.

He repeated this claim more than once, and turned it into a command, adding a grim warning: "Unless you eat the flesh of the Son of Man and drink his blood, you have no life in you; he who eats my flesh and drinks my blood abides in me, and I in him. . ."

Holy Communion is the grandest and most perfect form of worship that any creature on this earth can offer to his Creator. Communion is meant to do for men in the spiritual world what food does for them in the material world, and we can easily understand how such spiritual food can act with divine power, inspiring countless manifestations of holiness throughout the whole human family.

It is a terrifying thing to have to admit with the "Eagle of Meaux", Monseigneur Bénigne Bossuet, that no Christian can be perfect without Communion.

Holy Communion has a greater splendour than any human glory, or greatness, or dignity.

20 APRIL

BENEDICTION OF THE BLESSED SACRAMENT

This may be called the evening sacrifice, because Benediction is generally in the evening, while the Holy Mass, at least according to the custom which prevailed until a short time ago, was always celebrated in the morning hours.

St Philip Neri, in an ecstasy during Benediction, saw in the Sacred Host a crowd of kneeling people and Jesus blessing them, as if this were his usual habit, the customary expression of his kindness shown in the Blessed Sacrament.

Oh what graces Jesus, ever present with us, showers upon us during Benediction! From my earliest childhood I was taught to make the sign of the cross three times when the priest blessed us with the holy monstrance.

In fact, in the Gospel Jesus is seen three times in the act of blessing. He blessed the children; he blessed the bread and the cup at the Last Supper; he blessed his disciples when he was about to leave them and ascend to heaven, as a pledge of the great blessing they would receive at the Last Judgment.

The eucharistic blessing shows us how close Jesus is to us in our humble lives. "God with us." His blessing falls upon our troubles and afflictions, our anxieties and temptations, our failings and weaknesses, which in that moment we do not try to hide from him, and also upon all the frailties of our spirit, upon circumstances the dangers of which are not yet apparent to us; upon the evil spirits who try to scare and bewilder us; and upon our beloved and faithful Guardian Angels, as if to reward them for their loving care.

THE LORD'S TRUTH ENDURES FOR EVER

We must meditate upon the truth and honour it, tell the truth and act according to the truth; when we assert these elementary needs of human and Christian life a sigh rises from our hearts to our lips: where in this world do we find respect for truth? Are we not sometimes, and indeed too often, confronted with an insolent and impious anti-Decalogue, which abolishes the words "Thou shalt *not*", that introduce every one of the five clear commandments following immediately after the "Honour thy father and thy mother"? Is not the life passing before our eyes today in effect a deliberate exercise in contradiction: the fifth, kill; the sixth, fornicate; the seventh, steal; the eighth, bear false witness—as if inspired by a devilish conspiracy against the truth?

And yet the divine commandment which Moses heard on the mountain is still clear and authoritative: "Thou shalt not bear false witness against thy neighbour" (Ex. 20. 16; Deut. 5. 20). . .

We are living between two different conceptions of human society, on the one hand the reality of this world discovered, studied and practised as it exists in the mind of God; on the other hand—we are not afraid to repeat— the falsification of this same reality, facilitated by scientific techniques and by the skill of modern and contemporary man.

Faced with the fourfold ideal of meditating, honouring, speaking the truth and acting according to the truth, and the daily spectacle of the betrayal, open or covert, of this ideal, our heart overflows with anguish and our voice trembles.

In spite of all this the Lord's truth, "the faithfulness of the Lord", endures for ever (Ps. 116 (117). 2), and will shine ever more brightly before men's eyes and be heard speaking in their hearts.

22 APRIL

THE LESSON OF EASTER

The lesson of Easter and all its spiritual treasures will be a powerful stimulus to us, in the resolute effort that we must all make to climb more energetically up to those noble heights to which the voice of conscience and the good inspirations that come from the Lord are calling us. And they will also set us on our guard, for we must all be prudent—against human falsehood, contagious frailties, and individual and collective disobedience against the sacred laws of life.

The Lord's Easter. Repetition does not invalidate it. The words of Jesus by the half-shut tomb of his friend: "I am the resurrection and the life", had the same meaning at Bethany as they do now when they are gently murmured in the conscience of all sincere Christians, even when they are harassed by temptation. And they become the happy inspiration for a re-found and most joyful interior peace, and for true nobility of soul.

Oh! what liberation and blessing in the words which Holy Church reserves at Easter for her children, who still recall the innocent joys of their happiest years: "I absolve you from your sins, sin no more".

And there are those other words referring to the sublime mystery of the great Christian Sacrament: "The peace and communion of the Body and Blood of Christ". The Holy Eucharistic Communion raises every soul at all times towards the heights of that spiritual life which is inspired and nourished by Christ.

23 APRIL

CHRISTIAN FORGIVENESS

The first word after Holy Week is one of particular significance: forgiveness. Christ, triumphing from his Cross and from his glorious sepulchre which bore witness to his resurrection, is forgiveness granted to all mankind.

To everyone we may say: My child, you have sinned, you have acknowledged that you have sinned against the Lord, against your family and your duties and responsibilities; you have repented of your wrong-doing and you have paid homage to Jesus Christ the Son of God, who became man in order to obtain forgiveness for all men.

What joy to be forgiven! What joy to come away from the conversation with our father confessor, to whom we presented ourselves humbly and trustfully, and to have heard him say: "Go, my child, take heart, go on your way with a good will. I absolve you from your sins.

Christ is before you, Christ who died for you; go and receive the precious drops of his Blood in the Sacrament of his love, and then, in your private life as in your social, professional and domestic activity, wherever you go and whoever you are with, do honour to our Lord Jesus Christ, who has brought down pardon to this earth.''

Forgiveness is a great joy, a great treasure; the man who has humbled himself to obtain it has understood that he must become a better man, that he must set a good example, sanctifying himself and all around him.

The Pope wishes to remind you of your own duty: to forgive others, and to have compassion on them. From earliest childhood and in youth all must learn to obey this law of forgiveness, this great rule which the Lord brought to us here below.

24 APRIL

THE SIGNS OF THE RESURRECTION

My beloved brothers and children, think of what Christ said in the Gospel to the man he had healed: "See, you are well! Sin no more, that nothing worse befall you" (John 5. 14).

The warning that accompanies the command is added deliberately to deter us from falling back into sin.

The Lord's mercy, it is true, never fails his own.

Jesus tells his faithful that they are not to forget the daily prayer: forgive us our trespasses as we forgive them that trespass against us. This willingness to forgive and be forgiven does not however by any means imply that we may with impunity go on offending God and his holy law, or that we may resign ourselves to our sins and failings.

We must not make friends of our sins: we must avoid them, we must hate them, so as not to return to them like a dog that returns to its vomit, to use the Scriptural expression (Prov. 26. 11).

The effort we make to resist vice, to mortify lust and to wage battle against devils and the spirits that tempt us is the first sign of our spiritual resurrection, after the pattern of Christ's.

The other and most glorious sign is the endeavour to raise ourselves to a greater resemblance with Christ, with Christ the Teacher, Christ the Sufferer, Christ the "fountain of life and holiness", Christ the Conqueror.

25 APRIL

The Patriarch of Venice often spoke of the City's patron Saint, whose Feast we celebrate today.

ST MARK THE EVANGELIST

Viva San Marco! I want to remind you of two things: St Mark's faith, and his devotion to St Peter, two characteristics of the good Christian of all ages, a profound and living faith and devotion to Holy Church.

St Mark. . . stands for the treasure of truth which you guard in your hearts, a sacred inheritance—the religious faith, the Catholic faith, which your fathers bequeathed to you, and to which they did great honour, not considering it merely as a superficial embellishment of their warlike or diplomatic enterprises, but as an inexhaustible source of wisdom, of Christian and civil virtues.

Unlike so many ideologies that come and go, none of which has ever succeeded in giving peace to men's souls, faith in Jesus, the Son of God and Son of Mary, is still a great and never failing light to the mind and comfort to the heart. The tainted atmosphere of the spirit of this world gravely disturbs the tranquillity of souls thirsty for truth and peace, and must stir the consciences of all not to allow themselves to be lured by the various utopias which are merely deceit and delusion.

26 APRIL

TRUE BROTHERHOOD

To expect everything here below from this world alone, this poor world which is merely a passage way, or a place of trial, is an illusion. For here we have no lasting city for our sojourn, and we must look for our true fatherland that is to come.

One of the commonest illusions is that we can settle down here below as if we were permanent landlords of the tiny plot of ground on which we stand, living and behaving as if we were the owners and not simply the custodians of what is provided for the common good of all men, according to the laws of divine and human justice. And even when justice is well applied, it does not affect the need for all men to obey the Lord's command to love their neighbours in a spirit of gentle and sincere brotherliness.

In St Augustine we find a moving evangelical passage which illustrates the value of human labour and effort, as an expression of our trust in the divine promises, and our confident hope that the Lord will faithfully reward the efforts of the sincere and virtuous man.

Frequently the good things of this life, he says, their possession and their enjoyment, and even bodily health itself, elude the worker's grasp. But the man of honourable purpose and firm resolution, who is honest in his behaviour and faithful to the rule of "yours" and "mine", according to Christ's Gospel which is true brotherliness, is never alarmed by the uncertainties of life.

27 APRIL

THE MEANING OF EASTER

Christianity is not that complex system of oppressive rules which the unbeliever describes; it is peace, joy, love, and a life which is continually renewed, like the mysterious pulse of nature at the beginning of Spring. We must assert this truth as confidently as the Apostles did, and you. . . must be convinced of it, for it is your greatest treasure, which alone can give meaning and serenity to your daily life.

The source of this joy is in the Risen Christ, who has set man free from the slavery of sin and invites him to become a new creature with Him, and to look forward to an eternity of joy.

The joyful mystery has a meaning which affects every single Christian in the innermost sanctuary of his spiritual life, with power to make him become like the Risen Christ. Easter is for all a mystery of death and life; therefore, according to the clearly expressed commandment of the Church, every Catholic is at this time urged to purify his conscience with the Sacrament of Penitence, steeping it in the Blood of Jesus. He is asked to draw near to the Eucharistic Feast with greater faith, to nourish himself with the life-giving flesh of the Immaculate Lamb. The mystery of Easter is therefore a mystery of death and resurrection for every believer.

Throughout the whole of Eastertide the Church will proclaim the joyful truth: "The Lord is risen indeed!" This must be said also of every member of the Lord's family: "The man who was a sinner is risen indeed!" The doubting, the distrustful, the diffident, the timorous, the lukewarm have risen again, together with those who have been sorely tried, and those who suffer, the poor and the oppressed.

28 APRIL

DIVINE PATIENCE

The Lord's Passion and his Resurrection show us that there are two lives: one which we barely live, the other for which we long. Is not Jesus, who deigned to bear this poor earthly life for our sake, able to give us the life we desire? He wants us to believe this, to believe in his love for us, and in his eagerness to share with us his own riches, as once he chose to share our poverty. It was because we all have to die that he chose to die too.

We all know this already: our end and our beginning, birth and death. This is common knowledge and clear for all to see in our own sphere. Our sphere is this earth: the sphere of the angels is heaven. Our Lord came from one sphere to the other, from the realm of life to the realm of death; from the land of bliss to the land of toil and sorrow.

He came to bring us his gifts, and to bear with patience our sufferings—to bring us his gifts in secret, and publicly to bear our wretched lot, to show himself as a man and to conceal his divinity, to appear in the flesh, while the Divine Word was hidden from our eyes. The Word was hidden but it was not silent: it taught us to endure in patience.

29 APRIL

EASTER, THAT IS, THE "PASSING OVER"

On the altar the divine Book and the Chalice are the loftiest and most sacred signs of communion and intercourse between the divine and the human. The priest's voice reads and chants from the Book; his hands hold and bless the Chalice.

It is on the altar that the two testaments are joined and fulfilled. Beween them Jesus, the Word of God made man, is enthroned as eternal Priest, perpetuating a rite sealed by the sacrifice of his Blood, mysteriously continued through the centuries by the ministry of priests, applying the immense spiritual significance of the Redemption to the benefit of individuals and peoples.

It is right that Easter should be called the Pasch, that is, the Passover of the Lord. . . Every Mass that is celebrated is the sign of this Passover, so that every day is Easter in the temple of the Lord. It is indeed around the altar, and the Holy Mass, that the religious life of individuals, parishes, cities and nations revolves. It is from the altar that there irradiate those other forms or expressions of worship which make up the whole of the sacred liturgy.

30 APRIL

FEAST OF ST CATHERINE OF SIENA

I love to lift my eyes to the glorious light that streams from the figure, the life and the teaching of St Catherine. It is the light of Christ Jesus which penetrates and absorbs her, transforming her from the humble daughter of a tanner and his wife, Monna Lapa, into a heroic virgin—a bride of Christ, champion of Holy Church, Mother of the people and angel of peace. These titles represent all that most aptly corresponds to the modern needs of the Christian spirit which lives by faith and strives to draw nearer to religious perfection.

Today co-operation in the effort to establish world peace is becoming a dedicated service, the third devotion which is linked with the devotions to the Blood of Christ and to Holy Church. But peace must truly be the "peace of Christ". The peace which passes all understanding is founded upon conscientious self-examination and the determination to be at peace with ourselves, with our nearest neighbour and, in the wider sense, with our neighbours in the national and international order, with clear-sightedness, simplicity and evangelical honesty of purpose: with fewer trumpets and shouts, complications and subterfuges.

An "angel of peace"—our Holy Father Pius XII hails the heroic virgin of Siena under this title. Let us all imitate her by being angels of peace, with pure and honest hearts: angels full of sincerity and light: not spirits of confusion and violence.

MAY

1 MAY

The month chosen by the Church in which to extol the virtues of Our Lady. It begins, however, with a day dedicated to her husband, Joseph.

FEAST OF ST JOSEPH THE WORKER

Today, 1 May, we celebrate . . . the Feast of St Joseph "the Worker", the chaste husband of Mary and patron of the immense throng of artisans and working men, and of all workers in every field—and we are all workers—because he too knew the humble, secret joy of duty done, and of all the trials and hardships of daily toil endured.

For today, the Feast of all workers, we consider most fitting the greeting we placed at the head of our Encyclical Letter of 15 May 1961, published on the seventieth anniversary of Pope Leo XIII's *Rerum Novarum: Mater et Magistra!* Mother and Teacher! The Church, as in the age of the Apostles, is still the mother and teacher of truth and justice, liberty and peace, a mother and teacher whose kind voice we love to hear, and from whom we expect assistance in our efforts to make peace between the various conflicting interests of national, economic and social groups.

In the sphere of public life, in the harmony and co-operation of the various forces of production and re-distribution of the good things of this world, and in the collaboration of all within the framework of social peace, we are more and more conscious of the presence of

Christian social teaching, which springs from the Gospel of Jesus, and is proclaimed with endless practical applications by the teaching office of the Church.

This watchful, sensitive presence, alert in all spheres of activity, is a providential reality which brings joy to all, and kindles hope.

2 MAY

Prayer to Our Lady composed by Pope John for Boy Scouts.

MOTHER OF GOOD COUNSEL

O Mary, your name has been on my lips and in my heart from my early infancy.

When I was a child I learnt to love you as a Mother, turn to you in danger, and trust to your intercession.

You see in my heart the desire to know the truth, to practise virtue, to be prudent and just, strong and patient, a brother to all.

O Mary, help me to keep my purpose of living as a faithful disciple of Jesus, for the building up of Christian society and the joy of the Holy Catholic Church.

I greet you, Mother, morning and evening; I pray to you as I go upon my way; from you I hope for the inspiration and encouragement that will enable me to fulfil the sacred promises of my earthly vocation, give glory to God, and win eternal salvation.

O Mary! Like you in Bethlehem and on Golgotha, I too wish to stay always close to Jesus. He is the eternal King of all ages and all peoples.

Amen.

3 MAY

THE SWEET NAME OF MARY

We are in the month of May: what could be found more beautiful and more encouraging than a visit to the altar of Mary, there to join our voices with the songs of spring—with the birds of the air, the murmur of the wind, the blossoming of nature, and above all with the chants of these innocent children of our families? Nothing is more joyful than this vision of youth, which is the promise of a sure future and an augury and fountain of blessings, because pure young people who have flowered in innocence are the pledge of the Lord's most wonderful graces.

The Pope recalls his Lenten visits to some parishes of his diocese of Rome, in newly built areas. He knew then that all felt in their innermost hearts the sweetness of this meeting of Christians, and welcomed the Pope's endeavour to bring to everyone the name of Mary and the blessing of Jesus, to describe to them and recall to their minds the great wonders and miracles which, by the Lord's grace, the Catholic faith and the practice of virtue bring into the world.

So all feel greatly comforted: even when the road is sown with thorns we have more courage to remove these thorns and to endure them with patience, turning our mind and heart to heaven, to what are true inspirations from on high, and a source of blessing.

4 MAY

The Feast of St Monica, the mother of St Augustine, a shining example of Christian motherhood.

THE WATCHFUL GUARDIAN OF THE FAMILY

The family is a most precious gift. Founded by divine decree on the differing and complementary characteristics of the husband and wife, it finds in the wife a watchful guardian. We beg women therefore to love the family, understood as the natural setting for the growth of the human personality, and the God-given shelter in which the passions of life are soothed and sweetened, the stirrings of unruly desires are stilled, and the influence of evil example opposed.

This sanctuary is threatened by so many insidious attacks. Propaganda, at times unrestrained, makes use of the formidable power of the press, of entertainments and of amusements, to scatter the fatal seeds of corruption, especially among our young people. The family must defend itself, and the women must play their part in this struggle courageously, with a sense of their responsibility, never wearied of watching and correcting, and teaching the difference between good and evil. When necessary, they must avail themselves of the protection offered by the laws of the State.

The Gospel . . . records the words of an unknown

woman . . . "Blessed is the womb that bore you, and the breasts that you sucked!" (Luke 11. 28). These words very rightly referred to Mary, but the same might be said of all mothers if their children, on the hard, rough ways of this life, know how to bear themselves like true Christians, in accordance with the teaching they have received.

5 MAY

MARY IMMACULATE

The splendour of dawn is called immaculate, unstained. Mary, preserved from all stain of original sin, was full of grace from the first moment of her conception. While she was still in her mother's womb the divine light had entered into her soul. After the long night of the centuries which had passed since the sin of our first fathers, this morning star arose, pure and bright, transparent and inviolate, while the sky glowed with the promise of the coming dawn.

Friendship with God, granted to Adam when he was created, and so soon lost, was restored in all its original perfection in Mary, and already men had heard the good news of the coming of the Sun of Justice (Mal. 4. 2), of him who, by giving his life, has restored friendship and union with God for men of good will.

The Christian soul must feel this throb of supernatural life which begins with baptism. We say to you, in the words of the apostle: "Walk as children of light (for the fruit of light is found in all that is good and right and true), and try to learn what is pleasing to the Lord. Take no part in the unfruitful works of darkness" (Eph. 5. 8-11).

6 MAY

Mary's consent: "Be it unto me according to thy word".

THE IMMACULATE VIRGIN IS THE PROMISE AND WHITE FLOWER OF REDEMPTION

She who was preserved from original sin through the merits of her Son the Redeemer was granted this privilege because she was predestined for the sublime mission of being the Mother of God. She who was to clothe in mortal flesh the eternal Word of the Father could not be contaminated, even for an instant, by the shadow of sin. So she is immaculate through the power of Christ, because all that was granted to the Mother was granted through her Son. The blooming of this snow white flower on our soil is a sure pledge of the reconciliation of mankind with God.

How apt are the words of the liturgy that we sing on the Feast of the Nativity of the Virgin: "Thy nativity, O Virgin Mother of God, was the herald of joy to the whole world".

But this joy is also a purple flower of sacrifice: the sacrifice of the blessed Mother of Jesus who, when she gave her consent: "Be it unto me...", accepted her share in the destinies of her Son, from the poverty of Bethlehem to the self-denials of the secluded life in Nazareth, and the martyrdom of Calvary.

So we may not consider ourselves the beloved children of Our Lord and of his Mother if our life is without sacrifice and self-denial.

May this reference to the requirement of sacrifice be then a loving and thoughtful reminder of the strong and solid Christian virtues of self-denial, patience and penitence.

7 MAY

THE SHINING CROWN

"Immaculate" suggests order and beauty: the natural order, raised to a state of grace as soon as it left its Creator's hands, and therefore ever obedient to his will and his commands, and the beauty which is the shining crown of this order.

But everyone of us must begin in this way: by contemplating this vision of serenity and light, God's masterpiece, we must draw the strength to rise to the heights of perfection, whether of the individual or of the family, of institutions or of Holy Church.

Everyone must try to set his own soul in perfect order, for this is true supernatural beauty; and the special gifts of individuals are then reflected and reproduced on an ever wider scale, in order to enrich with increasing joy and beauty the great family of believers.

And, finally, "Immaculate" suggests the vision of heaven. The perfect and supreme grace bestowed on

Mary from the first moment of her earthly life is granted to us also, though, to be sure, to a lesser degree, and only as a pledge of future happiness: for the day when faith will be stripped of the veils which hide the vision of God, and we shall see the Lord face to face.

8 MAY

GATE OF HEAVEN

The Immaculate Virgin heralds the dawn of eternal day, and guides and sustains us on the long road that still stretches before us. The liturgical hymn "Hail, Star of the Sea" contains the loving prayer:

"Still as on we journey,
Help our weak endeavour,
Till with thee and Jesus
We rejoice for ever."

We must look forward to this final goal, the coming of the life of grace, with eager hearts and more persevering Christian fidelity.

Let us take courage, beloved children: we shall not be lost for ever. O Immaculate Mary, you are our strength.

Immaculate Virgin, radiant image of purity and grace, whose appearance scatters the shades of overhanging night and restores to us the splendours of heaven, look graciously down upon your children and all who love you and gather around you. Star of the dawn, prepare us to welcome the Sun of Justice, whom you brought into the world.

Gate of heaven, teach our hearts to desire the things of heaven. Mirror of Justice, preserve in us the love of divine grace so that, living humbly and happily in obedience to our Christian calling, we may always enjoy the Lord's friendship and your motherly consolations.

9 MAY

"SHOW YOU ARE OUR MOTHER"

The glorification of Mary, as it shines in the gentle radiance of this month's celebrations, is simply a reminder of her mission, of all God's purpose for her.

It is a mission of mercy and salvation, which springs from her other supreme privilege, divine motherhood. God's purpose is one of forgiveness and reconciliation, because the Heavenly Father, when he sent his Son to redeem the world, chose Mary as his first collaborator in his plan for our redemption. In her heaven and earth were joined, and through her the Divine Saviour was offered to mankind.

What harmonies of piety and love are awakened by the hymn *Salve Regina*, one of the oldest and dearest of all canticles, which sings with trustful longing of this motherly role of Mary! From beginning to end this prayer: "Hail, Holy Queen, Mother of mercy", is the lyrical cry of all who, disturbed by sin and subject to tears, pain and death, still look to her as their "life, sweetness and hope". To her they address their imploring prayer, a supreme expression of shining and unconquerable faith: "Show unto us Jesus, the blessed fruit of thy womb, O clement, O loving, O sweet virgin Mary".

10 MAY

OUR MOTHER

In this earthly life of ours, in the exercise of our individual and collective freedom, in mutual respect and in the common striving for charity and brotherliness—in all these things which make up our earthly life that shines in the light of God, the light of truth and love—we have as our loving and guiding star Mary the Mother of Jesus Christ whom he, when about to die, left to us to be our Mother, and whom we love with such warmth of filial affection that we wish to glorify her as our Queen.

But there must be no confusion of ideas. Christ Jesus is King by his very nature. He is seated upon the throne because he is himself the Lord, the Holy One, the Most High. That is why he is enthroned. But we like to think of his Mother and ours as standing beside him, in her golden robe, surrounded by a great throng, as Psalm 44 (45) described her centuries before her birth: "At your right hand stands the Queen, with her virgin companions, her escort, in her train".

O Queen of the Universe, remain for ever with us . . . All our voices will mingle with the voice of the Holy

Father, and those of the whole Catholic world: "Hear us, O Mary, O Mother and Queen; we pray to you, O sweet, O merciful, O loving, Immaculate Virgin Mary".

11 MAY

THE TEACHING OF THE APOSTOLATE

Oh how the gift of grace ennobles and gives life to the bonds of nature, of flesh and blood! It is so in the Gospel, it is so in the life of the Church of all ages. Let us together bless our Saviour for this sweetness of the love of Jesus, which is given to us all and encourages us to learn the lessons of the apostolate.

An apostolate of learning. "So faith comes from what is heard and what is heard comes by the preaching of Christ!" says St Paul (Rom. 10. 17). My brothers, our ears are open always to the voice of the world; why should we not keep them open to the appeals of holy preaching which, thanks be to God, still continues in the Church?

An apostolate of teaching. As in ancient times, to the special ministry of the bishops and clergy is today joined the co-operation of the faithful, naturally always under the direction of the bishops and priests, invited to join in the propagation of the Gospel, the Word of God, in these forms of Catholic action.

An apostolate of dying: with every day that passes, with the cross honourably borne, in all the manifestations of our lives and even, and above all, in the face of death.

12 MAY

TO JESUS THROUGH MARY

The simple words of the first page of Matthew's Gospel: "Mary, of whom Jesus was born, who is called Christ" (Matt. 1. 16) suffice for me to establish the fundamental principle of all the great theological teaching which illustrates the connection between the Blessed Sacrament and Our Lady.

Christian piety has rejoiced to learn from the Book of Acts that Mary was present at the first gatherings of the faithful, when they broke bread together as brothers and spent long hours in prayer. And modern art has often portrayed the heavenly Mother in the act of receiving from the hand of St John, the beloved disciple, the Communion of the Body and Blood of her Son. But all this is superfluous and unnecessary for our convinced belief.

When we say that in the Eucharist we have the Son and in Mary we have his Mother, have we not said all? The great genius of Hippo, St Augustine, with his eagle-eyed power of vision, found the words which so brilliantly contain the doctrine: *Ave corpo vero, nato de Maria Virgine:* Hail, true body, born of the Virgin Mary.

In this way—a delightful thing to say, a sublime thing to contemplate—the terms of this twofold mystery are merged into one, so that Mary appears to us radiant in the light of the Eucharistic mystery; they are merged, and yet they are the two extreme points between which is evolved and developed the whole Catholic dogma of the Incarnation and of the continuing life of the Church.

13 MAY

Feast of St Robert Bellarmine.

'' BEHOLD YOUR MOTHER ''

Shortly before his death Jesus, seeing his Mother with the beloved disciple by her side, said to Mary, indicating John: "Behold your son". Then he said to his disciple: "Behold your Mother".

As if enraptured by the infinite generosity of God, St Robert Bellarmine asserts that whoever draws near to the most high God with a frank and open heart may obtain grace and salvation. In fact Jesus, who wanted us to be co-heirs with him of his Father's kingdom, invites us too to share in the kindness of his perfect Mother, and she herself loves to carry on her work of mercy and solicitude for all who have been redeemed by her Son's precious Blood.

"Let us then", says Bellarmine, "hasten with confidence to Christ's throne of grace, and with prayers and profound contrition let us beg him to repeat for every one of us the words he said to his Mother: 'Behold your son'. In the same way, as he looks at Mary, may he repeat to every one of us the wonderful invitation: 'Behold your Mother'."

In short, here we find our true relationship, already established on earth, with Jesus our Redeemer and our brother, and our relationship with Mary, the Mother of Jesus and of all who belong to the human race redeemed by the Saviour. It is therefore a glory of Catholic worship, and of the Christian doctrine which always presents the Lord Jesus to us with his Mother by his side.

How eternally happy are those faithful who invoke the heavenly Queen by the sweet name of Mother, and faithfully follow her counsel, her inspiration and her example!

14 MAY

PRAYING WITH OUR MOTHER

My dear brothers in Christ and in the love of Mary! The sacred altar is the meeting point of all that is for the Christian and the Catholic a vision of heavenly doctrine, inspired by divine grace, the inexhaustible source of strength, holiness and joy in our life here below, in the certainty of the eternal life to come.

Follow me then to this blessed altar of my sacrifice which is a sacrifice offered for you and with you: for all that is dearest to you in the innermost sanctuary of your souls, and in your family life, and in the various relationships of your civil and social activity.

The land where we were born, which is so dear to us, is always, even when resplendent with natural beauty, full of thorns and of things which cause us distress and pain.

True comfort is found only in union with the Cross of Christ and his sufferings, united with the sorrows of his Mother, who is our Mother too.

Oh how beautiful it is, and how consoling, to believe, live and pray with our Mother, sharing in her love with her Son, the Word of God made man for us, as a sign of blessing, prosperity and peace amid the uncertainties of this present life, in the certain hope of the eternal joys which await us.

15 MAY

FEAST OF ST JOHN BAPTIST DE LA SALLE

The Feast of St John Baptist de La Salle reminds us of

his spiritual sons, scattered throughout the world.

Although they are not priests they live in the observance of a religious rule, they seek perfection, and do a great deal of good among children and young people, especially among those of the less well-to-do classes, caring for their upbringing and education.

When the Holy Father was Apostolic Nuncio in France, he paid a visit to Rheims and saw not only the Cathedral, one of the most magnificent of all Christian churches, but also the house where St John Baptist de La Salle was born, an apostle among the people and for the people's good. The Church is always present among men, and her most loving care is for the poor and humble. We see the Saint's sons, the Brothers of the Christian Schools, demonstrating this love by "giving a Christian education to the poor and confirming youths in the way of truth" (Collect).

This is really one of the loftiest aims of human life, and a most meritorious answer to one of the noblest calls in the Lord's service.

The Holy Father therefore begs you all to honour St John Baptist de La Salle and the Religious of his Congregation. It is evident that among the many problems of social life, and the great needs which we must try to satisfy, it is particularly important to ensure liberty of instruction, and make it easier for all to draw near to the sources of grace.

16 MAY

THE ANGELUS

It is the custom in Catholic countries for the bells to ring the Angelus at dawn. . . "The angel of the Lord declared unto Mary". This peal of bells, after the darkness of the night, represents the light that returns in splendour, while the heavens bow down to meet the earth. The angel's greeting is answered by our prayer which recalls the wonderful truth: "and she conceived of the Holy Ghost".

The woman, daughter of Eve, chosen before all ages for this privilege, is called to a unique motherhood, to become, by a divine miracle, the Mother of Jesus. How our hearts throb with joy as we repeat together a prayer in which Mary is invoked as our Mother too! . . .

These are simple and familiar words—but it is good to meditate on all they stand for, in recollection and peace of mind. . .

The Son of God has become the Son of Mary, our brother, and has lived among us—and we know well what this means for us. First of all thirty years of silence, work and obedience. Then three years of the apostolate: teaching, miracles, all-conquering light. Then the hour of humiliation and sacrifice; but in the end the triumph.

17 MAY

Feast of St Pascha Baylon, Apostle of the Eucharist.

MOTHER OF THE EUCHARIST

The Christian heart understands certain harmonies at once, in a surprising and miraculous way; and this mystery which fuses together the dearest objects of Catholic worship, the Eucharist and Our Lady, is one of the most consoling and delightful harmonies of our faith.

It is a doctrine, and it is a fact . . . I open the Old Testament and find the Song of Songs presents me with two most beautiful comparisons (cf. Song of Solomon 2. 2-3): "As a lily among brambles, so is my love among maidens". Can we not all see here, in the delicate image of the lily, Mary the Immaculate, beautiful and resplendent?

In the same passage I find: "As an apple tree among the trees of the wild forest, so is my beloved among young men". What is this tree, laden with fruit, which resembles the beloved? This apple tree that grows among the trees of the wild forest, the fruit of which is wholesome, and sweet to the taste? Obviously it is Jesus—the fruit of the tree is the Sacrament of his Body and Blood.

Oh what a wonderfully apt association of images! The lily and the tree: Mary and the Eucharist! The Church is compared to a lovely garden, a "garden locked". In it the fountains play, and herbs and fruits make it pleasant and perfumed like a garden of Paradise. And see! beside the fountain blooms the lily; near at hand is the tree. The faithful soul seeks for himself a place between the fragrant lily and the fruit-laden tree, between Mary and the Holy Sacrament, and lingers with great delight in the shade of the tree, enjoying the odour of the lily, and eating the divine fruit. "I sat in his shadow. . ."

O Mary, pure lily, tender and delicate flower! O Holy Sacrament! O mysterious tree, truly the most beautiful of all the trees in the wild forest, because you are the Christ!

18 MAY

FOUNTAIN OF LIFE

There is a passage from the pen of a distinguished English writer on religious subjects (F. W. Faber, *The Blessed Sacrament*, London, Burns and Oates, 1855) which is so wonderful that I am sorry I can do no more than briefly trace the main line of his thought.

The Immaculate Virgin is with us. We still enjoy hearing our fathers describe the delight felt by the whole Catholic world in the middle of last century, when the ancient doctrine of Mary having been preserved from all taint of original sin was defined as dogma.

That doctrine is like the mountain spring, purer than the waters of Sion, from which flow all the other mysteries of the Incarnation. The whole Church gathers around this source to gaze at its reflection in the clear deep waters. Kneeling on the bank is the supreme Pontiff; the teachers who thirst for the truth hasten to drink from the spring. Mitred and crowned heads, and humble children of the people, the poor and afflicted of all classes, a whole multitude of pious folk, stoop down, drink and rise again: sight is restored, Mary shines more brightly than before.

Look well, my brothers, at those waters. They are the elements of the Precious Blood of Jesus. They flow mysteriously in the sanctified breast of Anna, they appear again, transfigured into the blood of Mary, the fair child, the maiden of fifteen years, the Bride of the Holy Spirit. Through the power of the Spirit that overshadows her this blood gathers into itself the elements of the sacred humanity of Christ. Behold the Spring, and then the Blood! Oh what a miracle occurs! The Blood is already beating in the Sacred Heart, it crimsons the cheeks of the Divine Child—it is sweated out from every pore of Jesus, in his Passion.

MOTHER OF GOD

My thoughts turn once more to the words of the humble daughter of Israel who still speaks for our own hearts and lips, words which we repeat with enthusiasm to the blessed Mother of Jesus, who is our own Mother too: *Beata, beata viscera Mariæ Virginis quæ portaverunt Æterni Patris Filium!* O blessed indeed the womb that bore you! And I place my confident trust in the reply of Jesus which is the renewed assurance for you, children of the Catholic Church, that we may find here below on earth, as a pledge of our eternal happiness in heaven, prosperity, joy and peace, in proportion to our unconquerable fidelity to the teaching of the divine Word, always better understood and better guarded: Blessed rather are those who hear the word of God and keep it.

O Mary, Mother of Jesus and our Mother too! We hail you with this cry that all generations of men repeat, contemplating the mysteries of your life and the splendour of your Assumption. Once more we hail you as blessed, *beata;* intercede for us, O glorious Queen of the world, and be ever mindful of us, particularly in the dangers and needs of the present hour.

O Jesus, Son of Mary, our Brother and our Saviour, by the mystery of the body and blood which you deigned to assume from the Virgin's pure womb and which we today renew on our altar, preserve for us the gift of faith for the salvation of our souls, for the prosperity and greatness of our people and for the glory of your name, which will be at the same time our glory and our joy, in this present life and in eternity. Amen.

20 MAY

Feast of St Bernadine of Siena, chosen as Patron Saint of those who work in a new field of labour in our modern world, the field of public relations.

THE RIGHT USE OF MODERN INVENTIONS

We wish to address our priestly exhortation to all who hold positions of the highest responsibility, who preside over the organization of civil order, to heads of State and directors of regional or municipal administrations, indeed to all workers in general. We speak to teachers, parents and instructors, to all those who work with their heads, their hearts and their hands, and especially to those responsible for public opinion, which is formed through the medium of the press, the wireless and television, the cinema, competitions and displays of all kinds, literary and artistic—to writers, artists, producers, directors and choreographers.

Beloved children—we beg you never to use talents to falsify the truth: may the mere thought of doing so inspire you with horror!

Do not make use of these wonderful gifts of God, light, sound, colour, and their technical and artistic applications, whether typographical, journalistic, or used in wireless and television, to turn aside man's natural inclination towards the truth, on which his nobility and greatness are founded; do not use these means to corrupt consciences which are still unformed or wavering.

Have a holy fear of spreading those germs which desecrate love, dissolve families, make a mock of religion, and shake the foundation of that moral order which is built upon the control of selfish impulses, and on peaceful brotherhood which respects the rights of others. Instead, you must work together to make the air we breathe purer and less tainted, for its first victims are the innocent and the weak: learn how to construct with calm perseverance and indefatigable efforts the foundations of a better age to come, more healthy, more honest and more safe for all.

21 MAY

MOTHER OF THE CHURCH

Mary is with us, among us; she protects and helps us; she leads us along a sure road.

More than once the Pope has heard the wistful cry of some souls—among those brothers of ours who, since the beginning of the sixteenth century, have been cut off from the unity of the Church—who exclaim with profound sadness: is it possible not to love one's own mother? And yet, some of them have managed to forget her altogether, or at least to keep her at a distance, as sometimes happens, alas! in certain families, in which the mother, when advanced in years, is borne with as a burden instead of still being cherished with loving care.

We, however, by the grace of God, honour Mary as Mother of Jesus and Mother of the Catholic Church. She not only receives the homage of an exquisite art, which testifies to her in every place, but the ever fervent, beautiful and profound veneration felt for one who never for a moment fails in her motherly care.

Let us always share in the sorrows of Mary, when we see her beside the Cross of Jesus. Let us pour out our tears to her in the saddest moments of our life, remembering the first announcement God's angel made to the most holy Virgin: "The angel of the Lord declared unto Mary, and she conceived of the Holy Ghost", which is like a synthesis of the whole story of the Incarnation of the Word, and the Redemption brought by the Son of God: the glory which, here below, is the beginning of the eternal glory of Paradise.

22 MAY

MOTHER OF THE YOUNG

For all of us Mary is guide, refuge and strength. Turning to her we have all found comfort; and on the last day of our earthly life which is also the first day of eternity—it is good for us to think of this frequently—it will be an infinitely precious consolation to be able to turn to such a gracious Mother, and feel her near us in that grave hour. With what intensity of love we shall say our last "Hail Mary", in which will be gathered up the fervour of all the others we have said throughout our earthly life, and which will be the finest greeting for us to utter as we go to meet Our Lord.

The devotion to Mary is a valid and unfailing support for all believers; it is a pledge of inward peace, and inspires a firm determination to do our duty. This truth must be carefully impressed upon young people, especially on those just beginning a new chapter in their lives. This is the right time to remind them of the good instructions they have received, and of their daily prayer to Our Lady, Mother of Jesus and Mother of us all—so that they may behave in a manner worthy of their early training.

THE SOURCE OF COMFORT

Motives for melancholy are never in short supply—and when were they ever lacking in the history of the world? —because of the inexorable alternation in human life of sadness and joy. Sometimes these mix and merge together, and when that happens we would try in vain to separate them.

A wise man, a wise Christian, must do all he can to free himself from sad thoughts, and at all times have recourse to those sources of comfort which transform suffering into motives of love, of merit, of present and eternal joy.

The Mother of Jesus, who is our Mother too—oh how I love to associate these two titles!—is one of the richest sources of our consolation, the richest after Jesus, who is of his very nature light and life: she is rich in comfort and joy and encouragement for all the children of Eve, who have become her own children through the redemptive sacrifice and will of Christ.

This explains the whole world's devotion to the Virgin whom her saintly cousin Elizabeth truly hailed as "Blessed", in reply to Mary's confession of humility in the *Magnificat*, which remains the everlasting canticle of mankind redeemed, the song of the past, present and future.

OUR LOVE FOR MARY

All the world knows the Gospel story of the Lord's last testament in which, at the supreme moment of death, he left his Mother to the world as the universal Mother of all who believe in him and form his Church, one, holy, catholic and apostolic. He who was the witness and heir of this testament takes care to add that from that moment " the disciple took her to his own home" (John 19. 26-27).

This welcoming of the Mother of Jesus as our Mother is characteristic of the moving and glorious history of the Church's continual devotion to Mary. Every altar, every chapel, every church built in honour of the Mother of God anywhere in the world testifies to the historic fidelity of the Church's children to the example of the beloved disciple.

Holy Immaculate Mary, help all who are in trouble.

Give courage to the faint-hearted, console the sad, heal the infirm, pray for the people, intercede for the clergy, have a special care for nuns; may all feel, all enjoy your kind and powerful assistance, all who now and always render and will render you honour, and will offer you their petitions . . . Hear all our prayers, O Mother, and grant them all. We are all your children: "Grant the prayers of your children". Amen for ever.

25 MAY

THE SUPERNATURAL ORDER

The honour you pay to Mary, the Mother of Jesus, Queen of heaven and earth, shines more brightly through a more ardent Catholic faith, the Catholic faith in the thought and life of the people of Christ.

We must take note of some very sad and disconcerting truths. The dividing line, my dear brothers, between the different conceptions of truth and falsity, good and evil, war and peace, with which the modern world is concerned, is here before us: are we to admit or to deny the existence of a supernatural order which satisfies the loftiest aspirations of the soul, in the vision of a final and eternal world which awaits us all, at the end of our lives, and which the chosen will spend in an eternity of bliss?

Today men have reached the point of wondering whether the heavens are empty, and whether all the teaching that has produced twenty centuries of the history of our race and given us so much to admire in the social and architectural order was not indeed a universal illusion, which must be abolished if we are to rebuild everything on the basis of a new world—a world without God, and without the moral law of justice and charity, set up upon an imposed egalitarian system, which would have nothing in common with the brotherhood of individuals and peoples.

26 MAY

In 1907 the young priest Angelo Roncalli gave a lecture for the third centenary of the death of Cardinal Cesare Baronius. On many occasions in later years he spoke about this extraordinary priest, the disciple of St Philip Neri, whose feast occurs today.

OBEDIENCE AND PEACE

Cardinal Cesare Baronius was well known throughout the world for his *Annales Ecclesiastici*, which were like twelve stones plucked from the torrent and slung against the editors of the *Centurie di Magdebourg*. Every evening he used to go to the Chiesa Nuova near St Peter's, and once inside he would go straight to the bronze statue of St Peter, which was then near the door, and kiss the apostle's foot, always pronouncing these two words: *Pax et Obœdientia;* Peace and Obedience. In this brief and simple gesture, so constantly repeated, the whole man comes to life for us. Such words have a profound meaning and, if I mistake not, explain and interpret his whole life. Peace for his own soul, peace for his brethren, for the Church troubled with heresy, and for the whole of human society, was the dream and ideal which always cheered him in his unending labours and in the transports of his soul. Obedience of the humblest and blindest sort, a childlike obedience to his Father Philip Neri as long as he lived, and obedience to the Pope, whoever he was and whatever his character, and in his epoch there was in the Chair of Peter a succession of men, attitudes and ambitions of the most varied kinds. That was his only rule of conduct and the real secret of his success.

My very dear brothers, I have revealed to you the little secret of my episcopal motto, which I hold very dear, and which has kept me such good company for twenty years.

In this hour of uplifting and encouraging prayer, a prayer which answers the supreme appeal of Jesus "that they may be one", I wish to ask you to seek your peace and inspiration in the obedience and peace of Baronius. He who remains faithful to the spirit which inspires the apostolic activity of the Church, strengthened by a joyful obedience and firm peace of mind, possesses the gift of ensuring domestic and civic order. It is in this order that we find the example and the symbol of peace between nations and in the international relations of peoples.

27 MAY

THE LIGHT COMES FROM THE ALTAR

When he ascended into heaven the majestic flow of the

Blood of Jesus did not cease on this earth; it still flows in an ever-widening stream through untold centuries of grace: the vision which began with the Immaculate Conception ends in the Blessed Sacrament.

In this way one mystery corresponds to the other; the one illuminates, completes and confirms the other. From the Eucharist back to the Passion, from the Passion to the public life and, further back, to the hidden life of Jesus in Nazareth, from this hidden life to his birth—from far beyond the Annunciation to the heights of the Conception and back to us again—it is a continual rising and redescending, unutterable, divine. Because of this we see Mary Immaculate present at every Mass and in every Communion. The light of the Immaculate which streams upon us comes from the altar, from the tabernacle; and in the same way, when we draw near to the altar and the tabernacle it is almost as if we hear Mary's voice inviting us: "Eat, O friends and drink: drink deeply, O lovers" (Song of Solomon 5. 1).

This, my brothers, is the doctrine.

On this foundation is built the reality, the great and thrilling reality which reassumes so fully in all ages the best Christian piety of the whole world.

In fact, when persecution rages, the Christians draw strength to resist and to extend their conquering apostolate, and, if need be, even to die, from the Bread of the strong, from the inebriating chalice offered over the tombs of martyrs in our ancient cemeteries, under the kind eyes of Mary whose roughly drawn image smiles among the symbols and ornaments of primitive Christian art.

28 MAY

OUR STRIVING AFTER PERFECTION

To have a special devotion to Mary means that we are trying to perfect our own spiritual lives, in imitation of our heavenly Mother and with the help of her grace. In this effort, which we must all make, we must strive to obtain purity, and be constant in our search for what is best, and in our endeavour to improve our conduct. We must find the sure and decisive way of attaining the bright goal of our desires, with the sure hope of finally sharing with Mary in the joy of Jesus Christ, the fountain of eternal bliss.

We turn to you, O blessed Virgin Mary, Mother of Jesus and our Mother too. How could we, with trembling hearts, concern ourselves with the greatest problem of all, that of life and death, now overshadowing all mankind, without trusting ourselves to your intercession to preserve us from all dangers?

This is your hour, O Mary. Our blessed Jesus entrusted us to you in the final hour of his bloody sacrifice. We are sure that you will intervene.

And now indeed we beseech you for peace, O most sweet Mother and Queen of the world. The world does not need victorious wars or defeated peoples, but renewed and strengthened health of mind, and peace which brings prosperity and tranquillity; this is what it needs and what it is crying out for: the beginning of salvation and lasting peace. Amen. Amen.

29 MAY

QUEEN OF THE WORLD

An eloquent passage written by St Peter Canisius, as a commentary on the Gospel of St Luke, contains these admirable reflections: "Oh blessed day that saw the humble Handmaid of the Lord raised and borne aloft to such great glory, made queen of heaven and mistress of the world! She could rise no higher than this, being destined to reign in glory by the side of Christ, enthroned in the kingdom of the blessed."

. . . This is one of the characteristic conceptions of the Christian faith. When we think of the Mother we know we are all brothers of the Son; we know that the Spirit, the divinity, of our Brother passes mysteriously into us, and enables us to understand these hidden and wonderful truths, with the help of the sublime and magnificent indications of the sacred liturgy.

We must therefore try in every way we can to foster these feelings in ourselves, and make them more profound, ever adding new warmth to our love for Mary. This helps us to love our Lord Jesus Christ, the beginning, the continuation and the end of all, and also to love his Gospel and his Church.

Everything must always be placed in the light of this supernatural doctrine, and under the protection of the Mother of God who, having risen to eternal glory, has

not withdrawn herself from us, and does not lose sight
of us. She is always willing and anxious to listen to our
prayers and receive the trustful petitions we offer to her
with profound humility, so that she may present them
to her Son.

30 MAY

MARY, MOTHER AND QUEEN

We crown you together with your divine Son, O Mother,
we crown you as our Queen, and may the golden crown
that encircles your brow glow as a sign of the highest
holiness to which a human creature may rise, as an
"ornament of honour that surpasses all other dignity
and merit in the Church, both militant and triumphant,
and finally as a symbol of your most powerful intercession with your Son for our needs. These are the individual needs of every one of us, and of our families . . . "

The crown is of purest gold, like the hearts of your
children who offer it to you: " . . . a crown of gold upon
her head".

We beg you for two special graces: peace of mind and
the spirit of peace in our families, in our parishes, and
in this diocese which loves and honours you; peace in
our own blessed land, and in all her endeavours to
achieve the loftiest ideals of human and social life in the
light of the Gospel and in faithfulness to the teaching of
the apostles, today, yesterday and always the shining
beacon of truth, justice and true Christian brotherhood.

Ah, my brothers! I speak of true Christian brotherhood
and, after peace, this is the second grace for which I
intend to pray, and for which I ask you all to pray to
Jesus. . . under the auspices and with the help of the
prayers of our newly crowned Queen.

31 MAY

The last General Audience held by Pope John in the Vatican Basilica (15 May 1963) before his death. He exhorted us to

LOOK TO MARY

Is it possible for a Christian not to love the holy Mother
of Jesus, whom he has regarded with affection since his
childhood, to whom he prayed with the first words he

ever uttered, and to whom he has trustfully turned for help in the difficult moments of life ? All find in her and for her a tender expression of confidence and gentleness; this is a great comfort to us, a great comfort at all times.

In this month of May good Christians increase a hundredfold their tributes of profound veneration for Mary. . .

We must cherish in our hearts a fervour that will strengthen us and enable us to look to Jesus and to Our Lady with great confidence, so that we may not only await but hasten the triumph of the Lord's charity and grace, by our enthusiasm and virtuous living and through our apostolate. This fervour must promote brotherly love and induce us to reject all motives for division among us. We must be impelled, in short, to love all that unites us, because the Lord came to redeem the whole world, and he is always continuing his work of salvation, mercy and peace.

JUNE

1 JUNE

The month dedicated to the Sacred Heart.

A DEVOTION TO THE HEART OF JESUS WHICH BRINGS MANY BLESSINGS

In the various activities of our lives and of our Christian piety, what is there more delightful than a fervent and enlightened devotion to the Heart of Jesus, the great devotion of our own times?

You should associate the devotion to the Heart of Jesus with zeal and enthusiasm for works of missionary co-operation. There is nothing more useful for our well-being and for the enjoyment of peace in this present life; there is nothing more sweetly reassuring for our last day on this earth, and our final rising in glory, to be with our Lord and Saviour for ever and ever.

To him, the immortal King of all worlds and all ages, be honour, thankfulness and blessings. Amen. Amen.

2 JUNE

THE DIVINE ORIGIN OF MARRIAGE

In jealously guarding the indissolubility of the bond of marriage and the sanctity of the "Great Sacrament", the Church is defending a law which is not only ecclesiastical and civil but above all natural and divine.

These two great and necessary principles, which the veil of passion and prejudice at times obscures so much that they are easily forgotten, are established, the one by natural law engraved indelibly on the human conscience, and the other by the divine law of our Lord Jesus Christ. So it is not a question of decrees and regulations which circumstances require and which succeeding generations may modify; it is a question of the divine will, of the inviolable order established by God himself to safeguard the first fundamental nucleus of civilized society. It is the primordial divine law, which in the fullness of time Christ himself restored to its original integrity, "but from the beginning it was not so" (Matt. 19. 8).

The Church does not defend class interests or obsolete customs. Her glorious hymn, her title of honour, is heard in the Lord's Prayer, Our Father: thy will be done, on earth as it is in heaven.

What she preaches and defends in this world is the will of God, in which will be found the peace, serenity, and even the material welfare, of all his children.

3 JUNE

THE DOCTRINE ABOUT MARRIAGE

It is necessary that the Church's teaching about marriage should be made known and widely diffused by every possible means. I have already told you what I think about this . . . :

"Considering the gravity of the danger which threatens us", I have said, " . . . the appeal rises spontaneously to our lips, and we repeat it most urgently 'with all the affection of Jesus Christ', and first of all to shepherds of souls—that they should use every means, in instruction and in catechism, by word of mouth and by the wide distribution of the written word, to enlighten consciences. . . And we appeal also to all who have the will and means to influence public opinion, so that they may intervene in this question, not to cause more confusion of ideas but to clarify and to encourage right living, and respect for the greatest and most precious element of social life: the integrity of marriage" (A.A.S., 160, pp. 900 - 901).

We renew this appeal today, and it comes from our heart, because everyone is now aware of the present danger, primarily due to the lack of solid teaching and frank instruction. People are writing and speaking, to say the least, light-heartedly, about subjects which require profound study, ripeness of judgment and a sincere conscience, and it is most necessary, therefore, that the faithful, indeed the whole social body, should be enlightened, warned and well instructed.

New methods must be thought of, to enable this teaching to reach all those who are thinking of marriage, and particularly young people and the betrothed.

4 JUNE

THE SANCTITY OF THE FAMILY

God's own eternal creative activity is in a certain way reflected in the happy and industrious lives of those sons of men who are raised to the supreme dignity and duty of sharing in his work of creation.

In the family we see the closest and most wonderful co-operation of man with God: the two human persons, created in the image and likeness of God, are called not only to the great function of prolonging the work of creation by giving physical life to new beings, in whom the life-giving spirit infuses the powerful principle of immortality, but also to the nobler task which perfects the other, that of giving a civilized and Christian upbringing to their children.

This firm conviction, based on such a sublime truth, is enough to ensure the permanence of the bond of every marriage, and to make parents aware of the responsibility they assume before God and men.

Teachers and shepherds of souls know by experience what feelings of holy enthusiasm and gratitude to God these thoughts arouse in young people who are preparing for marriage, and how earnestly their generous souls give their assent and form their own good resolutions.

So let there be spread abroad, by all available means, the joyful knowledge of the nobility conferred by God on man, on the fathers and mothers of families, who become God's first collaborators in the continuation of his work in the world, by giving new members to the Mystical Body of Christ, and by peopling the heavens with chosen souls who will for ever sing of the Lord's glory.

FAITH IN CHRIST'S VICTORY

Before he left this world Jesus, the conqueror of death, said: "Be of good cheer; I have overcome the world". It is true: a dead body was left lying on that grim field of battle. We often mention him by name: he is a Prince. The divine Teacher of Nazareth called him "the ruler of this world".

Christ wages war against him, gently but effectively, for the assertion of justice and the triumph of peace.

The infernal enemy, for his part, hates justice and throws every obstacle in the way of peace, peace for the nations of the whole world. Sometimes his attacks and his manœuvres cause such confusion as to tempt the defenders to surrender.

Every good Christian puts his trust in Christ; he does his duty according to the various demands of his conscience: his religious conscience and his social conscience, in the sight of God and in the sight of man. The Christian never gives way, and is wary of compromise: he goes on his way fearless and confident. He does what he can to further the solution of the problems of peace.

In Christ Jesus "death and life in a strange conflict strove". The Master of life triumphed over death, and his victory is the victory of the Church in all ages. Let us then free our souls from all dismay, and open our hearts to the finest hopes for the future. We may meet with opposition from the world—indeed, we can be sure of this. . .

SUCCESS OF THE LAY APOSTOLATE

Men and women and their children are the sacred ground, and the flower, of the Christian family, all the members of which are intent on training themselves, with conscientious and devout prayer and study, to take their place in the world.

We must seize every opportunity of pointing out the significance of the presence of the family in the Church and in the world.

The Pope who now speaks to you loves to refresh his soul with the thought of the enthusiastic laity, whose precious collaboration with the Catholic hierarchy ensures a more rapid extension of the kingdom of God on earth.

Playing their part in the manifold life of the parishes and dioceses, these valiant apostles offer to the Church, and to the national community to which they belong, the energy they put into intelligent activity, and the example of their stainless characters. But in them we see also the working of divine grace which springs from the Redemption brought by Jesus, influencing individual souls with the efficacy of sacramental action.

Only under the primacy of a supernatural life, thus understood, can men be sure of honest intentions, sincere and solid virtues, and an increase of zeal for the glory of God; only this supernatural inspiration can have a constructive and beneficial influence in the domestic, civil and social life of every individual, and so strengthen in this world the foundations of real progress and ordered tranquillity.

7 JUNE

SING TO GOD

St Paul encouraged his faithful Colossians, who were rather remote from the great centres, to find joy in the singing of the Psalms: "Sing psalms and hymns and spiritual songs with thankfulness in your hearts to God" (Col. 3. 16).

In fact, in the early centuries the Christian communities were heartened by the Old Testament canticles, and by those prayers said in common which were afterwards added to the Psalter, and which are alive with the same inspiration and express a more extended effort to rise towards Jesus, the Divine Word that has become the first member of the human family, reformed and regenerated in the sacrifice of the divine Blood.

When this way of praying, which is all contemplation, was set in an order better adapted to the increasingly numerous and extended opportunities of the Christian ministry, the Psalms kept all their liturgical importance, thus demonstrating the truth of what St Ambrose had so well described in his admirable introduction to his commentary on the first Psalm (Migne, PL, 14, 963). . .:

"The Psalm is the people's blessing, the praise of God,

the exaltation of humble folk, the joyful song of the Church, the ancient avowal of faith, the height of happiness. It calms anger, soothes anxiety, alleviates suffering. It is our safety by night, our guide in daylight hours: a pledge of peace and concord, like the lyre which mingles many notes in a single chord. It greets the rising day and makes the evening holy.''

8 JUNE

JUSTICE

Justice is born of divine wisdom, and consists in giving every man his due. Our first duty then is to render to God what belongs to God—to acknowledge him as Creator, Redeemer and Source of all life. Then we must put into practice what he taught his disciples, telling them to carry this teaching of his to the ends of the world. Two thousand years have gone by since then, and this gracious message is still passed on from one man to another, though the communication is at times interrupted or halted here and there, and often stained with the blood of the Confessors of the Faith. But the teaching is still alive and with us, and can never be abolished.

After our duty to God we must remember our obligation to give to Cæsar what belongs to Cæsar. This means that, when we have first of all paid our respectful homage to the Lord in the practice of our religion, we must give due consideration to our social relations.

We live on this earth; but we live by faith, and herein lies our strength. We are working for eternity, which is not of this world, but while we prepare for this final end we must learn how to live with dignity amid the trials of this present life, always subordinating all other things to what the Lord offers us in the future life. And our hope of arriving safely in eternity rests very largely on our constant respect for the rights of our fellow men.

9 JUNE

THE FOUNTAIN OF YOUTH

To give pride of place to the requirements of the supernatural life, which is nourished by an eager participation in the Sacraments, especially in the Eucharist. . .: this is the fountain of perpetual youth, and gives us strength to resist the enticements of the world and courage to endure mockery and disbelief; from this there springs the fervour of the purest charity, the living force which forms the new nature, created after the likeness of God in true righteousness and holiness (cf. Eph. 4. 24).

Thus sustained by prayer and strengthened by a robust supernatural life, you will have that convinced faith which is clearly seen in your words and demeanour, in all you do and in your work. No one can help feeling the fascination of a soul that knows what it wants, and lives by faith.

Beloved children! Continue on this sure way, which forms sincere Christians and good citizens, because by so doing you will be putting in the forefront of your life man's essential duty: to love God, pray to him and, through grace, share in his own life.

Do not let yourselves be influenced by the mentality of this world which finds no peace because it has forgotten how to pray: but learn to perfume all your actions with the life-giving breath of prayer. In this way, we are sure, your life will be full of harmony and peace, full of all the blessings of heaven and earth, and you will be able to pass on to other men the power of those ideals which strengthen your heart.

10 JUNE

OUR FATHER

The great mystery of life, and the story of individual man and all mankind are all contained and ever present in the words of the "Lord's Prayer", the "Our Father", which Jesus came from heaven to teach us, and which sums up the whole philosophy of the life and history of every soul, every people and every age, past, present and future. In fact, all is there: the triumph of the Name of God, the Kingdom of God, and the Will of God. In the realm of ordinary human life we find the daily bread for the soul and body of all, the intimate sense of personal humility, and of the need for mutual forgiveness, and of God the Father's forgiveness for each and all of us, with perfect liberty of thought and life, in the light of Christ and of his Gospel, and the certainty of eternal happiness and eternal blessing.

11 JUNE
Feast of St Barnabas

RESPECT FOR THE OPINION OF OTHERS

Beware of misunderstandings: they arise, challenge each other and come to blows. We must be on our guard against them; if they cannot be avoided, at least let us not cultivate them, or allow them to be exaggerated in our imagination. Let us try, unashamedly, to be the first to explain them away, to put things right once more, to disentangle them and to keep ourselves free from any feeling of resentment.

Even among cultured and spiritual people there may be a variety of opinions and views in matters open to discussion. This does no harm to charity and peace, as long as we preserve moderation of manner and harmony of minds. I will add moreover that the Lord makes use of these misunderstandings to bring about in other ways some great good. Thus Paul and Barnabas separated because of young John Mark. . . and yet they were both equally righteous and holy. With souls like these everything is set right by the Lord's grace. But this does not alter the fact that we must beware of misunderstandings and must try to clear them away.

We can never forget those words of our Lord's which so surprised the world, when he said that it gives more joy and peace to the heart to believe and to renounce than to demand and receive.

12 JUNE

CHARITY, THE QUEEN OF VIRTUES

Charity is indeed the precious gold, refined in the fire, which enriches all who possess it and makes them beloved when they dispense it to others. Whatever you offer... without charity, will be neither pleasing to God nor profitable to yourself. You must have charity, for it surpasses in dignity all other virtues. May charity set your heart on fire, inspire your soul, rule your life and enrich your prayer.

And now for your prayers: these are truly precious only when they are afire with the love of the Holy Spirit. Their fragrance rises from the earth, and is sweetly diffused before God's throne in the kingdom of heaven. The great prophet and singer used to pray: "Let my prayer be counted as incense before thee" (Psalm 140 (141). 2). But, just as even the loveliest thing can emit no fragrance until it has been touched by fire, so the incense of prayer is not pleasing until it has been burnt in the flame of charity.

Now we come to the question of penitence and mortification. This is the myrrh that is also needed for our correction and preservation. Charity and prayer support each other. Prayer falters and becomes drowsy if the love of charity does not sustain it. Charity inspires prayer, and the flame of charity is itself fed on prayer. So whoever wishes to make progress in prayer must make a strict self-examination and discipline himself, so that the lust of the flesh may be speedily curbed and mortified.

13 JUNE

THE FEAST OF ST ANTHONY OF PADUA

The seed of grace sown in St Anthony of Padua at his baptism, and the infused virtues and the Gifts of the Holy Spirit which he later received—as all Christians do—bore most abundant fruit for God. Ever faithful to the indelible mark he had received, he became transformed into the likeness of God, proceeding "from one degree of glory to the other, for this comes from the Lord who is the Spirit" (cf. II Cor. 3. 18), so that everyone felt the compelling charm of his personality, of one who lived for Christ. As the Apostle said: "We are the aroma of Christ to God, among those who are being saved and among those who are perishing" (II Cor. 2. 15).

So this is for you too an essential duty: to live according to the promises made when you were baptized, in willing fidelity to divine grace, and to draw all to Christ, who is the source of truth, of purification and of perfection.

Everyone must act according to the promptings of grace and his own personal calling, but all must share the same firm resolve to bear witness to the Divine Founder of Christianity, and this is essentially the life of God in men, and men's expectation of the life of heaven.

Anthony's mission was pleasing to God. The proof of this is seen in the extraordinary manifestations of divine power which were visible throughout his life. We cannot all expect this for ourselves, but certainly to be allowed to share in the work for the kingdom of heaven is already a great privilege, and a miracle in itself. And this is what the Church expects from you; this is the mandate entrusted to you today by St Peter's humble successor.

You will always be able to carry on the apostolate of a good example, in a world that is not ashamed to offer bad examples but needs good ones, and very good ones, from all who profess the Christian faith. Do this without fear, and graciously, in order to spread around you the warmth of your convictions and the serenity of your faith.

14 JUNE

FEAST OF ST BASIL THE GREAT

What an admirable Saint and Doctor of the Church we have in St Basil, one of the most splendid figures of the fourth century! He died in 379, at the early age of forty-nine, but his brief life was an example of all the best that Christian perfection can offer. He belonged to a family that was distinguished by its service for God: among them was a brother of his, also a bishop, as was also one of his mother's brothers. St Basil therefore stands for the importance of the family, and for the blessing which heaven bestows upon the families over which the Lord reigns supreme with his grace and his law. When he went to Athens to follow a course of higher studies he had for his fellow disciple and beloved friend another illustrious Father of the Church, St Gregory Nazianzen. In 370 he was elected Bishop of Cæsarea and Cappadocia, and he initiated numerous works and organizations for the defence of the faith and of the integrity of doctrine, the increase of monastic vocations and the apostolate of charity.

Here lies a great lesson for us all! First of all for priests, then for the young, and finally for those of us who are more advanced in years, for it is very pleasant to refresh our minds and hearts in the work of those who have left behind them such wonderful proofs of how we can and must direct our mind and will, our youth and all our life, to God.

15 JUNE

TO FIGHT FOR JUSTICE

It is said that the primary exercise of charity is to honour justice and act accordingly, to give every man his due, not to deny the worker his just reward, to provide for our brothers' needs and also, if need arises, and at the cost of any personal sacrifice, to fight for justice. But charity to the poor, according to the Gospel commandment, must never lose its distinctive role of preceding, accompanying, inspiring and completing the work of justice.

Even after the much desired triumph of social justice there will always remain a wide margin for charity to the poor, for our Lord said: "You always have the poor with you".

For help given to the poor the Lord reserves his special blessings: the grace of forgiveness, and the treasures of his mercy. . . There is nothing more noble and more edifying than dying poor, and doing good to others even in the act of dying.

16 JUNE

WE ARE ALL CALLED TO BE SAINTS

The daily anxious thought of the great importance, or rather the necessity, that the souls entrusted to our care should be directed to the purest sources of human and Christian perfection is always near to our heart. They should turn back to the most solid foundations of the spiritual life, for safe guidance in the ways of righteousness, evangelical charity and holiness. Yes, of holiness too, for we are all called to be saints.

Every one of us has heard, and still hears, ringing in his conscience, the command: "Climb higher"; higher, ever higher, until while we are still on this earth we can reach up to grasp the heavens, until we can join our saints, whether they be the venerable saints of old or the wonderful saints of modern times, who were our own contemporaries, and in whom our Mother the Church already rejoices.

17 JUNE

THE VICTORY THAT OVERCOMES THE WORLD

"Whatever is born of God overcomes the world; and this is the victory that overcomes the world, our faith" (I John 5. 4).

Only the man who has faith and is inspired by charity can rise above the miseries, the meannesses and the malice of this world; instead, the man who lets himself be overcome by the spirit of illicit gain, of overweening hatred, and of impurity, is doomed to suffer, first here below, because he can never be entirely satisfied, and later on in the other world.

Nourish your faith then, my dear children, faith in God who is just and merciful, without whom your life would be like a day without the sun, a world without light—faith in the Church which, by divine decree, leads men gently and surely to heaven.

If you have these ideals your heart will be full of that peace which Jesus, as we read in the Gospel, gave to his Apostles, when he showed them his hands and his pierced side (cf. John 20. 20). Notice that after he had said "Peace be with you" Jesus showed them the open wounds in his sacred body. For true peace is born of doing the will of God, and bearing with patience the sufferings of this life, and does not come from following one's own whim or selfish desire, for this always brings, not peace and serenity, but disorder and discontent.

We beg you to be faithful to the Lord's Law, and constantly obedient to his holy commands... always apostles of good news, of happiness and good will, in your own houses and with your companions, so that in all may reign the grace and joy of the Risen Christ.

18 JUNE

THE ASSURANCE OF THINGS HOPED FOR

The Christian faith is well defined as the "assurance of things hoped for, the conviction of things not seen" (Heb. 11. 1). Certainly, to judge by the violence of anti-

143

Christian propaganda, and the widely spread illusions that spring from the new conception of earthly well-being, there is much to sadden the soul. This propaganda is pushed to the point of persuading quite a few mortals that the heavens are empty, and that there remains for man's enjoyment nothing else but the Earthly Paradise, which may be enjoyed to the full, at least by the boldest and most evil-minded of those people who assert that here below our only aim should be the triumph of the three lusts. Indeed, the soul is saddened and the resolve to live a good life seems to weaken, subjected as it is to such strong temptations to discouragement. This is what happens to the weak, the tired and the indolent.

But the words of Christ have filled the pages of the Gospel and have inspired the world with courage, and with the happiness that comes to every man who lives a good life, with the consciousness of Christian duty done, and trust in the solemn promise given by Jesus Christ: "He who belives and is baptized"—that is, he who has passed through the holy door of redemption—"will be saved; but he who does not believe will be condemned" (Mark 16. 16).

We who are children of the light have no fear of death, for our faith in God teaches us to trust in all confidence to the promises of Jesus: and our hope is a certainty. "I am the resurrection and the life" (John 11. 25). What words these are! "Whoever lives and believes in me shall never die" (John 11. 26).

19 JUNE

THE MATURE CHRISTIAN

A superficial observer of modern trends and movements concludes that everywhere in the world is to be seen nothing but the triumph of absurd, almost crazy, anti-Christian ideas. In fact, we cannot deny the progress made by atheistic materialism, which has become a state dogma for some nations, and the progress of practical materialism, which crushes men with the slavery of business and politics, carried on in a soulless and heart-less manner. But we consider as a proof of valid resist-ance to evil, and of the certainty of future victories, the strengthened bond of discipline, charity and apostolic labour which unites the whole episcopate to the Vicar of

Christ, and the clergy and faithful to their own bishops, in a communion of faith and of apostolic action which is slowly reassuming the characteristics of the primitive Church. These characteristics are: the study and knowledge of Christ and of the Gospel, the catechetical, not polemical, explanation of revealed truths and of Christian culture, an intense liturgical-eucharistic activity, firmness of moral conduct in the face of worldly temptations, and fervour of industrious and generous charity.

This is what we must say to our men and women, to our graduates. . . to teachers, and also to our dear children. The Christian lives on this earth, and tries to improve human relations, but because he is Christian . . . , although he does not neglect but gives due importance to the social and communal aspects of life, he is above all a man of faith, prayer and grace, convinced that every day fidelity to his baptismal vows is the first and truest foundation for civilization and for a better world.

20 JUNE

SUPERNATURAL LIFE

It is supernatural life, nourished with the great means of sanctification at your disposal, which gives to every one of you clear ideas, strong convictions, and generous energies. And I need not describe all that flows from this attitude of mind: delicacy of feeling and a gracious manner, ripeness of judgment, ready obedience and the warmth of charity. This is the secret of the true and lasting success of the apostolate; from this spring all worthy initiatives, to receive the blessing of God.

This supernatural life is the active fulfilment of the great petitions suggested by Jesus in the "Our Father": "hallowed be thy name, thy kingdom come, thy will be done". You know how earnestly and insistently we recommend for your meditation the prayer we learnt from Jesus. The holy name of God, revered, loved and taught, that is, his light and his love which "shine in our hearts to give the light of the knowledge of the glory of God in the face of Christ" (II Cor. 4. 6), his kingdom extended and enlarged, in an outpouring of enlightened and joyful enthusiasm, and his will, that will which works our sanctification (cf. I Thess. 4. 3), understood and obeyed.

145

His name is resplendent in the light which makes every Christian a dedicated worker in the good cause of God's holy Church; his kingdom is the purpose of every apostolate, including that of lay people co-operating with the ecclesiastical hierarchy; in the divine will is our mandate for action, which we cannot refuse to obey.

Therefore you must guard in your heart this anxious care for the interests of God and of souls, in the search for the "one thing which is needful" (Luke 10. 42).

21 JUNE

PRAYER FOR THOSE WHO SUFFER

Let us remember in prayer the everyday problems of the lives of some peoples, problems the solution of which statesmen have sought for so long to find. May the Lord enlighten the minds of all and strengthen their wills, so that all in positions of responsibility may understand that in their good will, their endeavour to establish friendly agreements, and in their loyalty to these, lies the secret of success for their efforts.

When hatred has been quenched and disagreements smoothed away, may the divine Redeemer bring about the final triumph of that justice which is invoked by so many of our fellow men; may there reign that spirit of sincere collaboration which alone can guarantee true peace and ordered progress for all the peoples of the world.

Finally, let us pray for the immense multitude of those who suffer in body and soul: for the sick, for prisoners and the unemployed, and for the exiles who, driven by dire necessity, wander far from their own lands, leading hard and anxious lives. Let us pray for all those who in their own lands are oppressed by irksome restrictions or constrained to do things contrary to their consciences and to the teaching of Holy Church. We implore Jesus to grant that they too may finally be allowed freely to confess their faith, to practise their holy religion and to live in complete serenity of mind.

We entrust these petitions of ours to the intercession of the Virgin, the most holy Mother of Jesus, who is our Mother too.

22 JUNE

NECESSITY OF GOOD WORKS

Confidence, indeed certainty, of victory in the Name of Jesus, of spirit over matter, of his Gospel over the seductive power of the "prince of this world", as he more than once described the devil he had encountered upon his path, does not mean that, after our first feeling of dismay, we may turn over on the other side and go to sleep again. God wants us to be saved, and he can save us and his Church even when we do not deserve this. But the Lord does not want to save us without our willing and convinced co-operation. To every soul setting out on the path of life he has given a good coin, that is, free will, which must be profitably employed, and with this every one of God's creatures holds his salvation and his perdition in his own hands. This is a crucial point of doctrine and of human life.

Let us ponder well, my children, and frequently, this responsibility laid on every one of us. To possess freedom of choice, enlightened by a clear discriminatory sense of good and evil, right and wrong, justice and oppression, and not to honour ourselves by using this freedom rightly and defending it in the sight of God, who is ready to help us and to carry us forward to the final triumph, would mean great stupidity, and great unhappiness!

23 JUNE

REST IN CHRIST JESUS

"Come to me, all you who labour and are heavy laden" (Matt. 11. 28). St Augustine comments: "We are all tired and heavy laden, because we are all mortal, frail, infirm, bearers of earthen vessels. But if the flesh is frail, or suffering, we can enlarge our charity. It is God who calls us, who is always ready to raise us up again and strengthen us, for life, for joy, for glory" (Augustine, *De verbis Domini in Mt.*).

"Come to me, all you...", and this does not necessarily mean on foot and on a pilgrimage, which can sometimes be undertaken more as a recreation than as a devout religious exercise, but with faith, confidence, piety and love.

"I will give you rest." This is what Jesus did during his mortal life, and this is what he still does in his continuing life in his Church. How strongly and gently he received, corrected and raised up Mary Magdalen, Matthew, Peter and Paul! With what humility and love he continues to receive countless millions of souls in the Eucharistic Communion which marks the highest point of union between the human and the divine!

24 JUNE

Angelo Roncalli, Nuncio in Paris, speaks at Lyons for the seventh centenary of the First Council of Lyons, 24 June 1945. The war had barely ended.

FEAST OF ST JOHN BAPTIST

The days of wrath, calamity and universal misery have passed over our own heads. But God has abased the proud who wanted to conquer the world. He has struck down those who were responsible, and their formidable armies. Now new horizons are opening before us, and new opportunities are presenting themselves for the improvement and progress of the social order.

Let us gather up all the blessed tapers which the terrible hurricane has extinguished. Let us light them again with a new flame, and, gathered joyfully around our father, the august Pontiff Pius XII, like the soldier pilgrims of old, re-form the procession of the Church and march forward, to the music of our hymns.

The Feast of St John the Baptist, the forerunner of our Saviour, to whom this great cathedral church is consecrated, offers us the lyrical inspiration and the melodious notes of the canticle of Zechariah: "...we, being delivered from the hand of our enemies, may serve him without fear: in holiness and righteousness before him, all the days of our life".

The centuries pass, my beloved brothers of Lyons, but the Church, like truth, is one and eternal. God's light shines on us from on high. Let us work, here below, nobly and indefatigably for the triumph of true liberty, in all senses of the word. Let us share in works of edification and the apostolate. Let us direct our steps in the paths of peace, so that Christ may be exalted, to his glory and our joy. Let us work for the glory, the prosperity and the blessing of France and all peoples in all ages. Amen.

WORKS THAT ARE MERELY HUMAN DO NOT LAST

How to put a stop to this internal corrosion, the stripping of the supernatural element from the mind and customs of modern life in all its aspects—this is undoubtedly the central problem of the religious apostolate of our day. It is equally necessary to restore to their rightful place and honour the Christian principles contained in the Gospel, for the most part unknown to the world or set aside, and here and there, even in our own land, treated as absurd or discreditable, or relegated to dismal oblivion.

Man's destiny is to seek his heavenly fatherland. Instead, alas! we see him struggling convulsively to take possession of the Earthly Paradise, forgetting the great disillusionment, the tragic experiment which stains with tears and blood the first chapters of the Divine Book. Ever since the failure of that first experiment, when man's will, free and sacred, was turned to licence and falsehood, the story of mankind has been a long alternation of wretchedness and recovery.

The wretchedness is of men abandoned to themselves, to fallacious knowledge and the prodigies of a technical skill that is undoubtedly admirable and powerful, but not conducive to the triumph of the Spirit; the recovery is due to the Lord, with the collaboration of his priests and saints, in whom the apostolate of the Church is perpetuated, according to the promise of Jesus, who assured us of his presence with us until the end of the world.

26 JUNE

THE DIVINE EXAMPLES

The gifts of God are of priceless worth to those who know they have received them from their Creator, and use them humbly and without boastfulness.

Instead, to give way to vanity or to show oneself eager to possess these gifts, perhaps merely in order to cut a good figure in the eyes of the world, is a sign of great spiritual poverty, which excites both pity and scorn.

In the Catholic Church everything which is great and truly glorious is a reflection of the divine examples of

Jesus and his Blessed Mother. This heavenly doctrine is expressed and exalted in the Gospel, when Jesus tells his disciples to learn from him, their Master, "for I am gentle and lowly in heart" (Matt. 11. 29), and when Mary replies to the Angel: "Behold, I am the handmaid of the Lord: let it be to me according to your word" (Luke 1. 38).

27 JUNE

PATIENCE IN EVERYDAY LIFE

Good Christians . . . know that the practice of patience means first of all rejecting the frivolous pleasures of the world and always cherishing in our hearts the commandments of God's Son, with the help of his grace which is distilled through his most precious Blood; and it means receiving in our souls the marks of his passion and indescribable sufferings—a sure sign of great blessing.

This then is the good and fruitful task set before you; everyone of you, returning to his habitual residence, must carry away, in remembrance of his meeting with the Pope, the great and splendid truth enshrined in the sublime word: patience!

Sometimes we think we can solve in all sorts of ways the ordinary problems and difficulties of our lives. We have recourse to complicated and even to difficult means, forgetting that just a little patience is required to arrange everything in perfect order and restore calm and serenity. The Christian must treat the virtue of patience with constant and loving care, until it has become a real and excellent habit, which will result in many advantages and generous rewards.

We all remember having heard, from our early childhood, that in every house, behind the front door (with the disadvantage that it is always being moved to and fro!), hangs a cross. In fact there is no family that has not some trial or suffering to bear. However, every good Christian might add that in the eyes of faith a trial is considered a necessary cross, a clear sign that Christ himself died upon the Cross and wants us to be near him: he calls us and awaits us.

28 JUNE

PATIENCE IS A MOST NECESSARY POSSESSION

"May the Lord direct our hearts and our bodies to the

love of God and to the steadfastness of Christ" (cf. II Thess. 3. 5).

May the Lord watch over our bodies. To be sure, physical health is a great blessing, but if it should fail, may the Lord assist us to set a greater value on what physical strength may yet achieve in his service.

May he watch over our hearts! This is what concerns us most. We must direct and control our affections according to the Lord's wishes and commands, so that we may be fully united with him. And may he always preserve in us the supreme gift of charity: the source, even on this earth, of true happiness and nobility. Jesus wants all men, scattered throughout the world and divided into so many peoples and nations, to be united in him. He said so in the wonderful prayer he uttered before going to die for us: "Father,. . . that they may all be one; even as thou, Father, art in me, and I in thee, that they also may be in us, so that the world may believe that thou hast sent me" (John 17. 21).

Finally, in the grace of Christ, we must have patience with everyone, and in all suffering. Indeed patience is a most necessary possession, if we wish to live well. A Father of the Church observed, very rightly, and encouragingly: "Where there is patience, there is happiness". When patience fails we become a prey to wrath, disquiet, irritability and bitterness. With the Lord's patience, especially if it becomes a permanent habit with us, we are sure of receiving every blessing. Then the Lord is one with us, and within us.

So, even if he lays upon our shoulders some part of his own Cross, he is there to help us to bear it with self-sacrifice and with love.

29 JUNE

FEAST OF THE HOLY APOSTLES PETER AND PAUL

There are two Gospel passages upon which are laid the foundations of the Catholic Church. One of these is the brief dialogue between the Angel and Mary in the holy seclusion of Nazareth, which expresses the whole mystery of the Incarnation and Redemption of the world. The other is Peter's cry of faith: "You are the Christ, the Son of the living God", followed by the promise of Jesus: "You are Peter, and upon this rock I will build my church".

In fact, through the divine motherhood of Mary the Word of God is made man, and the work of the redemption and salvation of the world begins. The avowal of faith in Christ, the Son of the living God, is answered by Christ's words: "You are Peter. . ." and with these words the Church is founded.

So the salvation of the world is brought about. . . .

Let us praise God and rejoice in the glory of St Peter and of the other apostles who by divine power and grace have gone out to the ends of the earth, and continue through the centuries to preach the liberation and salvation of all men.

O St Peter, Prince of the Apostles, first Pope of the universal Church, how our heart rejoices when we bow our forehead over your blessed foot and repeat, as we did in the early years of our priesthood, the holy words: "Obedience and peace".

Here we are united in this liturgical homage to you, O Peter, Son of John, most holy saint, with the Apostle of the Gentiles, the incomparable Paul, that "chosen vessel" of sanctification, your partner in death and a sharer in your crown. You are both lamps to guide our feet, lights and ornaments of the universal Church.

30 JUNE

Commemoration of St Paul.

RENEWAL OF THE SPIRIT

In these days we are always hearing the cry: "We must make all things new" (cf. Rev. 21. 5). Everything must be brought up to date: the advance of scientific knowledge has transformed old ways of living, thinking and acting.

Now we, that is the Church, give a cordial welcome to all technical progress, and willingly avail ourselves of improvements in our food and drink, in rest and recreation, in all the requirements of our social life. But the apostle's command is twofold; he says also: Do not seek to follow the fashion of the day, which is changeable and fleeting, but transform yourselves into what is always new, into Christ Jesus. St Augustine comments with characteristic subtlety: "We must be changed, not in order to conform to the fashion of this world, but in order to grow more like the Son of God. Therefore do not put on the clothing of this world, like the worldly, the vain, the proud and ambitious, and those who seek only what is of this earth, indifferent or hostile to what is heavenly and eternal. 'But put on the Lord Jesus Christ' " (Rom. 13. 14).

This eagerness to clothe ourselves in Christ must be felt every day. Pope St Gregory has something brilliant to say about this: "The love of God which burns in our hearts is of such splendour and beauty that it increases in fervour with every new dawn. The spirit never grows old with the passing years, and is always in time to renew itself."

JULY

1 JULY

FEAST OF THE PRECIOUS BLOOD OF JESUS

The devotion to the most precious Blood of Jesus, by the virtue of which we humbly beg the Lord to forgive us our sins, is an excellent devotion for both clergy and laity.

We read about this priceless treasure in the Liturgy, in the New Testament—remembering what St Paul wrote about it—and even in the Old Testament too.

The Blood of Christ is his Sacrifice applied to us; it enters the souls of the redeemed; it is the inextinguishable source of all heroism. Even in the face of everyday events which seem to threaten our security, we know where to find strength, perseverance and certainty. This we have learnt from those who, responding generously to the Saviour's call and offering him their own lives and blood, have striven to find and keep that peace which the world refuses to understand, which is the work of God.

2 JULY

Feast of the Visitation.

THE HUMBLE OF HEART

The Son of God, who came to earth to teach men, left us no instruction clearer and more precise than this: we are to be humble in heart, mind, speech and behaviour.

This humility is often expressed in silence; this gentleness may seem weakness. But, on the contrary, it is strength of character and dignity of life; it is of great importance, even for the future of peaceful relations between men.

Success is always assured and granted to the humble in heart. The man who has no humility, who yields to the temptations of presumptuous arrogance, is doomed to live bitter days, to find himself before long empty-handed, and to live years of great unhappiness.

This strength of character finds its most glorious expression in the spirit of sacrifice, which is the mortification and annihilation of the self offered in sacrifice to the Lord's will, for the purification of souls.

3 JULY

THE DANGERS OF THE ROAD

In this question of the use and abuse of the road there is . . . a mystery of life and death, a responsibility laid on every one, which no one can refuse to bear.

The civil laws of human society rightly support the great commandment: "Thou shalt not kill", clearly set forth in the Decalogue that speaks to all generations, and for us all it is a sacred precept given us by our Lord.

Permit me now to remind you all of your moral obligations with regard to the dangers of the road, and we will also indicate to you a sure and most precious heavenly protection, the help of our Guardian Angels.

Among their other tasks they were entrusted with that of guiding our steps. Remembering this, how can we fail to feel rightly dismayed when we are faced with the daily spectacle of blood upon our roads?

Do you not think, my beloved children, that this appeal for the help of the angels who were given us to guard our childhood steps and all our wanderings, in every age and circumstance of our life and work—do you not think that this appeal will touch the hearts of those who have fallen under the deceitful and intoxicating spell of speed, so as finally to bring about absolute and universal obedience to the regulations controlling the traffic?

PRAYER FOR THE MOTORIST

Protect us, O Lord, from all danger to men that may arise from the difficulties of travelling, the weariness of the body, or from inconsiderate speed. . . . And as, O Lord, you graciously sent the Archangel Raphael to be a travelling companion and protector to the young Tobias, so save all your children from all perils of soul and body, so that, journeying along the ways of this world in your sight, they may deserve to reach the haven of eternal salvation. Through Christ our Lord. Amen. Amen.

4 JULY

THE LOVE OF OUR OWN LAND

The love of our own land is a ray of the Lord's love shining on all who are brothers under the same sky. . .

Our country's welfare is based, not merely on the material prosperity of trade and business, on the success of military enterprises and diplomatic treaties, or on the predominance of one element or another in the development of economic relations—but, above all, on the firmness of the fundamental principles which uphold the constitution of the State, and on the cultivation of those Christian and social virtues which make up what is generally known as justice, and which are the greatness and glory of individuals and nations.

While every citizen must find some way to co-operate for his country's good, it is the duty of the bishops and clergy to uphold and preach these principles, in their apostolate of word and example, in order to foster the growth and practice of those virtues without which any society falls into decay.

Leave us then the holy freedom of our peaceful and noble ministry. Leave us at our altars, where we may intercede with God for Christian people and their rulers. Leave us to guard the fundamental principles of law and civilization, contained in the Decalogue and in the Gospel. . .

And ask nothing else of us. . . To remain faithful to God and to the Church, and not to meddle in confused and changing political activity, to keep ourselves above all worldly interests, watchful and eager only in the constant work of dispensing charity. . . this is the most precious service we can give to our country.

5 JULY

THE VALUE OF SPORT

The great value of sport lies in its particular effectiveness for the improvement of your spiritual powers, achieved through the external discipline with which you earnestly and continually train your bodies.

We trust that you will never forget, beloved children, that the efforts you make are not an end in themselves; the body which serves you reflects, in its agility and harmony of movement, a ray of the beauty and almighty power of your Creator; it is only an instrument which you must keep under control and sensitive to the powerful influence of your soul.

Your exercises and competitions, which are like pleasant interludes in the monotony of study and daily work, must serve to enhance the spiritual and immortal part of you. If they were to have a harmful effect, if in your athletic career you were to find not a safeguard but a danger for your souls, or an obstacle in the way of the practice of your religion, then you would have gone astray, like the cross-country runner who, because he did not follow the right course, could not win the race.

Courage then, dear children. Aim always at that goal to which we are all called, the eternal life that must be won with good works, and the practice of Christian virtues.

6 JULY

To the members of the *Centro Sportivo Italiano* Pope John spoke of another prize to be won, beyond this material world.

SPORT AS AN EXERCISE IN VIRTUE

Sport is of very great value in your lives, as an exercise in moral virtue.

You are always in training, so that your muscles may not lose their agility, suppleness, or strength. This continual preparation, although its chief aim is the reward of physical and technical prowess, must nevertheless have a lasting and beneficial effect on the soul, which has much to gain from the precious habits thus formed.

In fact, sport too may develop the true and sturdy Christian virtues which, by the grace of God, may become permanent and fruitful. In the spirit of self-discipline you learn and practise obedience, humility and unselfishness; in your team work and competitions you learn charity, brotherly affection, mutual respect, generosity, sometimes even forgiveness: in the strict discipline of your training you must be chaste, modest, self-controlled and prudent.

Oh what a great blessing it is for you to be able to practise with youthful enthusiasm these ancient virtues, without which you may be great, but not truly Christian, athletes!

The spiritual value of sport is enhanced also by that noble discontent which, shown in the effort to do better every time, characterizes every competition.

So we learn that, as in the physical world, so, and particularly, in the world of spiritual endeavour, we must learn never to be content with the level we have reached but, with the help of God and with our own determined efforts, we must aim at ever greater heights, at continual improvement, so that we may in the end reach mature manhood, "the measure of the stature of the fullness of Christ" (Eph. 4. 13).

7 JULY

FEAST OF ST CYRIL AND ST METHODIUS

Today's liturgy commemorates those two apostles of the Slavonic world, St Cyril and St Methodius, in whose glory Pope Leo XIII appointed a special Feast in the calendar of the Universal Church.

The shining figures of these two great saints remind us of our duty to care, with ever increasing affection, for our separated brothers, and to try in every way to draw them into that unity for which we all pray today.

We rejoice to think that, through our prayers and sacrifices, Divine Providence is working one of the greatest mysteries of history, the mystery of his mercy poured out upon all peoples.

To care for others. . . this is good and meritorious; this is the true and holy Catholic apostolate.

8 JULY

THE USE OF LEISURE

We draw your attention to the right use of leisure, which

the new conditions of social life are making increasingly available to us all. We must thank Providence for having enabled modern science to make this possible. In the Christian view of life the whole of our time—not only that given to work, but what is set apart for recreation also—is God's gift to man, to be used for His glory, in the integral development of the whole personality. Leisure must give us the opportunity not only for recreation, but also for a renewal of our physical and spiritual energies.

First of all, we must make a more strenuous endeavour to restore to the Lord's Day its sacred character, that is, we must "remember the Sabbath day, to keep it holy" (cf. Ex. 20. 8).

The failure of the collective conscience to observe this obligation has an adverse effect on public morality and can impede the progress of grace, influencing society in favour of religious indifferentism, which is sad and harmful. On the Lord's Day the faithful must stop being men of machines and worldly business; they must really abstain from work, not only from what is called "servile" work, but from other labours also, because they rob the mind of its rest, which it needs in order to be able to rise to heavenly things in prayer, to take an active share in the liturgical life of the Church, and to meditate upon the word of God.

9 JULY

PURITY OF LIFE

The stainless glory of the Catholic priesthood all over the world and in all the labours of the apostolate, especially in these modern times (as undoubtedly also in the future), consists in this: a clean life, that is, purity of mind and heart, the spirit of meekness and humility, and bright unconquerable enthusiasm for action and sacrifice.

Do not let yourselves be led astray or corrupted by every new doctrine, or every attempt to assail the integrity of this principle, which is fundamental. Any yielding on this point, or even any slightest compromise, is always a snare and a delusion.

Ah, my dear sons! withered flowers are a dismal sight! We were expecting to enjoy their perfume, diffused for the edification and admiration of all. Instead, a gust of wind has laid them low.

Youth is joyless once this flower has withered; the man who has failed to honour his great vow of total consecration to God goes forward, sometimes for many years, with heavy, dragging steps.

A stainless life is poetry and freshness, joy and enthusiasm, and has an irresistible fascination for the souls of men.

10 JULY

A JOYFUL SOUL

These three gifts, simplicity, alertness of mind, and a cheerful spirit may, in different measure, be applied to the actions and behaviour of all.

The apostle Paul begs us. . . to give all we have, without making a great fuss about it, without a long pealing of bells, but with simplicity, that is, naturally and graciously.

We must know how to direct ourselves and others, and this direction must be very carefully imparted. Everyone has his own temperament and character. Some are in a hurry, others not; some are slow to move, while others act speedily and rashly, endangering themselves and others. Moreover, it may happen that some, insufficiently trained in the discipline of Christian perfection, let themselves be dominated by what is defective or excessive in their own characters, and so become at times strong and overbearing, at other times weak and inert.

Finally, we must bear all cheerfully. Our life, especially that part of it which we spend in the company of others, must not be sad and gloomy; we must not let our own boredom, restlessness and melancholy depress those who are near to us and depend upon us.

In this life we have to lift ourselves ever higher. There are various kinds of poetry: but the supreme poetry of this life is found in a joyful soul.

11 JULY

CHRISTIANS ON HOLIDAY

The open air, the sunlight and the sea remind us of the

160

sick and suffering, and consequently . . .lead us to reflect on the great importance of physical health which, although in itself so precarious, is indispensable for the accomplishment of our daily tasks.

"You shall not ruin your health" is the necessary corollary of the commandment: Six days you shall labour. . . It would seem quite unnecessary to have to remind people of this, when they are using their holidays to restore their physical health, were it not that experience has shown us that holiday-makers often run the risk of tiring themselves out, or of becoming restless, and at times even expose themselves to real dangers to their body and soul.

You must remind town dwellers, who go to the seaside, the lakes, the mountains and the great open plains, that these expeditions must not be taken as opportunities for spiritual laxity, or as pretexts for unbridled licence, made more easy by the feeling that they are far away from their customary activities.

Make them understand that during these holiday periods of free and legitimate recreation men must and can enter into the life of nature, in order to recover the serenity, calm and harmony of their spiritual nature, and also in order to resume the conversation with God which enlarges the horizons of the supernatural life of grace.

This is the final purpose of all sight-seeing and wandering, and of the enjoyment of the beauties our heavenly Father has created for us, as a foretaste of his eternal wisdom and beauty: "Thou openest thy hand, thou satisfiest the desire of every living thing" (Psalm 144 (145). 16).

12 JULY

GOODNESS

Nothing is more excellent than goodness. The human mind may look for other eminent gifts, but none of these can be compared with goodness. It is of the same nature as the Son of God himself, who became man, and it is the essence of all he taught us by word and example: the exercise of brotherly love and of patience, constancy in compassion and forbearance, in the interior discipline of our own characters and in the relationships of social life, just as he told us.

Jesus did not say to us: Learn from me for I am the Son of the heavenly Father. He did not show us how to create heaven and earth, or to clothe the sun in its mantle of splendour, but how to be meek and lowly of heart. This is the very foundation of goodness. When we understand the secret of goodness and have made it our own we shall have found the surest way of overcoming the difficulties and failures of our earthly life.

13 JULY

CHRISTIAN CHARITY

Charity is at the summit of human and Christian virtue ... at the point of union between earth and heaven, which is sublimely expressed in Christ Jesus, the Word of the Father, who became man to save mankind. The Creator of the world, in order to save fallen man, took on a human body and "made us partakers in his divine nature" (cf. II Peter 1. 4).

These are moving and mysterious words, enshrining in celestial light the doctrine of the redemption of the world and of the divine institution of Christ's Church.

In this holy Church we have all received, and continue to receive, life from Jesus who, by becoming our Brother, has laid the foundation of the great precept of neighbourly charity, of which the Saviour said, foretelling the terms of the Last Judgment: "As you did it to one of the least of these my brethren, the poor, the abandoned and the needy, you did it to me" (cf. Matt. 25. 40).

These words demand a corresponding charity from all Christians as if by way of repaying Jesus himself for making us "partakers of his divine nature".

Oh how wonderful is the story of Christian charity, which continues to shine through all the centuries!

14 JULY

THE LIGHT OF THE WORLD

The light of truth, which springs from the divine Word, illuminates the past and inspires the present. It is like the breath and promise of a future life, beyond the last coming of God for the final judgment here below, the judgment which will decide the eternal destiny of every man.

What is most important to understand and remember is that man's capacity to know the truth implies a very grave and sacred responsibility of co-operation in the plan of our Redeemer, our Saviour. And this is an even graver responsibility for the Christian who, by his reception of the grace of the sacraments, shows that he belongs to the family of God.

This is the greatest dignity and obligation ever laid on man, and particularly on every Christian: the obligation to do honour to the Son of God, the "Word made flesh", who gives life to all mankind and all human society. Jesus left us the example of his thirty years of silence, so that we might learn to see the truth in him, and his three years of unwearied and persuasive ministry, so that we might find in him an example and a rule of life.

The Divine Book teaches us this doctrine and makes us rejoice in it.

Union with Christ, since he proclaimed himself to be our Lord and Master, is therefore the triumph of truth, supreme knowledge, the supreme doctrine. . .

The divine Teacher said: "I am the light of the world: he who follows me will not walk in darkness" (John 8. 12).

15 JULY

Feast of St Henry II, Emperor of the Holy Roman Empire.

THE RIGHT USE OF AUTHORITY

Authority is not an uncontrolled force; it is the right to rule according to reason. Therefore it derives its power to command from the moral order which is founded on God, its first principle and its last end.

Authority which is based mainly or only on the threats and fear of punishment, or on the promise and expectation of reward, is not an effective means of making human beings work for the common good. Even if it were to succeed the result would not be consonant with the personal dignity of the subject, that of a free and reasonable being. Authority is essentially a moral force; therefore it must make its appeal primarily to the conscience, the sense of duty which every one must willingly obey as his contribution to the good of all. Human beings are all equal in their natural dignity: none may penetrate to the interior life of another. This only God can do, because he alone sees and judges the intentions of our innermost soul.

Human authority can therefore be a moral obligation only if it is instrinsically in harmony with the authority of God and has a share in this. In this way the personal dignity of citizens is safeguarded, since their obedience to the public authorities is not the subjection of one man to another but, in its true significance, an act of homage to God, our provident Creator, who has decreed that the conditions of social life shall be regulated according to an order he himself has instituted. There is no humiliation in rendering homage to God; in fact this raises and ennobles us, for "to serve God is to reign".

16 JULY

THE CHURCH IN THE MODERN WORLD

Nearly all contemporary writers are full of pessimism, and the rulers of this earth now confess their powerlessness to raise man to greater heights, or to create for him that realm of happiness and prosperity which he always so ardently desires.

The Catholic Church has never said she wishes to dispense men from the hard law of suffering and death. She has not tried to deceive them, or to drug them with the compassionate opium of illusion. Instead, she has always insisted that our life here is a pilgrimage, but she has taught her children to join in that song of hope which, in spite of all, is still heard in this world.

Man is now, as it were, bewildered by the scientific progress he has made and is at last aware that none of these conquests can bring him happiness. He sees the continual appearances and disappearances of all those who promised eternal youth and easy prosperity. It is therefore right and natural that the Church should raise her authoritative and persuasive voice, to offer all men the comfort of her doctrine, and of truly Christian brotherhood which prepares the splendour of the eternal day for which man was made.

Undaunted by the difficulties which her children are encountering, and which impede the service she wishes to render to truth, justice and love, still faithful to the orders of her divine Founder, she wishes to speak to men about him, about Christ Jesus as Master, Christ Jesus as Shepherd, and about Christ Jesus as victim and expiatory sacrifice for our redemption.

17 JULY

THE TRIUMPH OF CIVILIZATION

In their mutual relations men have learnt from the natural law, and from the nobler law of their Creator, the sacred obligation of caring for one another. "And he gave to every one of them commandments concerning his neighbour" (Exodus 17. 12). And this is a fundamental law.

Indeed a great obligation is laid upon us all, to honour our brotherhood, in the sense of sharing with all others, every man with his fellow men, the good things necessary for social life—for the individual alone is incapable of providing, out of his own resources, for his bodily spiritual needs.

This exchange of brotherly assistance produces what we usually call civilized or social life. We might describe it more worthily as the perfection and beauty of human partnership, the triumph of civilization.

It is obvious that human society can live and prosper when regulated by this basic law which obliges the human conscience of one and all to draw inspiration and strength for a good life from the consideration of our sublime end. This law is engraved by the Creator on the heart of every one on whom he has bestowed the august gift of life. It is inscribed in the pages of the Bible—the Old Testament—where all forty-five books repeat it under various forms, all exalting the human spirit for its incomparable wisdom and beauty.

But this law is perfected in the New Testament, the Gospel of Christ, with its corollary of apostolic writings, familiar to all good Christians and all educated people.

18 JULY

Feast of St Camillus de Lellis, Apostle of the Sick.

CHRISTIAN SUFFERING

In order to receive from our meditation upon the Cross

all the spiritual consolation promised to Christian suffering, you must have within you the gift of grace, which is the very life of the Christian soul. In grace you will find strength, not only to accept suffering with resignation, but to welcome it as did the saints. Your sufferings will not be wasted: they will be united with the sufferings of the Crucified and the sufferings of the Virgin Mary, most innocent of creatures, and so your life will grow in conformity with the likeness of the Son of God, the king of suffering, and become a means of reaching heaven.

But there is more to it than that. The Passion of Jesus will teach you also the immense value of suffering for the sanctification of souls and the salvation of the world. Look again at our divine Saviour on the Cross! He taught men by his words and example, and healed them with his miracles, but it was above all through his Passion and Cross that he saved the world. Do you wish to be like Jesus? Do you wish to transform yourselves into him? Do you wish to help him to save souls? In your infirmities you have the instrument given you by Providence to "complete what is lacking in Christ's afflictions for the sake of his body, that is, the Church".

Is this not what the Immaculate Virgin requested of us all with such insistence at Lourdes, when she asked St Bernadette for "prayer and penitence"? Work and suffering were the first penance set mankind by God: mankind that had fallen through sin. Just as sin calls down God's wrath, so the sanctification of work and suffering brings God's mercy to all mankind.

19 JULY

Feast of St Vincent de Paul, whose name is for ever associated with works of charity.

SUFFICIENT MEANS

In human society all an individual's natural rights bring with them corresponding duties towards others, in fact, the duty of recognizing and respecting these rights in other people too. Every fundamental individual right derives its irrepressible moral authority from the natural law which confers it, and which exacts a corresponding duty. Therefore those who claim their rights but forget or fail to attach due importance to their corresponding duties run the risk of building up with one hand and pulling down with the other.

Human beings are persons, and therefore by nature social beings. So they are born to live together and to work for the common good. This requires an ordered society, with the recognition and observance of one another's rights and duties, but it also requires the generous contribution of everyone in the work of creating human groups in which the rights and duties have an increasingly richer content.

For example, it is not enough to recognize and respect the right of every human being to his means of subsistence; it is also necessary that, according to our different capacities, we should all strive to ensure that every human being actually receives sufficient means to satisfy his requirements.

20 JULY

MODESTY IN DRESS

"When women begin to dress immodestly, and men to make fun of religion, it is the beginning of the end." So said the philosopher Seneca.

It is not my habit to look at the world through dark coloured spectacles, but now I consider it is necessary to call everyone's attention to this question of moral conduct, and to try to reform public opinion, which seems to have gone to sleep.

We must unite all our good intentions, representing every point of view, religious, moral and civic—and I would add also the æsthetic point of view and the question of good taste—in the common effort to erect some barriers, if we can do no more, in the path of this alarming landslide.

We can do no more than protest, but we must, above all, avoid giving the impression that we connive at such a spectacular attempt to undermine moral values.

On this occasion, as at other times and frequently, I remind you of the prophet's lament, and ask: "If the foundations are destroyed, what can the righteous do?" (Psalm 10 (11). 3).

Faced with the indifference which arises in a bewildered mind and corrupts the heart, what can, what must the righteous man do?

In fact, many parents and teachers have given up the struggle: the guardians of order and decency seem at a loss; the magistrates sometimes lack, we must admit, the support of precise legislation on this matter.

My children, the Psalm goes on, with terrible words: "the Lord's throne is in heaven . . . his eyes behold the children of men... The Lord tests the righteous and the wicked. On the wicked he will rain coals of fire and brimstone."

21 JULY

AN INALIENABLE POSSESSION

There is a television programme which, I am told, is very interesting, and which is intended to prevent fatal accidents and to appeal for moderation of speed: "The road belongs to everyone".

I wish to repeat these words with reference to the subject of morality, which demands mutual respect, with especial reverence for children. Woe to whoever violates the innocence which naturally belongs to every one of them, and so sends them out unarmed into the great battles of life!

It is not a question of severity or intolerance, but of fundamental principles, without which families and nations alike fall into ruin. It is enough to have common sense (and every man worth his salt has this), it is enough to respect the noble values of a civilization which is based on the religious aspect of life and its duties, it is enough to appeal to the principles of natural morality, in order to find ourselves in agreement about this.

And as for the Christian: he is the temple of the Holy Spirit, a member of the Mystical Body of Jesus; he is a follower of that doctrine which preaches self-denial, and purity of heart, speech and behaviour, in order to make men healthier, freer and more noble.

Innocence is of its own nature inalienable, and where our children are concerned, we are its keepers and guardians.

22 JULY

Feast of St Mary Magdalen.

THE SACRAMENT OF FORGIVENESS

A strange episode is described in St Luke's Gospel. Mary Magdalen, a poor sinful woman, falls penitent at the feet of the Lord, who has been invited to the home of one of the chief Pharisees, Simon; she weeps bitterly over her sins. She trusts in the Saviour, Son of God, and from him she receives words of indescribable comfort, of real renewal of life: "Your faith has saved you: go in peace".

Naturally the fellow guests begin to murmur at this unusual occurrence, and above all at the Lord's words. And Jesus, hearing their murmurings and understanding, through his divine power, what his host was thinking, took the opportunity of explaining to him his law of goodness, compassion and forgiveness. In this conversation we see how the Lord pities repentant sinners, accepts their sorrow and raises them, leading them to salvation, telling them to go in peace and sin no more.

Many souls, like St Mary Magdalen, have been able to enjoy the consolation of God's infinite mercy.

It is the same mercy which, in the sacrament of repentance, absolves all sins, great or small, and has its roots in what the divine Master, shortly before this recorded episode, had taught his apostles and disciples, when he told them to pray:

"Our Father, who art in heaven . . . forgive us our sins as we forgive those who sin against us".

23 JULY

THE CONSEQUENCES OF COMPROMISE

By now you know me well, my beloved brothers and sons. My temperament and my long spiritual training, for which I thank the Lord, have prevented me from being inclined towards pessimism. I like to repeat what a recent Pope used to say: "I am glad to have been born in this present hour, rather than in any period of the past. I prefer the times that are to the times that were. . ."

Our eyes, shocked by the misery of present troubles, prefer to turn to the contemplation of the great deal of good still being done in the world, in the universal Catholic Church, by millions and millions of souls who have answered the call to grace and holiness. . .

But all this cannot disguise the horror we feel for the

vast extent and gravity of present evils, and does not affect the sorrowful reality . . . We are concerned with the danger of the growing power of error and evil, studied, organized and full of menace. We see the vulnerability of poor human nature disconcerted by the irridescent brilliance of modern life, and every day exposed to the temptation of compromise—I repeat this word—compromise between spirit and matter. The consequences of compromise are distressing and deplorable: the mind is clouded and the will to perform the most sacred duties of human and Christian life become weakened.

We look all around us to see whether there may be new ways of defending the religious, doctrinal and moral inheritance we have received from our forefathers, and whether it is still possible to prevent a universal collapse of principles.

24 JULY

THE DECALOGUE

What a marvellous passage this is in the 20th chapter of Exodus! The principles we are looking for are all here. In every man's heart there is a reflection of God, and the germ of his Law. It is the natural law corresponding to the nature of created things, of which Providence makes use to rule the world. . .

In Exodus, in the commandments God gave to Moses so that he might deliver them to his people, the natural law is confirmed and amplified in an impressive list of precepts concerning the relations between man and God, thus becoming the purest kind of religion, and then, still in the light of God, the relations to which I have already referred, those between man and man, for man was made for civil and social life, that is, to live for the family, the nation and the rest of mankind.

This is the most solemn and sacred drama of the Old Testament. The people, trembling with awe, had stayed at the foot of the mountain. Moses alone had passed through the whirlwind and the thunder, the smoke and the fire, into God's presence, and had received the Law, formulated in ten Commandments, written "by the finger of God" on two stone tablets. The first tablet contained the law regulating our attitude to God, in three articles; the second tablet, in seven articles, contained the principles of the moral law that governs man in his civil and social life.

"Honour your father and your mother, that your days may be long in the land which the Lord your God gives you. You shall not kill. You shall not commit adultery. You shall not steal. You shall not bear false witness. . . you shall not covet your neighbour's house. . . or his wife, or his manservant or his maidservant. . . ."

25 JULY

Feast of St James the Apostle.

"YOU SHALL BE MY WITNESSES"

The kingdom of Christ Jesus, the Son of God, the Word made flesh, the Lord of the Universe, began when these words were said: "You shall be my witnesses" (Acts 1. 8). From that moment the Catholic and Apostolic Church, One and Holy, began its onward march. Twenty centuries have gone by. Grave and dangerous crises resulting from human weakness have often, here and there, threatened the survival of this wonderful institution; difficulties have beset its path, and trials and uncertainties, due to the infidelity and desertion of some, have at times seemed gravely to endanger its unity. But the apostolic succession has never been broken. . .

The word of Jesus is still with us to give life to his Church. The miracle is renewed in the faithful outpouring of grace on every faithful disciple, and sometimes, in an impressive and mysterious way, over the whole social body.

Beloved children! The encouraging words: "You shall bear testimony to me" are a divine link between the two Testaments, explaining the mysterious association of past, present and future. Jesus, the divine Teacher, is still in our midst, and in his own person, his teaching, and the sacrament of his Body and Blood there shines the glory of his kingship.

"You shall be my witnesses." The testimony was twofold, for Jesus bore witness to himself, showing himself to his disciples always as Lord and Master, in the evidence of his sublime doctrine, in the series of miracles he accomplished, in his bloody Sacrifice and victorious Resurrection, and in the endless outpouring of grace and love to man forgiven, and to all mankind redeemed and raised to the height of kinship with God! "Born of a virgin, he has shared with us, that is, with the world, his divine nature."

26 JULY

FEAST OF ST ANNE, THE MOTHER OF MARY

St Anne was the mother of the blessed Virgin Mary. The sweet and venerable figure of this highly privileged woman cannot be separated from that of her husband, St Joachim, equally loved and revered by all Christians. We do not know much about them, but from an ancient tradition we learn that they were already advanced in years when the Lord bestowed on them the gift of the stainless lily chosen to be the Mother of the Word of God made man, and the Spiritual Mother of all the redeemed.

We can all learn a twofold lesson from the recurrence of the Feast of St Anne.

The first is for children and young people, and perhaps for older folk too. It is that we must always treat elderly people with great respect and affectionate care. They possess a real treasure of gifts and graces which the Lord has showered upon them on the long way they have come, and this treasure will be of priceless value to them when they reach the end of their earthly pilgrimage.

You must then respect the old, and during the years of youth and maturity you must be generous in service to God. In this way we can be sure that the young people of today will enjoy a serene and trustful old age, strengthened by fine memories of the good they have done.

27 JULY

THE NATURAL LAW

In practice a moral code independent of God is only effective in so far as it is founded on a sense of justice contained in the very conception of humanity.

But if justice is based merely on everyone's interests,

or on the interests of the various groups that make up human society, it is very natural that the principle of mutual respect, which is invoked as the first and noblest characteristic mark of a respectable moral code, should always run the risk of being interpreted and applied in different ways. There is also the danger that human appetites will inevitably usurp the place of any other power which moves and directs the will, and these appetites will war fiercely against each other. It is this contradiction that leads to war. When one party says: "We have all we want, and justice is on our side", and the other party says: "We are hungry, and justice must come to our help and feed us", the bloody struggle begins. Where shall we find justice if all justice begins and ends with man? What will our duty be if, by virtue of the above principle, all contenders seek to keep or to take what they consider is theirs by right?

All this shows how far modern thought has strayed from the sacred principles of Christian morality. The way in which contemporary life has abandoned the rules of human and Christian morality is an even more serious matter. False principles, in the service of what is worthless and ephemeral, can only produce evil results.

28 JULY

ALL MEN ARE BROTHERS

The Church does not shut herself up in an ivory tower, or remain indifferent in the face of so much need, but goes eagerly about her great mission of love and peace. For are not all men brothers, since all are redeemed by the same precious Blood of our Lord Jesus Christ? And is Mary, his Mother and ours, not also the Mother of the whole human race? Even if, during the centuries that have passed, some have left their Father's home, this does not prevent the Church from holding out her arms to them, and showing kindness, understanding and affection to all.

That is why ... those who work in accordance with the intentions of the Church of God, that is, to extend the kingdom of God in all the various fields of the apostolate, beginning with that of education, have good reason for new hope.

What we must do, in fact, is to listen to the Spirit of God which, as we read in the first Book of Genesis, is "moving over the face of the waters". We must gather our inspirations from the Lord and live according to these in our present circumstances, and try to understand them better by means of constant prayer and persevering fidelity.

29 JULY

Feast of St Martha.

THE FAITH OF MARTHA

A few days before his death Jesus told his disciples that the hour was approaching when he would have to suffer greatly: "The Son of man. . . will be mocked and shamefully treated, . . .they will kill him, and on the third day he will rise" (Luke 18. 32-33).

And so it came to pass: he rose indeed "on the third day". In the last hours of his sojourn on this earth he foretold what would happen to his Church: the trials and opposition she would encounter, and the bloody battles. And he went on to say that he had overcome the world, and would be with them until the end of time. Since then many centuries have gone by, with all their history, but we are sure that at the end of time will be seen the eternal glory of Christ the Son of God, and of all those who have believed in him. "Martha. . . I am the Resurrection and the Life . . . do you believe this?" (John 11. 25-26).

The faith of a humble woman was considered worthy to represent the faith of all mankind in Christ the Saviour. Our memories of Holy Week make us more confident about the mystery of Jesus Christ our divine Brother, the Word of God made Man, "for us men and for our salvation"; the target of all human malice, the "sign that is spoken against" throughout the centuries, despised and rejected, yet always glorious and all-conquering.

30 JULY

THE DIFFUSION OF GOODNESS

It is sad to have to deplore evil, and its deprecation does

not suffice to eliminate it. Instead, we must desire goodness, and express it in our lives, and exalt it in every way. Goodness must be proclaimed in the face of the world, so that it may be widely diffused, and penetrate every form of individual and social life.

The single man must be good. He must give an example of a pure conscience, without deceit or cunning or hardness of heart. He is good because he tries constantly to attain purity of soul and true perfection, good because he is loyal to an unbreakable resolve, to which all his thoughts and deeds are subjected.

The family must be good. In it mutual love must throb like a flame, in the exercise of all the virtues. Goodness sweetens and strengthens the father's authority and is taught through the mother's tender care; it makes the children obedient, tempers their high spirits and teaches them to make the necessary sacrifices.

St Leo the Great says: "To commit an injustice, or to repay this in kind is the prudence of this world: not to render evil for evil is the innocent expression of Christian forbearance... Let us then love humility, and let the faithful avoid any kind of arrogance. Let everyone put his brother before himself, and no one seek his own interests but those of others, so that when kind affections abound in all the poison of hatred will be found in none" (*Sermo XXXVII, In Epiphaniæ solemn.* VII, Migne PL 54, 259).

Mankind must be good. This teaching that comes down to us from time long past, and yet speaks to us now in the accents of our own day, reminds all men of their obligation to be good: that is, to be just, righteous, generous, disinterested, ready to understand and to make allowances, willing to show forbearance and forgiveness.

31 JULY

FEAST OF ST IGNATIUS OF LOYOLA

St Ignatius has taught and still teaches all that perfection, as an exercise in Christian living, means poverty, obedience and the apostolate. Not destitution but poverty, that is, indifference to worldly wealth, which is to be desired only in so far as it is conducive to salvation; obedience which makes us similar to Christ Jesus who was obedient to death; the apostolate which is expressed in manifold ways, in teaching, in works of charity, in social assistance, or in the civilization which endeavours to raise life and ennoble it.

To Christ Jesus the glory. He is truly to be "admired in his saints", and supremely admired in St Ignatius of Loyola whose example is set before us today. First of all St Ignatius teaches us not to fear for the holy Church of Christ, for the Lord sustains her, and preserves in her the very fountain of life, of the apostolate and of its success. In some countries the Church meets with opposition; sometimes she has much to endure. But storms are followed by calm weather.

What matters is that all should work together for their own sanctification, for the sanctification of the family and of the civic and social order. To difficulties and crises we must respond with the calm of the Gospel. Opposition must always be expected from those who do not believe in Christ.

Let them rage. We shall continue to bless the name of the Lord Jesus, and to bless his saints. To him be supreme honour, glory and blessing in his saints. Amen.

AUGUST

1 AUGUST

SANCTIFICATION OF THE CHRISTIAN DAY

We are, alas, living in a world full of temptations and deceitful flattery. According to the ideals of this world all our activity should be directed to the search for amusements, wealth, and the enjoyment of success in all the various activities of earthly life.

When people pursue only this narrow and ephemeral aim they keep their gaze fixed on this earth and never lift their eyes to heaven. But when they live by faith, when every morning, at the first notes of the Angelus bell, they lift their minds to God and ask for his Mother's assistance, and then, through all the events of the day, encouraged by that help and those inspirations, do the duties of their work and proper state obediently, conscientiously and faithfully, then indeed can they be truly said to have understood the real meaning of life.

By thus endowing every human act with immense significance, and living under the influence of the Holy Spirit, even their sighs and groans are able to make their own meaningful contribution to their future abundant rewards.

2 AUGUST

Feast of St Alphonsus de Liguori, a great moral theologian.

THE DOORS ARE NEVER CLOSED

I would like to speak from my heart to every one of you. . .
The Son of God, in the sacrament of his love, has

sanctified your senses with the touch of his own pure body: he has stilled the desires of your flesh, has consoled you in your sorrows, soothed your angry heart and strengthened your wavering resolutions. How long have you still to live? You do not know. But, whether your road be long or short, the eucharistic food will, like Elijah's loaf, be your unfailing food and will keep you good company on your way up to the Lord's mountain.

There are some who, perhaps for a long time now, have failed to respond to the Lord's command, and for many years have even ignored his Easter. What message have I for them? Courage, take courage, my brother, my son.

The doors of the banqueting hall are never closed. Every day is the right day for the lost sheep to return to the care of the tender shepherd who calls to it and goes out to seek it with great longing.

Any day, any week, a sinner may return to God.

3 AUGUST

THE CONCEPT OF AUTHORITY

Whoever is invested with authority, understood in its true meaning of a mission and a service, must try to realize what God is asking of him, and to make God's will the mainspring of all his thoughts and actions.

This must be so: human life must be an expression of the will of God, shown in obedience to the commandments engraved on men's hearts, and revealed in the two Testaments which Christ entrusted to his Church.

And Christian living is living according to the will of God, sublimely revealed in the teaching of the Gospel, that "good news" which reverses our merely earthly way of judging things and events. What words these are, my dear people! "Blessed are the poor, blessed are the meek, blessed are the merciful, the pure in heart, the peacemakers; blessed are those who mourn and those who hunger and thirst for righteousness..." (cf. Matt. 5. 3-10).

These are the principles which offer the motives and ideals for a Christian life here below.

Human society means generous service to our fellows, a service which draws its inspiration from the order of the created world and is unwearied because it feels an imperative need to spend itself in accordance with the Pauline expression: "The love of Christ controls us" (II Cor. 5. 14). In this way it co-operates in that wise, liberal and willing evolution which is derived—allow me to say this—clearly and authoritatively from the social teaching of the Christian Church.

4 AUGUST

Feast of St Dominic, the apostle of the holy rosary.

THE BIBLE OF THE POOR

When our forefathers built their churches they adorned them with sacred imagery, paintings or stained glass illustrating the mysteries of the lives of Jesus and Mary. It was like having a Gospel open for everyone to read, easily understood by all and rightly called the Bible of the poor.

This is just what the rosary of Mary has been to us for seven hundred years, a joy to our eyes and hearts in the contemplation, in so many images, of the chief episodes in the life and mission of Jesus, and of Mary: of Jesus the Son of God, our Redeemer, of Mary the Mother of Jesus and our Mother too. It is a prayer that rises from our lips and our innermost hearts, begging for the divine gifts that may satisfy the needs of individuals and of the whole Church.

What a great and mysterious thing is human life too, Christian life! a sequence and interwoven pattern of its own joys, sorrows and triumphs. Is this not so, my brothers?

The altar that occupies the most sacred and central place in our churches bears in the missal and in the chalice all that is contained in the Gospel narrative and perpetuated in the eucharistic sacrifice.

5 AUGUST

Feast of the Dedication of the Basilica of

S. MARIA MAGGIORE

The Church is like the soul of the people, which soars like this stone building itself, raised by a common intention of prayer and piety, an intention which rises to the vaulted roof, sings and prays, groans and sighs.

The church is built to house the Eucharist, which throbs with life here among the precious stones and metals and the harmonies of worshipping hearts; and it is built for Our Lady whose mild eyes look down from her altars, the protectress of the pious concourse—and it is triumphant in the splendour of the lofty towers.

There are hundreds of cathedrals and churches, many of them dedicated to the glory of Mary, which have risen like miracles of art to enshrine the sacred Host and to express the people's fervent love for the Blessed Sacrament and for Our Lady.

Is it true that our modern times are degenerate, compared with former ages? Alas, there is some truth in this. Unbelief and indifference in private and public life poison our epoch and reduce it to a state of moral inferiority in comparison with preceding times.

Yet, for our common encouragement, we must add that perhaps the devotion to the Eucharist and to Mary was never so deeply felt before as now.

6 AUGUST

THE FEAST OF THE TRANSFIGURATION

Jesus and the three apostles Peter, James and John went up to the top of Mount Tabor. At a certain moment the divine Master disappeared from their sight to reappear all at once in a glory of light and splendour. Moses and Elijah stood on either side of him, and Jesus was talking to them. Moses represented the Law, Elijah the prophecies that had been made through the centuries, foretelling the Redemption of man. What was Jesus speaking about with these two personages of the Old Testament? Certainly not about human and worldly opinions and enterprises, nor about the enjoyment of this transient life, but about the fulfilment of the purpose of God's infinite goodness, in accordance with which the Son of God made man was about to suffer and die on the Cross in order to save mankind.

The three apostles were not yet capable of understanding all this; they were so entranced by the vision that they wished it could last for ever, so intense was the joy of their hearts. Stricken with awe they fell to the ground, but were soon raised again by Jesus who had re-assumed his ordinary human appearance. "Rise, and have no fear." That was the first order he gave them, and then, as they were coming down from the mountain, he said: "Tell no one the vision, until the Son of Man is raised from the dead".

In this episode described by St Matthew there is a profound and sublime lesson for all times, and for Christians of all sorts and conditions. In this earthly life we must not expect every hour to offer us joy, pleasures and glory, even if we seek these with an honest and legitimate purpose.

The Transfiguration was to be followed, very soon, by the Passion and Crucifixion of Jesus.

7 AUGUST

THE DESIRE FOR HEAVENLY THINGS

We must do all we can to foster a longing desire for our heavenly home.

The love of our earthly fatherland is a fine and enno-bling sentiment, and it has always been considered an act of meritorious love to sacrifice oneself for one's own land, even to give one's life for it. But this love must always be considered in the light of our heavenly fatherland, the radiance from which gives meaning and value to the trials and tribulations of our sojourn here below.

This constant familiarity with the thoughts of the eternal life which awaits us all, so that we may all, with Jesus in glory, enjoy the beatific vision together with those who were near to us in this human life, is a joy for all our days, and makes more perfect our service to our fellow men.

Let us love the Paradise that awaits us; let us familia-rize ourselves with the thought of heavenly glory, so that we shall be able better to endure and sanctify the sorrows and sacrifices which the circumstances of this present life impose upon us.

8 AUGUST

FEAST OF ST JOHN VIANNEY, THE CURÉ D'ARS

When we speak of St John Vianney we immediately re-call the figure of this extraordinarily saintly priest who, for the love of God and the conversion of sinners, went without food and sleep, imposed upon himself a harsh discipline and, above all, practised self-denial to a heroic degree. It is true that the faithful are not generally asked to follow this unusual way, but nevertheless divine Providence has seen to it that the Church should never be short of souls who, moved by the Holy Spirit, never hesitate to set out along this road, for it is these men, more than any others, who work miracles of conversion. The admirable example of self-denial set by the Curé d'Ars, "severe with himself and gentle with others", reminds everyone most eloquently and urgently of the primary importance of the ascetic life.

First of all, we must notice the poverty of the humble Curé d'Ars, a worthy imitator of St Francis of Assisi, and his faithful disciple in the Third Order. He was rich enough to give to others but poor for himself, and lived in such total detachment from the good things of the world that his heart was able, in perfect freedom, to give generously to all those in material and spiritual distress who came to him in great numbers. "My secret", he used to say, "is very simple: To give all and hold nothing back." His disinterestedness made him deeply solicitous for the poor, especially for those of his own parish, to whom he showed great tenderness, treating them "with delicate tact and consideration, indeed, with respect!" He used to remind people that one must never treat the poor with disrespect because in so doing we should be disrespectful to God. When beggars knocked on his door and were received with his usual kindness he was happy to be able to say to them: "I am as poor as you; today I am one of you!" At the end of his life he loved to repeat: "I am very happy; I have given everything away, and the good God may call me whenever he wishes".

9 AUGUST

PRE-EMINENCE OF THE SPIRITUAL VALUES

A heart set free! How movingly St Leo the Great pleads: "Do not let your hearts be cluttered with the transient vanities of this world, but let your constant wish be for all that will last for ever." He had already said: "The heart set free, and detached from all that appeals to the senses, must follow the light of the intelligence, as if it were a guiding star." This is the first requirement of the apostolate: a heart detached from the fleeting joys of this earth, disentangled from worldly compromise and interests, and stripped bare of meaningless vanities.

Of course we must endeavour to know and understand the reality of our daily lives, but our hearts must remain free, safely and surely anchored to the divine promises of Christ, and to a supernatural vision of life and of the world. The struggle for success may conceal a temptation to self-glorification, and in any case can hardly be reconciled with the manner in which divine Providence works, teaching us calmness, confidence and moderation.

As you see, it is still and always necessary to give supernatural values pride of place, and we are never tired of insisting on this truth when we speak to the Catholic clergy and laity.

10 AUGUST

TO SAFEGUARD THE FUNDAMENTAL PRINCIPLES

Every one should make a serious effort to safeguard those fundamental principles which rule and ennoble our lives: modesty, purity and Christian behaviour, which must be protected, not noisily or with violence but with the strength of profound conviction, in order to fortify robust virtues in individuals, families and society.

To the Christian the supernatural order is apparent in every moment of his daily life. In fact, it becomes very familiar to him, especially through his prayers, whether said privately or in public. . .

These are our ideals: modest behaviour, religious and social education, prayer and recollection in Christ Jesus, the Saviour of the world, the King to be enthroned in all hearts. . .

We must bear unfailing witness to the most holy Trinity, to God our Father and Creator, to Christ our Redeemer, and to the Holy Spirit which, continually sent forth into the world from Bethlehem, from Calvary and from our altars, inspires all hearts and moves whole races of men to bring about the coming of the kingdom of Christ.

11 AUGUST

THE APOSTOLATE AS THE DIFFUSION OF THE SPIRIT OF CHARITY

The apostolate seeks to diffuse God's love for man. It is like a flame of love that spreads to all parts of the world, seeking not to divide the world into spheres for selfish exploitation, but to prepare the harvests. The fields are irrigated with the sweat of the apostles, and sometimes with their blood.

With this great ideal before us every one plays his own part, and men work humbly and willingly, for their own good and for that of their fellows, knowing that they are all living parts of one and the same family, entrusted to the loving care of the heavenly Father, who desires us to co-operate with him in his purpose of infinite love. Hence the sense of order, of completion, and of dedication in the labour of that mission which everyone has to carry out in this world.

We must not try to do everything at once, but to do as much as circumstances permit; even when we are convinced that we are serving in a good cause, and we feel impelled by the most urgent necessity, discretion, wisdom and kindness must control the more vehement impulses of our nature.

12 AUGUST

THE CINEMA AND OTHER ENTERTAINMENTS

The atmosphere in which our young people are obliged to breathe is spoilt and contaminated by images, with their accompanying maxims, that present an everyday danger of perversion, and an incentive to licentious behaviour. This leads to the weakening and demoralization of our families, once so sturdy and now being gradually reduced to sterility and exhaustion. . .

The cinema may arouse emotions that excite the mind to good purpose; but often it merely poisons the imagination, the senses and the heart. The snake lies in wait in the long grass: one bite from its fangs is enough to extinguish that light of truth which shone serenely to encourage chaste thoughts and generous resolves.

We must be equally on our guard against a danger very

present to our mind just now: that is, the danger associated with holidays spent in the mountains and at the seaside. This habit, like so many others in our lives, is in itself harmless, and may be used to promote health of mind and body, but it also presents disquieting opportunities for sin: frail human nature finds many an encouragement to indulge in immoral behaviour.

13 AUGUST

Feast of St Hippolytus and St Cassian.

"THIS IS THE VICTORY. . ."

St Hippolytus was a martyr, and therefore a witness to Christ. Paul of Tarsus stood on guard over the cloaks of those who were stoning the young deacon Stephen: and this was the beginning of his conversion. Hippolytus, a soldier ordered to accompany and watch the tortures and torturers of St Lawrence, was enraptured by the splendour of the heavenly virtues of the young victim who was sacrificing himself for Christ: he too was converted and became a perfect Christian, and he converted all the members of his large family, which became an edifying centre of faith and holiness.

Those times were indeed sad, under the Emperors Decius and Valerian. When his hour came Hippolytus too was seized and subjected to pitiless cruelty which conferred on him the honour of joining that band of indomitable witnesses who form the purple crown of the Holy Catholic Church in all ages and among all peoples.

". . . This is the victory which overcomes the world": faith in Christ. Faith is above all a divine grace, and must be safeguarded, handed on and enriched with good works. It must be protected in our families so that it may permeate with its beneficial light all expressions of the domestic, civil and social order.

We must be ready, if need arises, to give our blood, or even our lives, rather than to deny or betray it.

14 AUGUST

TO LIVE WITH OUR EYES LOOKING TO HEAVEN

What is this earthly life? It cannot, to be sure, be compared with life in our heavenly home. Nevertheless, it is encouraging to see what man, in obedience to the Lord's will, has succeeded in doing, by remaining ever loyal to all those principles of truth, goodness and wisdom on which serene and tranquil peace is based: peace which must be sought, spread abroad and realized in every circumstance of our daily life.

The Christian life is not an antique dealers' fair. We are not called upon to study in an ancient museum or academy of bygone days. Undoubtedly, this also has its uses, like visits to ancient monuments, but it is not enough. Our aim in life is to move forward, but at the same time to cherish all that the past may offer us in the way of practical experience, as we press on along the paths opened up for us by Our Lord. . .

We are pilgrims here below; whether our way be long or short it surely has its end, and this end must be one of enjoyment, not of punishment.

What matters is not to live in comfort here, but to live in such a way as to prepare ourselves for that moment when the divine Judge will call us into the true life. We shall then be blessed indeed if he can say to us: "You have borne suffering with patience; you have con-scientiously followed the way of the Cross; when you encountered difficulties you did not let yourself be over-come by discouragement or despair; you have been loyal to the teaching of the Gospel. In a word, you have acquitted yourself honourably as a true Christian: now the moment has come for you to enter into the joy of eternity."

15 AUGUST

FEAST OF THE ASSUMPTION

This doctrine about the body of the blessed Virgin Mary being preserved by the Holy Trinity from all corruption, and immediately transfigured and spiritualized, does not merely represent a truth of faith; it exalts the eternal values of the spiritual world, with its intrinsic needs and irrepressible aspirations.

It renews our hope of a happier future.

It restores our faith in a more perfect justice which will re-establish the order disturbed by sin.

These are thoughts inspired by faith, and if we en-courage them they will direct our steps to our heavenly

Father's home, and help us to overcome the trials and uncertainties of our daily struggle.

The Dogma of the Assumption teaches us:

1. Earthly life is not an end in itself; its end is in heaven. Youth passes away, dreams and projects fail; the evening comes with its disillusionments and wistful regrets; but the Christian can never give way to melancholy.

2. The soul has pre-eminent and irrefutable rights over the body, and for its sake we must learn how to control our passions, renounce the seductive pleasures of the world and even, sometimes, make heroic decisions.

3. Humble submission to God is the secret of true happiness and peace.

The Feast of the Assumption, so understood, kindles in our hearts those holy enthusiasms which our religion is always capable of arousing in individuals and in peoples, and strengthens the resolve to renew our souls with the help of divine grace. Finally, it restores hope, which turns the bitterness and hardship of life into joy.

16 AUGUST

Feast of St Joachim, the father of Our Lady.

THE MISSION OF PARENTS

Every family is a gift from God; it implies a vocation which comes from above and for which we must be trained. The family is the beginning of true and right instruction; it is everything, or almost everything, to a man. It is here that the child begins to make his first unforgettable experiments in living: adolescents and young people find in their families examples to imitate and a bulwark against the evil spirit of wrongdoing. The parents themselves find in it a protection against the crises and perplexities they encounter; finally, elderly people can enjoy in family life the well deserved fruit of long faithfulness and constancy.

In this vision of the family the woman has her own indispensable part to play. In the home one voice is always listened to by everyone, if this voice has known how to make itself heard and respected: it is the anxious and prudent voice of the woman, wife and mother. She may take as her own the testament of the dying Moses and say to her children and through them to future generations: "I call heaven and earth to witness against you this day, that I have set before you life and death. . . therefore choose life, that you and your descendants may live, loving the Lord your God, obeying his voice, and cleaving to him. . ." (Deut. 30. 19—20).

My beloved daughters, try to teach parents the truth about this great mission; see that your work is deeply grounded in the faith and widely extended, so that generous and fervent bands of Christian families may respond to the need of undertaking a lasting reform of public and private morality, and an effective re-appraisal of family and social life in the light of what the Gospel teaches.

17 AUGUST

OUR DUTY TO OUR NEIGHBOUR

Justice is an admirable virtue. We hear it much spoken of and yet, in our daily lives, we live in the midst of great injustices, due to the manner in which so many people behave and act. The first flagrant injustice is apparent all around us. We have only to reflect on the huge number of people who take not the slightest interest in spiritual things, in all that reflects the Gospel message, dedicating themselves exclusively to profit-making, the pursuit of pleasure and the satisfaction of their own selfish desires.

When we have firm principles of right judgment and justice, we can make good and swift progress in God's company. Our duty is not to remain inert, but to lead active lives that do honour to our principles.

If you have a family, try to be worthy of this mission and responsibility. If you have uncommon talents or gifts, that you can use in higher spheres of educational or artistic activity, you must employ these talents for the purposes assigned by God's law. If you are rich in resources and material possessions, your first duty is to remember that whatever you do not need and have left over, you must, according to the noble Gospel doctrine, give to others who need your help.

We are dismayed when we read or hear about some aspects of modern life. Notwithstanding all that is done and said and organized, and all the progress made in scientific techniques and communications, there are still today millions of undernourished human beings, many of whom die of starvation. They die deprived of what they have a right to claim, for God created the heavens and the earth to satisfy the basic needs of life.

18 AUGUST

TO LIVE IN A STATE OF GRACE

All Christians—young people too will learn this more or less quickly from their own experience as they grow older—know that everyone has to endure trials, crosses and hardships; and that nevertheless we have been given a sublime spiritual food that will give us ever renewed strength and prepare us for that eternal life without which this temporal life would be vain and without purpose. It is significant that the day after the multiplication of the loaves the Lord Jesus foretold the institution of the Eucharist in those wonderful words: "I am the living bread which came down from heaven; if any one eats of this bread he will live for ever".

So you see that the Christian doctrine, instilled into our hearts from our earliest years, becomes a necessary, mysterious and indispensable means of happiness.

By virtue of this sublime truth all followers of Christ, beginning with fervent and generous young people, know what it means to live in a state of grace, to be pure, sincere, charitable and patient; in a word, as St Paul teaches us, to put on the new nature, in holiness and righteousness.

This cannot, to be sure, be effected in one day: we need long and arduous training, and we must learn how to overcome trials and opposition. But, in the end, we shall reach our shining goal.

Good discipline also, and the willingness to submit to authority—beginning in the home circle—is a sure pledge of an excellent future.

19 AUGUST

Feast of St John Eudes, Apostle of the Eucharist.

THE MYSTIC BANQUET

To partake of the Body of Jesus and drink his Blood, to

become one with him, enabled to share in his divinity by receiving this sacrament—this is the culminating joy of Easter, writes St Paul to the Corinthians. "Christ our paschal lamb has been sacrificed;" let us therefore celebrate the Festival not with the old leaven, the leaven of malice and evil, but with the unleavened bread of purity. . .

The hall of the mystical banquet has opened its doors and all the children of the Church are invited. Many, I would like to be able to say very many, answer the call. They come from all ranks of society and from the ends of the earth, from the regions of the radiant East and from the twilight lands of the setting sun. They are received without distinction of caste, education or opinion. They ask the Church, who treats all alike without exceptions, to clothe them in a wedding garment, and then they sit down at the festal board which is like a foretaste and introduction to the eternal banquet.

Alas! alas! Many, too many, decline the invitation or at least defer their answer: a sinful refusal, a dangerous deferment, for the Lord says: "Many will seek to enter and will not be able" (Luke 13. 24).

20 AUGUST

Feast of St Bernard.

THE HOLY NAME OF JESUS

When we read the Breviary with due care and interest we find it is full of wonderful and heart-warming treasures. About the Holy Name of Jesus there are inspired and delightful passages from St Bernard, and indeed he may be considered the supreme poet and singer of the Name of Jesus. (The ancient Fathers of the Church, although their writings were implicitly a defence of the faith, were generally more concerned with spreading the knowledge of it.) What St Bernard says in the Breviary prepares us for what is written in the proper liturgy for the Sunday after the Octave of Christmas, with all the useful and beneficial lessons we may derive from this.

God's providence is for all his children. Yet there are some who do not know, or do not wish to know, the truth about his Holy Name. We know too well what happens. The name of God is at the beginning of the Decalogue, which is the foundation, the principle, the law for all men and all things: instead, very many people in this world behave as if in obedience to an anti-Decalogue—their conduct is like the practical application of atheistic principles, even when they do not deliberately practise the doctrine actually taught in atheistic schools.

From the first commandment to the others: not to kill, not to commit adultery, not to steal. . . one might quote innumerable examples of obvious methodical transgressions of these laws. And what can we say about false witness, which means the service of falsehood? In fact, it becomes increasingly necessary to insist upon this commandment, so widely diffused, manifold and unbelievable is the distortion of truth.

21 AUGUST

A HIERARCHY OF VALUES

Scientific and technical progress, economic successes and improvements in living conditions are certainly positive elements in any civilization. We must, however, beware of ever considering them as supreme values, for in comparison with these they are essentially means to an end.

It is sad to note that in countries which have a high level of economic prosperity there are many human beings who have lost or inverted the right order of values: spiritual ends are neglected, forgotten or denied while progress made in science, technical skill, economic development and material well-being is welcomed and encouraged as if it were of supreme importance, or even the sole purpose of life. This attitude contains the danger of a most harmful corrupting influence in the work which the more economically advanced nations do for those which are still underdeveloped, among which it is by no means rare to find, handed down through ancient traditions, the consciousness of some of the most important human values, still alive and operative.

To interfere with this consciousness is essentially immoral. On the contrary, it must be respected and, wherever possible, illuminated and developed, so that it may remain what it surely is: the basis of true civilization.

FEAST OF THE IMMACULATE HEART OF MARY

As the Saviour's Mother, the Virgin Mary shared intimately in the work of redemption by which Christ made us members of himself and called us to "become children of God" (John 1. 12). Like a mother who always wants the best of everything for her own children she leads us, by her admirable example and powerful intercession, towards the perfection of love. In her body she is the Mother of Christ, and she is spiritually the Mother of his Mystical Body which is the Church, so she is truly the "Mother of God and our Mother too" (St Anselm, *Oratio* 52, PL 158, 957A).

Whatever may be the conditions of our life and our responsibilities, we are all enfolded in the motherly embrace of the Virgin Mary, who does for us what every mother does so lovingly for her own children: she loves us, watches over us, protects us and intercedes for us. To reward her, show yourselves always faithful Catholics in your love for the Virgin Mary, "the Holy Mother of all the members of Christ's Body" (Enc. *Mystici Corporis, Scritti e Discorsi di Pio XII*, 1943). All Catholics are therefore Our Lady's children, and their love for Mary obliges them to reflect upon their common membership of the family of God's children, and to share in the customary expressions of the devotion which the Church of Jesus Christ has, for so many centuries, felt for our Saviour's Mother.

Dear children, avoid everything which savours of singularity, and instead look for the traditional Marian devotions, handed down to us from the beginning through all the succeeding generations of Christians, both of the East and of the West.

Such a devotion to the most holy Virgin is the mark of a truly Catholic heart.

23 AUGUST

TRUST IN THE LORD

We often hear it said that our present difficulties are immense and that, besides encouraging good, we should be busy opposing evil.

There is some truth in this . . . the essential thing is to

know how to respond whole-heartedly to the Lord's call. It is true that we must live in the atmosphere of the past and present hour; but the Gospel still shines in all its splendour and power; grace is still poured out upon us. So one cannot deny that heaven and earth are still in touch, and we can easily discern what is the real life of the spirit and what is, instead, mere appearance; we can see what is but external illusion and what is, instead, our strength and vitality.

That is why, when we look at the Church, founded and instituted by God, we still feel immense confidence in the future.

As happens in the world of nature, stormy days precede and follow days of calm and sunshine. But we all know what we must do. As our souls are still living flames, we can still irradiate the truth to spread the kingdom of Christ and the virtues which belong to it.

Old and young must therefore join in the praise and service of the Lord, in this present hour and in that which is to come.

24 AUGUST

Feast of St Bartholomew the Apostle.

THE PERENNIAL SPRING OF HOLY CHURCH

This is the perennial spring of Holy Church. The consideration of this sublime reality has inspired the Pope to insert, in a personal letter sent during these days to every bishop in the Catholic world, his own fatherly appeal to remember that, while it is true that everyone is obliged to do his own duty, to sanctify himself, and to guard within himself the deposit of faith and Christian tradition, all are obliged also to contribute to the diffusion of that charity which makes us see others, whatever may be their origin, race or language, as so many brothers; and since human means offer us promising occasions for meetings, all must endeavour to use these entirely for the glory of our Lord Jesus Christ.

It is a fine thing to live and sacrifice oneself, to die if necessary, for such a sublime ideal, which is guaranteed by the Saviour's promise: "Lo, I am with you always, to the close of the age".

St John Chrysostom sums up the precious teaching that springs from such impressive splendours, with the following comment: "Remember, my brothers, that one day you will be called to give an account, not only of your own lives but of the life of the whole world".

25 AUGUST

The prayer of the faithful who belong to recently founded Churches, written by Pope John.

THE MYSTERY OF LOVE

O Jesus, Son of the living God, who became man and made the supreme sacrifice of yourself in order to reveal the mystery of the Father's love and his plan of mercy and salvation for all peoples, we adore you and praise you, because you have enlightened and redeemed us.

O Jesus, you who sent out your apostles to gather in the harvest from all the fields of the world and did promise to draw all men to yourself on the Cross, we thank you for having sent to us those who have taught us the truth and made us sharers in your grace.

We beg you to grant that, through the intercession of the Blessed Virgin Mary, your heavenly Mother and Mother of us all, the Queen of Angels and of Saints, we may be worthy children of your Church, faithful to your doctrine and to your commandments, and to your Vicar on earth, the father, protector and guide of our souls.

We beg you to make us obedient to our bishops and priests. We implore your grace for them also in order that they may be sanctified, and that their ministry may be faithful; in accordance with your divine will may they be as the salt, and the light, of our lands and our peoples.

26 AUGUST

THE GOOD SHEPHERD

Every page of the Gospel is sacred and resplendent with light, but certain passages reveal their innermost meaning to responsive souls, and diffuse a more powerful and widely spread radiance over the whole world.

There is, for example, the passage in the tenth chapter of St John, in which Jesus presents himself: "I and the Father are one", and a short time before this he had said: "I am the door of the sheep" (John 10. 7).

The shepherd enters the fold by the door. As soon as he comes the sheep hear his voice, for he calls them one by one; he goes before them and they follow him because they know his voice. "Yes, I am the door of the sheepfold", he tells us, "whoever enters by me will find pasture. I came so that through me the sheep might have life, abundant life." And he continued: "I am the good shepherd. I know my own and my own know me. I have so many sheep", he said, "and not all are here, or of this fold. I must bring them here; they will listen to my voice, and I promise you that one day there will be one fold and one shepherd."

Jesus insists once more: "I am the good shepherd" and then, directing his words and his gaze from the restricted landscape of Palestine to the whole wide world, he adds: "the sheep that are far away also belong to me, because there is only one fold and one shepherd".

27 AUGUST

THE PURPOSE OF LIFE

We are on this earth as wayfarers and pilgrims: there is a law and a destiny that control all our steps, according to the time, place and circumstances of our lives.

The end of our life is not here, but lies beyond the shores of the material world, stretching out to eternity; and eternity is the living substance of retribution, joyful or unhappy, according to the success or failure of our life and pilgrimage.

The practices of the religion which Jesus taught us are lit by the radiance from our heavenly fatherland for which we were born, and to which our souls feel drawn. So these practices are intended and ordered for the good of our souls.

The conditions of our life here, as it has evolved during the centuries, give rise also to anxieties of a material nature, for body and soul are intimately bound up together. But true religion is not directly concerned with our bodily enjoyments, except in order to control them and regulate their temperate use, so that material possessions may not be prejudicial to the truest and most sublime interests of human life.

FEAST OF ST AUGUSTINE OF HIPPO

Let us remember St Augustine, the incomparable glory of the universal Church.

In the past I have had the great joy of visiting his native land, the scenes of his pastoral activity, where shone the light of his powerful mind in its brightest splendour, at the time when he was preaching the power and truth of Christianity in the midst of a decadent pagan world, confronting the pride of false and erring teachers, and foretelling the certain resurrection of the peoples in the splendour of evangelical truth. Several times I have knelt before his glorious tomb in Pavia, and I have rejoiced to see the numerous careful treatises that have been published on the subject of the immortal bishop of Hippo and his teaching.

In my frequent and eager reading of the great Doctor's many works I have always found real and profoundly spiritual nourishment, and great help in my apostolic labours. Now I join with you in imploring for myself and for the whole world that charity which is the essence of St Augustine's doctrine, and which is still today the foretaste and sure pledge of happier days.

29 AUGUST

Commemoration of the Beheading of St John Baptist.

ST JOHN THE BAPTIST

Whereas June 24th is a Festival of rejoicing for the Forerunner's birth—and the Gospel story is full of joy—the Sacred Book contains even more vivid and expressive accounts of his martyrdom, no longer rejoicing in what came down from heaven, but deploring something which came about on this earth.

St John Baptist carried out his noble mission, preaching and baptizing on the banks of the Jordan; one day, among the crowds who were gathering around him, he recognized Jesus at once and hailed him: "Behold the lamb of God who takes away the sin of the world", thus confirming that the baptism which he had been conferring was an image of the more living and thorough purification to be worked in them by Jesus. In fact, the Saviour, whom John in this way revealed to all the people, was later on to complete his mission of world redemption by his sacrifice on the Cross.

John the Baptist also poured out his blood and in so doing bore witness to God's law. The story is well known. The head of the man who had so inflexibly repeated: "It is not lawful" to one of the mighty of this world was offered to the ridicule, scorn and horror of those who were disobeying every one of the Lord's commandments. Yet, as some of the Fathers have said, commenting on the Gospel story, those lifeless eyes still seemed to express their stern condemnation of evil: "It is not lawful".

Therefore, while his announcement of the Redemption to come was the great glory of the Baptist's mission, his final witness, given with the sacrifice of his life, confirms his indomitable loyalty to God and to his laws.

30 AUGUST

THE CHRISTIAN'S DUTY IN THE WORLD

It would be wrong for our children, and especially for the laity, to consider that prudence required a slackening of Christian activity in the world; on the contrary, they must renew and increase it.

The Lord, in his sublime prayer for the unity of his Church, did not implore his Father to remove his followers from the world, but to preserve them from evil. We must not create an artificial opposition where it does not exist, that is, between our own endeavour to sanctify ourselves and our active presence in the life of the world around us; it is not true, either that personal salvation can only be found in temporal activities, or that such activities fatally compromise the dignity of human beings, and particularly of believers.

Instead, it is perfectly in accordance with the design of Providence that every one should try to save his own soul through his daily work, which is for nearly all human beings work for a merely temporal purpose.

Our lay children must feel it is their duty to fulfil their professional obligations, as they are in honour bound to do, for this is a service to society, but at the same time to remain in spiritual communion with God and in Christ, working for his glory, as the Apostle Paul says: "So whether you eat or drink, or whatever you do, do all to the glory of God" (I Cor. 10. 31).

197

THE ORDER OF NATURE
AND THE ORDER OF GRACE

In the order of grace, man, by virtue of the Blood of Christ, is consecrated to a life that transcends ordinary human circumstances, and is called to share in the life of God. In fact, this is what makes us, by adoption, brothers of Jesus, the Son of the heavenly Father, and assures us that after this transitory life on earth we shall enter the life of joy and glory which is promised to man, to be granted to him in the Father's kingdom, which was prepared from the beginning of the world.

It is in the light of the Holy Spirit that these two rules, of nature and of grace, are understood by the good Christian.

According to their influence on the life of the body or the life of the soul, the earthly or heavenly life, they are distinguishable as temporal or eternal values.

Freedom, good health, physical and moral qualities, wealth inherited or gradually acquired, talents, important positions in society, and natural capacities exercised with wisdom and moderation are temporal values, intended to promote a respected and contented social life. But eternal values also may be found in these good things we have mentioned, provided that they are possessed and used with the aid of supernatural grace, and in order to attain the good things of eternal life.

SEPTEMBER

1 SEPTEMBER

THE LABOURER'S WAGE

The labourer deserves a just wage: this is what Our Lord Jesus Christ means when he said: "the labourer deserves his food" (Matt. 10. 10). A man's work is sacred, because it is the work of a rational being, raised to the dignity of a son of God. The Christian social doctrine is very clear on this point, and solemn papal pronouncements have testified to the Church's motherly solicitude for the conditions of the labourer.

First of all, you must have faith in God, without whose assistance it is impossible to achieve any lasting success even in this material world. "Unless the Lord builds the house, those who build it labour in vain. Unless the Lord watches over the city, the watchman stays awake in vain" (Psalm 126).

Faith in God then but also faith in yourselves, in the wonderful powers which the Lord has given to every man for the development of his personality, in his chosen way of life. In the first pages of the Sacred Book it is written that God created man in his own image and after his own likeness, and placed him in the Earthly Paradise so that he might cultivate it and watch over it. What dignity and strength come to man from this divine purpose, because of which he shines in the reflected splendour of the heavenly Father!

So you must have faith in yourselves: avoiding the dangers of selfish individualism, which isolates and paralyses every effort, and the cowardice which holds you back, and the habit of conformism. It is necessary also to cultivate a profound sense of solidarity, and mutual assistance, sharing in common your efforts and your successes.

2 SEPTEMBER

NOBILITY OF LABOUR

Jesus, who came to this world to save mankind, spent most of his life as a workman, and not, as we know, in a refined and superior order of activity, but in ordinary manual labour. We learn a sublime lesson from this: work is a noble thing, and the better a work, under all its various aspects, is done, the nobler it is. The fact is that here below everyone must work. Those who are concerned with heavenly things, to make them known and to invite all others to share in them, are doing supremely important work.

We have the priesthood: the contemplatives, the apostles, and the great writers. These are not directly concerned with the material things of life, but with what raises the mind to higher things and sets the heart on fire with the love that inspires zeal to spread true faith and true happiness, not only in family but in more widely extended communities. Work done for God in all humility—who could say that this is not worth doing? Indeed, it is a wonderful thing, and all work becomes supremely great when it is done in the spirit of our Lord.

3 SEPTEMBER

Feast of St Pius X

PRAYER TO POPE ST PIUS X

On the day of my first Mass your hands were laid on my head, the head of a newly ordained priest kneeling as you passed by in the Vatican.

I have always treasured in my heart the memory of that gesture and of the gentle words of good wishes and blessings which accompanied it.

Now fifty years have passed. You are a citizen of the heavenly Jerusalem, you rejoice in the glory of the saints, and all Christians pray to you.

The humble young priest of long ago has been placed in the Chair of St Mark, where you too presided with such splendour of doctrine, virtue and example.

O Holy Father Pius X, I put my trust in you. I do not fear to die. I do not refuse to work. May your powerful arm assist me, so that all that is still left for me to do in my life may be to the edification, the blessing and the joy of these beloved children of Venice, your children and mine, with whom it is sweet to live but still more precious and joyful to sacrifice myself in an outpouring of loving-kindness and pastoral care.

4 SEPTEMBER

A RIGHT INTENTION

The Bible tells us that Joseph was ill-treated and sold into slavery, and those who wished to get rid of him thought they had succeeded in their purpose. What did their father do ? At the first open signs of the older brothers' envy, Jacob pondered over it in silence, as if afraid that anything he might say would but add fuel to their disquieting animosity. Certainly the Lord must have given him to understand that all would end in justice. . .

What are we to learn from this story ? That unfortunately in the world of men even brothers are not always inspired by right feelings in their dealings one with another, and that they often have recourse to secret agreements and plots in order to do one another harm; and this is all the more serious when their purpose is to injure an innocent person. And yet we were all created to live according to a law already engraved on every man's conscience, one which moreover the Lord has revealed and explained to us with his precepts of salvation and grace.

There is, too, another vision, clearer and nobler. Opening the pages of the New Testament we meet with another Joseph, the pattern of the just man, the husband of Mary and foster-father of Jesus. In the holy family of Nazareth, too, work was the ruling factor of their lives: work, not in the open fields but in the humble restricted space of a carpenter's workshop. And together with this example of industrious toil we see the splendour of every virtue: the exaltation of innocence and the fundamental principles of a harmonious social life, obedience, humility and self-denial.

5 SEPTEMBER

CHRISTIAN ACTIVITY

Spend yourselves unweariedly in doing good work, in the practice of justice, equality and charity, and by so doing transform your labour into abundant merit for eternity. For this purpose we recommend the exercise of the Christian virtues, without which all human effort is maimed and fruitless, and we particularly recommend the practice of the works of mercy, the spirit of self-sacrifice, and the endeavour to set a good example.

Above all, may prayer be the breath and sustenance of your life, according to the maxim of Benedict of Norcia: *Pray and work*, always remembering that human activity, even the loftiest and most praiseworthy, does not find its end within the bounds of earthly life, but stretches out to the city of God. By so doing you will "lay up for yourselves treasures in heaven, where neither moth nor rust consumes, and where thieves do not break in and steal" (Matt. 6. 20). There all our labour will have an end, and everyone will receive his just reward from God, according to what he has done on this earth, in the pursuit of truth and righteousness.

6 SEPTEMBER

THE DIGNITY OF WORK

This is what Nazareth teaches us. We know very little about the hidden life of Jesus, but what we know about his thirty years of labour is enough. The example of Jesus has enabled twenty centuries of Christianity to teach man to be aware of his full stature, and to raise him to the consciousness of his dignity.

There may be work which is exclusively intellectual, and which must be supported by the physical efforts of other men. But there is no work which is exclusively material; the breath of the Holy Spirit, by means of which God created man in his own image and likeness (cf. Gen. 1. 24), must inspire all that man creates: the tools for agriculture, the marvellous new technical inventions, and the instruments for scholarly research.

Otherwise matter could get the upper hand and usurp man's dominion over the very laws he has succeeded in discovering. It is man who must dominate the universe, as we read in the old commandment: "Fill the earth and subdue it" (Gen. 1. 28).

7 SEPTEMBER

WORK AS A MEANS OF EDIFICATION

My dear children! I am speaking to you before all the majesty of heaven and earth but I want to talk to each one of you as if I were a guest in your own home, to open my heart to you trustfully and tenderly. All those present are busy with heart, mind and hands in all kinds of human activity, and all are in this way obeying the human and divine obligation to work.

I think of all of you who work with your hands, and I look at you wistfully to see if any of you remind me of my own dear ones, my father and my brothers, who all worked on the land. And I might have been a farm labourer myself if the Lord had not called me into another field, and if he had not made me obedient to his call.

In the Old Testament we learn that, because of sin, men were ordered to work, and that the first family gave birth to all the various races of mankind. How men have toiled, and struggled, even for their daily bread—but in the end joy has come of it!

In the New Testament he who came to redeem us gave us an example. Where did he go? Did he go to Athens, the centre of philosophic studies? Or to Alexandria? Or Rome? No. As far as we know, he spent thirty years of his life as a carpenter. Our dearest affections are founded in Christ, and from our earliest days we have found in him our purest joys.

8 SEPTEMBER

FEAST OF THE NATIVITY OF OUR LADY

Whoever believes in Our Lord Jesus Christ, whoever belongs to Holy Church has a Mother, Mary!

One of our most wonderful and appealing memories of family life is the recollection of a small child learning to say his first prayer, the Hail Mary. And nothing in the world is lovelier and more enchanting than the child's greeting to the most Holy Virgin.

Life is always unfolding: we leave our childhood behind, and our youth, and we still pray, and ever more frequently, to our Mother in heaven. . .

The child's Hail Mary is beautiful to hear, and deeply moving also is the Hail Mary of a dying man. So, throughout our lives, we have this ever present thought of Mary.

What marvellous offerings of faith can be seen in the whole Christian world! By the side of churches dedicated to Our Lord, and inside them, we find the presence and the memory of Our Lady.

And this has been so ever since the miraculous event of our Redemption. The New Testament, we might say, begins with the words of the divine messenger: "The Angel of the Lord announced to Mary". At the highest level of all communications between God and man is Jesus, the Redeemer of the world, who, shortly before his death on the Cross, entrusted Mary to his apostle John, saying to him: "Behold your Mother", and entrusted his disciple to Mary with the words: "Behold your son".

9 SEPTEMBER

THE GREATEST GIFT OF ALL

Always remember that faith is the greatest gift, greater even than life itself, because through faith we are united to him who is the creator and giver of life. This faith holds the certainty that heaven and earth will pass away, but the Lord's promises will not fail (cf. Luke 21. 33), and yet it lies within every man's power to accept it freely or to reject it.

So we see that to recognize God and to worship him require a serious spiritual effort and the free consent of the will. Therefore be firm in the faith and profess it freely and fearlessly, and do not weaken it by imposing on it conditions which may sometimes appear to be to your advantage in private or public life, but are derived from a materialistic conception of life and an opportunism which is becoming more and more widely diffused among those who, in order to disguise their own lukewarmness, try to make a distinction between faith in Christ and faith in his Church. But there is only one faith, and one Jesus Christ who in and through the Church continues his work of redemption until the end of time.

For this faith, and for the special grace of being allowed to profess it freely, let us at all times and in every place thank the Lord. In doing so we shall be united in brotherly union with the Apostles "in the breaking of bread and the prayers" (Acts 2. 42).

That is why the first Christians called the gifts they offered, which were transformed into the Lord's Body and Blood, the Eucharist, which means "thanksgiving".

The Holy Mass is the great sacrifice of thanksgiving offered by all who are redeemed by Christ.

10 SEPTEMBER

HOW TO OVERCOME DIFFICULTIES WITH FAITH

In the Divine Office every priest is familiar with the Book of Job. First of all Job is bereft of his wealth, and then his sons die; he suffers the direst, most wretched poverty. Then illness comes, terrible in the suffering it causes him, and in the horror, disgust and complaints it inspires even in his nearest and dearest. Nevertheless, the soul of that just and faithful man remains serene and imperturbable, firmly anchored to faith in God. "The Lord gave, and the Lord hath taken away", all has happened according to his will—blessed be the name of the Lord! (cf. Job 1. 21).

Such strength of mind, and such total obedience to the will of God, are rewarded even on this earth.

The Holy Father asks the faithful to read the Book of Job once more and attentively, from beginning to end. Everyone of us will find in it an indescribable encouragement, for this reading will confirm our faith in God . . .

There is earth, and there is heaven too. On earth we press forward amid difficulties, trials and disappointments, but we can overcome all these when we have faith in our hearts and confident courage, when we are sure that the Lord rules and directs all things and that our final and true goal is Paradise, towards the attainment of which all other things are directed and co-ordinated.

Misfortunes are by no means rare events in families— and cause many tears to flow. But faith is here to show us that if God has permitted us to suffer, he will help us to endure.

11 SEPTEMBER

KEEPING SUNDAY A HOLY DAY

From the first page of Genesis, which sanctifies the institution of the Sabbath—which is our Sunday—up to the most recent of Holy Church's provisions for interesting the faithful in the Sunday services, there is a whole epic of the life and union of souls with God: a true conversation of creatures with the Creator of heaven and earth, a raising of the soul towards the treasures of the supernatural order: all for the peace of souls here below, as the "beginning of future glory".

The Christian Sunday means:

(1) Absolute rest of body and mind, as the creature's homage to his Creator, and a pause in the expenditure of all physical energies.

(2) Close companionship of the soul with God, in communion with him in meditation, and in the rites of sacrifice, through which the whole man is renewed, and spiritual energy restored.

(3) Festival and song—the festival and song of the Christian life.

This is the divine and human law about rest and peace. But what a contrast we see in the present day distortion of the elementary principles of Christian and civilized living, what a profanation of Sunday's holy repose, what opposition between the customs of this world and the divine commandment: Remember the Sabbath day, to keep it holy!

12 SEPTEMBER

Feast of the Most Holy Name of Mary.

"TURN TO THE MORNING STAR, AND CALL ON MARY"

It is a magical name that moves heaven and earth, as

well we know. We have had proof of this every time Mary has come back among us, with her visible appearances in places that have since become centres of devotion to her.

Meanwhile we pray to her continually, and call upon her name. We have the holy rosary: a summary of the whole story of the Redemption in its fifteen pictures.

These are not events of yesterday—they go back two thousand years—yet they have preserved intact their meaning, their power and their lesson for every day.

That is why we ask you all to recite the rosary, not only with the mechanical movements of your lips, or of your fingers on the beads, but really pondering each individual mystery. By so doing we shall have unending peace in our hearts and the hope, nay, the certainty, that Mary hears us, blesses us and guides us to salvation.

In Mary's company age does not wither us; everyone may keep the freshness and charm of childhood, which induced a great writer to comment: "Nothing can be lovelier than a child reciting the Hail Mary". With the knowledge that this is the centuries old tradition of the Church, and the Catholic, Apostolic and Roman faith, we shall look forward also with serenity to our last hour on earth.

"Holy Mary, Mother of God, pray . . . now, and at the hour of our death." Our last thought and look will be for her, and she will return like the dawn of a new day: "Turn to the morning star, and call on Mary".

13 SEPTEMBER

REMEMBER TO KEEP SUNDAY HOLY

It is God's right to ask that man shall set apart for worship one day of the week, one day on which the soul, set free from material preoccupations, may rise to the thought and love of heavenly things, so that we may look into our innermost consciences and examine our bounden duty to our Creator.

But it is also lawful, and indeed necessary, for man to make a pause in the hard physical labour of the week, to refresh his tired limbs, and to enjoy honest recreation that is conducive to the unity of family life, for this needs frequent contacts and a peaceful life shared by all the members of the family.

With great sorrow we must point out and deplore the negligence, sometimes even the scornful rejection, of this holy law, with harmful consequences for the health of soul and body of the workers who are so dear to us.

In the name of God, and for the sake of the spiritual and material welfare of men, we beg all, authorities, employers and workers, to obey the commandment of God and of his Church, reminding all of their grave responsibility before God and before their fellow men.

14 SEPTEMBER

FEAST OF THE EXALTATION OF THE HOLY CROSS

The Fathers of the Church warn us that in every age and every place there are temptations . . . If we do not remain on the alert we may fall victims to their snares.

The three lusts assail and wound us. The more wealth we have the more we want; money brings unhappiness and yet it is hard to give it up. There are so many people who were once serenely happy in their work but who, acquiring wealth and using it wrongly, have become wretchedly unhappy. Even the thought of money can poison our lives. The same must be said of the other two great passions: that of pride, which breaks the bonds of brotherhood and simple affections and, aiming at power and domination at all costs, brings about injustice; and the lust of the flesh which mortifies and embitters the soul, destroying all possibility of raising the mind to God.

But we have our Lord Jesus Christ who . . . from his Cross purifies us, strengthens us and transforms our energies, neglected or ill used by evil lusts. He uses them to further our spiritual life and to train us in self-control.

Let us then follow Jesus who set us an example of humility, gentleness and kindness, and sacrificed himself for our good and our salvation.

At the end of life the door to eternity stands open: no one can pass through unless he carries a cross. The Lord keeps us company, in suffering and in bearing our cross. In this lie the hope and promise of our future life.

15 SEPTEMBER

FEAST OF OUR LADY OF SORROWS

The liturgy teaches us to meditate on the sorrows of Mary. So we turn once more to a memory of sadness, an example of patient endurance, to remind ourselves, for our own good, that our whole life here below is beset with trials and difficulties. It is a life of hardships, but at the end we shall receive the reward of eternal joy.

So we must always take courage: Jesus, Mary and Joseph give us the certainty of future triumph. In every moment of their earthly lives they knew sorrow, privations and suffering, and yet they always reflected the eternal splendour of heaven.

The lesson all the faithful may learn from such sublime examples is a continual encouragement and strength, by means of which, rising again after every failure, and correcting the faults of our temperaments, we may all seek to reach that shore where perfect peace and blessing are to be found.

16 SEPTEMBER

DISINTERESTEDNESS, HONESTY, SINCERITY

Purity of intention! That is the mark and indispensable condition of all interior freedom. St Leo the Great says in his sixth Sermon:

"He who ardently desires to know whether God dwells within him—that God who is called 'wonderful in his Saints' (Psalm 67. 36. Douai)—must scan the innermost recesses of his heart with perfect sincerity, and sternly ask himself to what extent he opposes humility to pride, and kindness to envy, whether he is indifferent to the praises of flatterers and rejoices in other men's prosperity."

It is in this spirit, beloved children, that we must treat our brothers, even those farthest away and least disposed to understand us. We cannot preach the word of God with truth and conviction if in our hearts there is envy or pride, foolish complacency, egoism or immoderate self-interest. The witness that all Christians are asked to bear must be above all disinterested, honest and sincere.

Sometimes it is just these failings, of which we may be unaware, which prejudice the results and impede the progress for which we have worked so hard.

17 SEPTEMBER

THE LOVE OF THE BIBLE

May the love of the Sacred Scriptures be ever more widely spread, and lead men to meditate on their message. All your efforts must be directed to this end. Even learned research, and the new light thrown on the Sacred Book by the contribution of the auxiliary sciences, find their final justification in this obligation to preach the revealed Word, and to guide souls to an understanding of its spiritual and didactic significance.

For this purpose we shall find ever new and indispensable assistance in the works of the Fathers of the Church, and the pronouncements of the Popes and Bishops through the centuries, even if they must now be read by eyes accustomed to the new knowledge derived from textual criticism.

More important than any display of erudition are the hunger and thirst for the Divine Word, because this is life to the soul, light to the mind, and the very breath of inspiration. Jesus proclaimed this in the words recorded by John: "The words that I have spoken to you are spirit and life" (John 6. 63).

The man of today, no less than the man who used to read the "Bible of the poor" on the walls of our ancient churches, has a great longing for the word of God. He awaits it and listens to it with the same reverence with which the Hebrews listened to Ezra reading to them the Sacred Book, after their perilous journey from captivity.

18 SEPTEMBER

THE BIBLE IS SACRED AND SUBLIME

This divine Book, the holy Bible, contains the two characteristic qualities of sublimity and sanctity, fused into one. To peruse these pages is like listening to the most beautiful and heart-stirring music. There is harmony between Holy Scripture and the general chronicle of ancient times, harmony in the style, and in the cross references to epochs in which the events narrated took place. There is harmony also between the various Books which, although differing in origin and subject matter, yet complete and confirm one another with their quotations, fulfilments of prophecies, and commentaries—a harmonious linking together of past ages.

Starting with the announcement which the Angel made to Mary, and moving back through time, the reader is led through long past epochs to the changeless eternity of God. "What marvels we have here!" writes Bossuet joyfully. "All the periods of the history of the chosen race are linked together. The period of the second Temple presupposes the age which preceded it and takes us back to Solomon. Thence through an age of endless warfare we go back to the Judges, to Joshua, and the flight from Egypt. The events of this miraculous escape take us still further back to the sad circumstances which led to the captivity. Thence we go to the Patriarchs, to Abraham, who might be said, through Sem, to have had one foot in Noah's ark. And these figures are linked to primitive man, to Adam and therefore to the Creator who breathed into him the breath of life."

These are the magnificent harmonies and visions of the Old Testament. But the central point at which sublimity and holiness meet and overflow in all their fullness is the New Testament, the Gospel of Jesus.

19 SEPTEMBER

THE SUBLIMITY OF THE GOSPEL

The sublimity of the Gospel is not like that of a torrent which rushes by, its great voice arousing the echoes of the mountains whence it sprang, but like that of a calm river, always full of water, and always wonderful in its majestic course. It is not the crash of thunder which precedes the storm, but the slow and peaceful diffusion of serene light, gradually increasing until it floods earth and heaven. This is the sublimity of the Gospel.

You do not expect it, but you feel with unutterable emotion that it is everywhere present. The begetting of the Word, the birth of Jesus, his childhood, his virtues, his miracles, his preaching to the crowds, his words: "Take and eat, this is my body; take and drink, this is my blood"; his groans and suffering, his dying—all is sublime.

Mary Magdalen at his feet, trembling and despised, the two sisters of Lazarus at their brother's tomb, the Angel's voice saying: "He is risen, he is not here"—nothing could surpass all this in grandeur. The Old Testament has its sublime moments; the New Testament is always sublime.

20 SEPTEMBER

THE GOSPEL: FULLNESS OF HOLINESS

The Gospel contains the fullness of holiness. It presents it to us in the most attractive light, gently tempered to our frail sight. In these pages we contemplate in fact the Man God, who is supreme, infinite perfection. To the pure and beautiful light already seen in the Old Testament saints, the Gospel now adds the most daring counsels, which raise virtue to the heights of heroism. It preaches worship in spirit and in truth, set free from the old observance, the old Law grown sterile; it preaches the love, rather than the fear, of God, the trustful love of a son for his father rather than the servant's trembling respect for his master. It teaches us to be "poor in spirit", to feel indifferent to wealth, to strip ourselves of possessions we might legitimately keep without ceasing to be good; it means giving our wealth to the poor.

It means simplicity, purity of heart and humility, even welcoming insults and rejoicing in suffering, forgiving offences, showing charity to our enemies, with forgetfulness of self and self-denial. It may even mean dying for those we love. In short, it is all that is most directly opposed to the faulty inclinations of our nature, all that most resembles and most nearly approaches the divine perfection. This is the Gospel; and besides giving us the fullness of sublimity and holiness it shows us also the continuation and harmonious fulfilment of the historical themes of the Old Testament.

21 SEPTEMBER

Generally, when we speak of the apostles, we think of the fishermen of the Lake of Tiberias, from among whom Jesus chose his first disciples, to form the initial nucleus of his Church.

St Matthew came from another social class. He was not a fisherman but a business man, expert in the handling of money. He himself tells us how Jesus called him, and how readily he obeyed the Master's peremptory and divine command to follow him. In fact, rising from his desk, he left everything at once and went to join him.

The newly chosen disciple had received such a profound impression of the Saviour's grace and kindness that, in order to find some way of showing him his devoted love, he at once invited him to his house. Jesus accepted his invitation and St Matthew tells us that many publicans and sinners sat down at the same table with the Lord, thus arousing the hypocritical indignation of the Pharisees, who were lying in wait to seize their chance of accusing the unusual Guest of causing scandal.

But when Jesus heard their outcry he told them very clearly and in memorable words the reason for his presence there. In fact, the kingdom of heaven does not consist in external forms and superficial conventions, but in the excellence of right and good feelings, and in true obedience to God's commandments, indeed, to put it shortly, in all those qualities which are essential for an apostle.

22 SEPTEMBER

TRUE WISDOM

The wise man knows how to see, to look and to study, in order that what he has to do may be done to perfection, with all that this implies. So he must not follow sudden irrational whims, or abandon himself to the impulses of his own nature, the nature we all like to carry around with us and treat with such clinging affection. It is instead absolutely necessary that everything be done with great discretion and prudence. We often hear the following judgment: He is a good fellow, he has a lot in him, but he is rather strange, rather moody, up one day and down the next. No, no, that will not do. It is essential to keep a sense of proportion, and to be serene with ourselves and with those around us. This is profound wisdom.

Now where are we to find this precious wisdom? We find it in abundance in the Lord's teaching, in his blessed Gospel, in the principles expounded in the Old Testament, and above all in the less numerous but more impressive principles of the New Testament.

Here we shall always find the way to acquire true wisdom. In this way, every time we have to make a decision, we shall feel naturally impelled to base it on the Lord's teaching, and we shall act righteously because the very name of Christ, his law and the reverence we feel in his presence, are the beginning of true wisdom.

23 SEPTEMBER

Feast of St Linus I, the second Pope.

THE POPE'S UNIVERSAL MISSION

The eagerness and anxieties of the missionary apostolate are most keenly felt at the very heart of the universal mission of Peter and his successors. They arise in the heart of Christ and he continues to pour them into the heart of his Vicar on earth, who is called to share intimately and painfully in his loving plan for the salvation of mankind.

There are the endless fields of the five continents where wait those sheep "who are not of this fold", but for whom—yes, for them too—was poured out the Precious Blood that stained Golgotha with its purple flow. They all belong to the scheme of universal Redemption: "I must lead them back to me", says Jesus, who wants them to enter, or re-enter, the fold.

But they must be drawn in with loving care, and it is from the Cross itself that the Lord Jesus seems to repeat to Peter and his successors the command to feed his sheep: "Feed my lambs, feed my sheep". And lest the weak shoulders should tremble and give way under so great a responsibility Jesus himself prays for Peter: "I have prayed for you", and Christ's prayer is the sure pledge of his help, that will last till the end of the world.

This help sustains Peter, giving him a robust and un-faltering faith, which is a source of courage and certainty for the whole Church: "Strengthen your brethren".

Oh what responsibility and what grandeur are here! What an onerous office is this of the Papacy, which we have accepted as a service, trusting ourselves to the Lord alone, to him who is "mighty . . . and holy is his name" (Luke 1. 49). What vast horizons unfold before us!

24 SEPTEMBER

THE EPISTLE OF THE FIRST POPE

The first Pope's message reaches us through the centu-ries, just as he addressed it on two occasions from Rome to the Christians who formed the first communities of the Eastern Church. It is still full of heavenly doctrine, spiritual direction and sound instruction . . .with wise and appropriate counsels for the circumstances of our life today.

These apostolic letters of St Peter—like those of St Paul, or indeed the whole of Sacred Scripture—should provide spiritual food for all the Catholics in the world.

When we reflect upon these Epistles we see that they deserve to be most closely studied, even learnt by heart . . . We invite you all to make a point of studying these two Encyclicals written by the first Pope. They contain the substantial food of doctrine, both sublime and practical, and are a real spiritual delight, coming as a surprise to most, but much cherished by all who are familiar with them. St Paul wrote to the Romans amaz-ing truths about lofty themes of universal interest. In-stead, St Peter wrote from Rome to encourage all the priests and faithful, dealing chiefly with subjects con-cerned with the practical life of the Church, and the Church in all ages.

For example, his first Letter speaks of the dignity of the Christian, and the sanctity of his life, and then of the duties, resplendent through grace, which were in-cumbent upon the chosen race, the royal priesthood, the holy nation, the ransomed people: the duty of obedience, the joys of family life and of charity. Then come the counsels to be followed while awaiting the end of life, and special recommendations for the elderly and the young.

25 SEPTEMBER

WOMEN'S WORK

There has been and still is much debate about this or that aspect of the advisability of women applying themselves to a given work or profession. It is necessary to consider the actual facts, which show that women are becoming more and more frequently employed, and more and more generally conscious of the need to undertake some activity which can make them financially independent and free from anxiety.

The problem interests us all, and especially parents, from the time when girls leave their childhood behind, and when the problems of existence and the urgent necessities of the family induce their parents to think of a source of profitable employment for them, or to prepare them by education for future professions and occupations.

But although the economic independence of the woman brings certain advantages, it also gives rise to many problems regarding her own fundamental mission in life, which is that of forming new creatures! Therefore new situations arise which urgently require solution and need preparation and a spirit of adaptability and self-denial.

26 SEPTEMBER

THE ETHICAL-RELIGIOUS ORDER

Mutual trust between men and between States can only arise and flourish in the recognition and respect of the moral order.

But the moral order can be based only on belief in God: when separated from God it disintegrates. In fact, man is not merely a material organism but a spirit endowed with thought and freedom. He therefore requires ethical-religious principles which must, more than any judgment based on material facts, decide the aims and solutions to be applied to the problems of individual life, the life of national communities, and the mutual relationship of all these.

It has been asserted that in this era of the triumph of science and technical skill men may set up their own civilization, leaving God out. But the truth is that scientific and technical progress itself gives rise to new human problems of world-wide dimensions which can only be resolved in the light of a sincere and active faith in God, the beginning and end of man and of the world.

The growing sense of unrest, which is spreading among the populations of those nations which enjoy a high standard of living, dispels the cherished illusion of an earthly Paradise.

27 SEPTEMBER

CHRISTIAN EDUCATION

A social doctrine must be not only preached but translated into concrete terms of reality. This is all the more true of the Christian social doctrine, for its light is Truth, its objective Justice and its motive power Love.

We therefore draw your attention to the need for our children to be not only educated in social doctrine, but also instructed about social problems.

Christian education must be integral, that is, it must extend to all kinds of duties, and it must also lead to the result that all the faithful shall feel increasingly bound to carry on their economic and social activity according to Christian principles.

The passage from theory to practice is, of its nature, hard, and all the harder when it is a case of translating into concrete terms a social doctrine like that of the Christian Church, because of the selfishness which is so deeply rooted in human beings, the materialism in which modern society is steeped, and the difficulties encountered in the way of deciding with clearness and precision the objective requirements of justice in individual cases.

Therefore education, besides arousing and developing the consciousness of our duty to act in a Christian way in the social and economic field, must also teach the methods by which this duty may be performed.

28 SEPTEMBER

THE DIVINE MESSAGE OF LOVE

A free heart and a pure intention give birth to generous love, which is the soul of every virtue and the strength of every sacrifice . . .

"Lest your careful self-examination", writes St Leo the Great, "should grow weary with too much questioning, seek in the secret recesses of your conscience the mother of all virtues, charity; if you find you are eager to love God and your neighbour with all your heart . . . be sure that God is leading you and dwelling within you . . . Follow charity, so that the hearts of all the faithful may be united in one great outpouring of chaste love. . . ."

After the all-powerful help of God and of his grace, the most effective means of overcoming the dangers of mutual distrust, theoretical and practical materialism, and religious indifference is to be found in the renewed and proven sense of the supernatural, allied to the practice of charity.

Love for God and our neighbour, whole-hearted, as St Leo would say: love for God so that his name may always be hallowed, his kingdom be extended, and his will made supreme by gentle means, on earth as in heaven; love for men, attentive to all their needs, with truth which never deceives them—but all in charity, tested and proved in real sacrifice for their good.

This is the message that will touch all hearts, and will recall to more intelligent fidelity to the Church those who think they can find without her and apart from her the answer to their longings for justice and peace.

29 SEPTEMBER

COVETING OTHER MEN'S POSSESSIONS

We are all brought face to face with this great commandment and the great temptation. We are not to steal, not to deprive workers of their just wages, not to oppress the poor, not to cherish immoderate desire for worldly wealth.

When we reflect upon it, this is the crucial problem of the whole world: in questions regarding political and economic order and disorder we do not assert that there are no longer any honest people to respect the rights of others—but in fact one of the greatest temptations of this life, and one to which a large number of people openly or secretly yield, is the temptation to covet and to steal.

Everything can lead to theft, or can seem to justify it. Everything is the object of desire and lust, and often of atrocious violence. Beginning with self-deceit and the subtle snare of the initial covetous desire of other men's possessions, people end by committing abominable crimes which can bring about the destruction of cities, nations and whole peoples.

30 SEPTEMBER

Feast of St Jerome

HOLY SCRIPTURE

The bishop, and all the priests in collaboration with him, perform the first characteristic task of the Church's pastoral mission: the teaching of the sacred doctrine. We have before our eyes in the Missal the two Testaments . . . The ancient Lawgiver appeared to his awestricken people with two rays of light shining on his brow; the first Gospel is, in fact, that of Moses, being the history and prophecy, direction and guide of souls and of the people . . .

Jesus, the divine Redeemer, Jesus the Shepherd, leads his flock by the light of heavenly doctrine and sets the whole world aflame with its fire.

The Fathers of the primitive Church, the writers of the great early centuries, and later on the two ancient and illustrious pontiffs of the Lateran, St Leo and St Gregory, together with two of the greatest geniuses of the Church, St Jerome and St Augustine, were all famous students and interpreters of Sacred Scripture to the whole world.

And here we wish above all to emphasize the sacred task of the pastoral ministry, the bold preaching of the faith, in all its light and power.

The law of goodness, the law of peace—all are taught in the doctrine contained in the Book, imparted by virtue of the Blood of Christ and through the close union of heart and mind of brothers in the faith.

Ah! this holy Church, one, catholic, apostolic and Roman! What charm, what sweetness and what joy we feel in all her manifestations of brotherly respect and love, of mutual co-operation not only in spiritual and religious matters but also in the relationships of civic and social life.

OCTOBER

1 OCTOBER

THE HOLY ROSARY

The real substance of the well meditated rosary consists in a threefold chord which gives its vocal expression unity and cohesion . . .

First of all the *contemplation*, pure, clear and immediate, of every Mystery, that is of those truths of the faith which speak to us of the redeeming mission of Christ. As we contemplate we find ourselves in close communion of thought and feeling with the teaching and life of Jesus, Son of God and Son of Mary, who lived on this earth redeeming, teaching, sanctifying : in the silence of his hidden life, all prayer and work, in the sufferings of his blessed Passion, in the triumph of his Resurrection, in the glory of heaven, where he sits on the right hand of the Father, ever assisting and with his Holy Spirit giving life to the Church founded by him, which proceeds on her way through the centuries.

The second element is *reflection*, which out of the fullness of Christ's Mysteries diffuses its bright radiance over the praying soul. Everyone finds in each Mystery a good and proper teaching for himself, for his sanctification and for the conditions of our life; under the constant guidance of the Holy Spirit, which from the depths of the soul in grace "intercedes for us with sighs too deep for words" (Romans 8. 26), everyone confronts his own life with the strength of the doctrine he has drawn from the depths of those same Mysteries, and finds them of inexhaustible application to his own spiritual needs and to the needs of his daily life too.

Finally there is the *intention* : that is, intercession for persons, institutions or necessities of a personal or social nature, which for a really active and pious Catholic forms part of his charity towards his neighbour, a charity which is diffused in our hearts as a living expression of our common sharing in the Mystical Body of Christ.

2 OCTOBER

FEAST OF OUR GUARDIAN ANGELS

According to the teaching of the Roman catechism, we must remember how admirable was the intention of divine Providence in entrusting to the angels the mission of watching over all mankind, and over individual human beings, lest they should fall victims to the grave dangers which they encounter. In this earthly life, when children have to make their way along a path beset with obstacles and snares, their fathers take care to call upon the help of those who can look after them and come to their aid in adversity. In the same way our Father in heaven has charged his angels to come to our assistance during our earthly journey which leads us to our blessed fatherland, so that, protected by the angels' help and care, we may avoid the snares upon our path, subdue our passions and, under this angelic guidance, follow always the straight and sure road which leads to Paradise . . .

Everyone of us is entrusted to the care of an angel.

That is why we must have a lively and profound devotion to our own Guardian Angel, and why we should often and trustfully repeat the dear prayer we were taught in the days of our childhood.

May we never fail in this devotion to the angels! During our earthly pilgrimage we may often run the risk of having to face the natural elements in turmoil, or the wrath of men who may seek to do us harm. But our Guardian Angel is always present. Let us never forget him and always remember to pray to him.

3 OCTOBER

Feast of St Teresa of the Child Jesus,
Universal Patroness of Missions.

THE MISSIONARY SPIRIT

"Let all the peoples praise thee, O God, let all the peoples praise thee!" (Psalm 66 (67). 3). These words from a Messianic psalm begin the Mass "for the Propagation of the Faith", and determine and explain the intentions of the World Missions Day, which every year so effectively appeals for spiritual and material offerings in aid of the propagation of the Gospel, and the brotherly union of all peoples.

We are faced with the melancholy and mysterious fact that millions of men do not yet know the true God, and so cannot pray to him. The thought of the divine plan of Redemption leaves us trembling and dismayed as we consider how much responsibility for its fulfilment has been left to us by Jesus.

The truth is that he wished us to co-operate with him in his redemptive work: he made us, as it were, sharers of his own responsibility, assistants in his own mission, in the time and way appointed by his divine love. In so far as we are able to grasp this mystery we are very conscious of our failure to collaborate . . .

So we still have a chance to make amends, and to prove our good will . . .

Earnest and confident prayer will be a first blessed step in the right direction, because it is written that blessed indeed are those who preach the Gospel.

Through the intercession of the Immaculate Virgin, of St Francis Xavier and of St Teresa of the Child Jesus, may God bless us all and give us cause to rejoice!

4 OCTOBER

ST FRANCIS OF ASSISI

Francis was called "another Christ", in the sense that he showed in his life and conduct the very pith and kernel of Our Lord's teaching.

We all have to fight against the lusts of the flesh. Many people also desire material wealth and dream of money, but St Francis teaches every one of us, whatever our social condition may be, to fight against "the lust of the eyes", which is full of deceit and vanity. The wealth of Christian life does not consist in money and all its cares and demands. To some extent it is necessary for our very existence, but we must not lose our hearts to it. In the presence of his father and of the Bishop, Francis gave up everything, even the clothes he was wearing — such was his love for poverty.

When Providence has enabled a man to possess more than sufficient for his needs, he is inviting him to re-distribute his wealth, to help the poor, and to contribute to the great works in aid of human brotherhood. This commandment is valid for all, and particularly for those who have dedicated their lives to God's service.

Therefore, whoever has more abundant wealth must give more generously, giving also for those who are unable to do so. The precept applies not only to two brothers, two families or two towns, but to the whole world. Sometimes a rich man may feel powerful, and boast of his resources, and shut his eyes and ears to the poverty of others who are condemned to live in want— whereas true brotherly feeling would see to it that the poor man had at least what he needed to live. If we wish to find a little spiritual joy on this earth we must follow after St Francis, who imitated the example of Christ, who even worked miracles in order to feed the hungry.

5 OCTOBER

RECITING THE ROSARY PRAYERS

The Our Father . . . gives the rosary its tone, substance and life and, coming as it does after the announcements of the individual mysteries, marks the passing from one decade to another; then the angel's greeting, echoing the joy of heaven and earth and accompanying the various scenes from the lives of Jesus and Mary; and finally the *Gloria*, repeated in profound worship of the Most Holy Trinity.

Oh how beautiful it always is when said in this way by innocent children and by the sick, by virgins consecrated to cloistered seclusion or to the apostolate of charity, always to a life of contemplative humility and self-denial; of men and women who are fathers and mothers of families, and are sustained by a lofty sense of their noble and Christian responsibilities, of humble families faithful to their old family traditions; of souls recollected in silence, aloof from the life of the world they have renounced, but in which they are still obliged to live, like anchorites, amidst doubts and temptations.

This is the rosary of pious souls, who are deeply conscious of their own particular lives and circumstances . . .

Oh blessed rosary of Mary! what joy to see it raised in the hands of innocent children, of holy priests, of the pure in heart, young and old, of all who understand the value and efficacy of prayer; raised aloft by countless pious multitudes as an emblem or standard of that peace in men's hearts and among peoples for which we all hope.

6 OCTOBER

MEMBERS OF THE MYSTICAL BODY

We are living members of the Mystical Body of Christ, which is his Church: "For just as the body is one . . ., and all the members of the body, though many, are one body, so it is with Christ" (I Cor. 12. 12).

With fatherly insistence we beg all our children, priests and laity alike, to be profoundly aware of the dignity and grandeur which are theirs because they are joined to Christ as the branches are joined to the vine: "I am the vine, you are the branches" (John 15. 5), and to remember that they are therefore called to share in his own life.

For this reason, in all their activity, even when this is of a temporal nature, provided that they are united to Jesus, the divine Redeemer, all their work becomes as it were a continuation of his work, full of redemptive power: "He who abides in me, and I in him, he it is that bears much fruit" (John 15. 5). Thus through their labours they will be working for their own supernatural perfection, and contribute to increase and to share with others the fruits of Redemption, while they leaven with their evangelical zeal the civilization in which they live and work.

7 OCTOBER

THE ROSARY DEFENDS US FROM ALL EVIL

The rosary is the Bible of the poor.

How I wish this devotion were ever more widely diffused in your souls, in your families . . . in all the churches of the world!

The rosary must be recited with profound spiritual understanding, not merely with lip service.

Every decade presents a picture of happiness or sorrow or glory: it must be the subject of contemplation. This contemplation, with the gentle repetition of the ten Hail Marys, must lead to prayer, so that the devotion may be for our edification and encouragement.

We are all brothers of Jesus. We are members of his Mystical Body: therefore we must try to grow like him.

We are children of Mary: therefore we must always try to please her and do her honour, and by this means to attain first of all graces of the spiritual order and then also graces of the material order, always in perfect accordance with the Lord's holy will.

Let us raise our hearts, let us raise our arms, holding aloft the holy rosary!

Mary, Help of Christians, give the Church victory and peace!

8 OCTOBER

JOYFUL MYSTERIES OF THE ROSARY

These are joyful themes: the angel's announcement to Mary, the song on the hills of Hebron to the most blessed among women, which answered her own song of joy for the wonders that were being wrought in her, the angels' chant of glory and peace around the cradle of Bethlehem, the joyful sigh of old Simeon when he welcomed to the Temple the Mother of God and the Child of Promise, and finally the firm and gentle voice of the Child himself, now a stripling, when on the threshold of the Temple he asserted the will of his heavenly Father and his glory: what motives these are for unutterable joy! Does not the joy of our own hearts respond to these, at the touch of grace which in Mary made us all brothers of Jesus: "The Angel of the Lord declared unto Mary", as we rejoice in the tender affections of our Christian families, rich in their children and in the satisfactions which surpass all the world's wealth ?

The intimate familiar love for the Child Jesus, who brings the gifts of innocence and purity to our homes, the serene certainty of the triumph of the kingdom of Christ . . . and finally the holy joy we feel in sharing in the apostolate for the defence of the kingdom of Christ, as Jesus defended it in the Temple—does not all this mingle in one true and joyful harmony for the follower of Jesus Christ ?

9 OCTOBER

THE SORROWFUL MYSTERIES OF THE ROSARY

These are themes of suffering: the agony of Jesus in the Garden of Gethsemane, the scourging of his body, the sharp pain of the crowning with thorns, his stumbling steps up the hill of Calvary, and the epilogue of his death with a final divine gesture of love for his Mother and her new son: do you not see that these images have much to tell us about the sufferings of everyone of us in the vicissitudes of human life ? Is this not true ?

Our ceaseless anguished prayer seems to meet with no reply, our weak bodies are tormented with pain, our poor heads suffer from uncertainties and poignant sorrows under the weight of the responsibilities and adversities of life, the long succession of melancholy days of physical and spiritual suffering as we climb the hill that is stained with the blood of Jesus—and at the end every one of us must die—death comes to us all. Ah! this dying, my dear brothers, what a grave and melancholy thought! Do we not all receive from the communion of our souls with Christ the strength to endure all these afflictions, as well as abundance of merit in heaven ?

10 OCTOBER

THE GLORIOUS MYSTERIES OF THE ROSARY

Themes of rejoicing and of triumph!

The triumphs of our poor human life here below are puny things: vain and fleeting satisfactions that bring joy one day and the next day are empty and gone.

Jesus is the real conqueror. He triumphs over death by rising again: his Father crowns him with this glory by associating him, in his human nature, with the eternal splendours of divinity. He triumphs in his Church through the constant outpouring of the Holy Spirit. He triumphs in his Mother through her Assumption and glorious crowning, when she is proclaimed Queen of all the angels and all the saints, and through the continuation of her glorious motherhood extended to include all the children of the Church, for they have become with Christ and by Christ's word her children too, the objects of her protective care and her great mercy.

It is the risen Christ, my brothers, who sets us free from our sins, Christ ascending to heaven to assure for every one of us a throne of glory there. And we have Holy Church, our Mother on this earth, inspired by the Spirit of Jesus and by the undying flame of the apostolate of her children, called to spiritual conquests in this world. Finally we have Mary, taken up body and soul into heaven, where she has become the loving object of our aspirations, our devotion and our filial affection, Mary who invites us to imitate her virtues and those of the saints in heaven.

11 OCTOBER

Feast of the Maternity of the Blessed Virgin Mary.

WOMAN'S MISSION

A woman's professional occupation must take into account those particular characteristics with which her Creator has endowed her. It is true that the conditions of our life tend in practice to establish almost absolute equality between man and woman. Nevertheless, although the rightly proclaimed equality of rights must be acknowledged in all that pertains to her human person and dignity, in no way does it imply similarity of function. The Creator has given woman talents, inclinations and natural dispositions which are proper to her, and differ from those he has given to man; this means that he has also assigned to her a particular function. If we did not clearly recognize the diversity of the respective functions of man and woman and the way in which they inevitably complement each other, we should be working against nature, and we should end by humiliating the woman and depriving her of the true foundation of her dignity.

. . . The special purpose to which the Creator has directed a woman's whole being is motherhood. This maternal vocation is so proper and natural to her that

228

it is present and active even when she does not actually give birth to children.

We must therefore give the woman all necessary assistance in the choice of her occupation, and in the training and perfection of her own gifts, and to do this it is necessary that she should find in the exercise of her profession the means of constantly developing and expressing her maternal affections.

Finally, we must always bear in mind the special needs of the family, the principal centre of a woman's activities, in which her presence is indispensable.

12 OCTOBER

THE ANGELUS FOR THE ASTRONAUT

The *Angelus* consecrates for all time the union of heaven and earth, the divine with the human. In this hour today we wish to associate with the intentions of our prayer the young pilot in space.

Beloved children, belonging to all races, you have come together like good brothers, while the pilot is proving, in an almost decisive and certainly a most scientific manner, the intellectual, moral and physical powers of man, and continuing that exploration of the created world which we were encouraged to make in the first pages of Sacred Scripture, when the Lord told man he was to multiply and fill the earth.

The nations, and especially the young generations, follow with enthusiasm the developments of the wonderful flights and navigations in space. Oh, how ardently we wish that these enterprises could assume the significance of homage rendered to God, the Creator and supreme Lawgiver!

May these historical events which will be recorded in the annals of the scientific exploration of the world become expressions of true and peaceful progress, the firm foundation of human brotherhood.

13 OCTOBER

Anniversary of the last apparition of Our Lady
at Fatima in 1917.

A SPECIAL ACT OF FAVOUR

This is neither the time nor the place to investigate or

study the three great secrets of Fatima, that were confided to the little seers.

We must respect this hidden mystery. What is clear to our eyes is this, that these frequent miracles and events that cannot be explained by human knowledge—especially supernatural miracles such as the spectacle of innumerable souls turned back from the evil roads that lead to hell—once more confront the modern world with one of those meeting points where heaven and earth are seen to meet, resplendent in the sovereign light of Jesus our Saviour, and the gracious light of his divine Mother who is our Mother too.

This is a great mystery of love, this familiar intimacy of Jesus with our human nature and with the souls he redeemed by his Blood. Jesus is still with us on this earth; his human and sentient form is concealed in the Eucharistic Sacrament wherein his Sacred Heart is also present.

But in the act of dying, as a final proof of his brotherly love, Jesus left to us his own Mother, as if he wished to grant her the right to visit us even visibly as a special act of favour, appearing now here and now there in her womanly and motherly form.

14 OCTOBER

NOT FEAR BUT LOVE

All men are gradually becoming convinced that eventual disputes among the peoples must be solved, not by recourse to arms but by negotiations.

It is true that in our present historical epoch this conviction is partly due to men's awareness of the terribly destructive power of modern weapons, and it is fostered by the horror aroused in their minds by the mere thought of the immense loss of life which the human family would suffer through their use. So it has become impossible to believe that in the atomic era war can be used as an instrument of justice.

Yet the nations, alas! are still living more or less under the law of fear. This drives them to pour out fabulous sums for armaments, not, so they assert, and we have no reason to doubt this, in order to prepare aggressive acts, but in order to dissuade others from doing so.

It is however legitimate to hope that as men meet and negotiate they may acquire a better knowledge of the links which bind them together, which are derived from their common humanity, and also that they may discover that one of the most profound needs of their common human nature is that all peoples should be ruled not by fear but by love, which tends to express itself in various forms of loyal collaboration, the source of so many benefits to mankind.

15 OCTOBER

FEAST OF ST TERESA OF AVILA

We permit ourselves once more to recall to our children's attention their duty to share actively in the life of the community, and to contribute to the common efforts for the welfare of the human family and of their own political society. They must therefore endeavour, by the light of faith and with the power of love, to ensure that economic, social, cultural and political institutions shall be such as will not impede but rather facilitate, by rendering less arduous, men's striving after perfection, as much in the natural as in the supernatural order.

Faith and good intentions alone are not enough to influence a civilization with wholesome principles and reform it in the spirit of the Gospel. For this purpose it is necessary to penetrate into these institutions and work effectively from within them. One must remember, however, that our civilization is above all characterized by its scientific and technical achievements. Therefore it is impossible to enter into its institutions, and work from within them, unless one is scientifically competent, technically skilful and professionally expert.

16 OCTOBER

A SYNTHESIS

We wish also to remind you that, although scientific competence, technical skill and professional expertness are necessary, they are not in themselves sufficient to reform the relationships of society in a truly human direction, that is, in an order founded on truth, with justice as its standard and objective, love as its motive power and freedom as the means of its realization.

For this end it is undoubtedly necessary for human beings to continue in their customary worldly occupations in obedience to the inherent requirements of these, and following methods consonant with their nature; but at the same time they must also perform their tasks according to the principles of the moral order, that is, as the exercise or vindication of a right, the performance of a duty and of a service. As their part of active co-operation in God's providential plan for our salvation, human beings must, in their own interior lives, carry out their worldly duties in the spirit of a synthesis of scientific, technical and professional elements, and spiritual values.

17 OCTOBER

THE ANNUNCIATION

This is the first shining point of union between heaven and earth: the first of those events which were to be the greatest of all time.

The Son of God, Word of the Father, "without whom was not anything made that was made" (John 1. 3) in the order of creation, in this mystery takes on human nature and becomes a man, in order to save and redeem all men, all mankind.

When Mary Immaculate, the finest and most fragrant flower of all creation, said in answer to the angel's greeting: "Behold the handmaid of the Lord" (Luke 1. 38) she accepted the honour of divine motherhood, which was in that moment realized within her. And we, born once in our father Adam, formerly the adopted sons of God but fallen from that high estate, are now once more brothers, adopted sons of the Father, restored to his adoption by the redemption which has already begun. At the foot of the Cross we shall all be children of Mary, with that same Jesus whom she has conceived today. From today onwards she will be Mother of God (*Mater Dei*) and our Mother (*Mater nostra*) too.

What sublimity, what tender love in this first mystery!

When we reflect on this we see that our chief and constant duty is to thank the Lord who deigned to come to save us and for this purpose made himself man, our brother man; he has joined us by becoming the son of a woman and by making us, at the foot of the Cross, the adopted sons of this woman. He wanted us, who were the adopted sons of his Heavenly Father, to be the sons of his own Mother.

Let the intention of our prayer, as we contemplate this first picture offered to our thoughts, be, besides a constant feeling of gratitude, a real and sincere effort to acquire humility, purity and ardent love for the Blessed Virgin who provides the most precious example of all these virtues.

18 OCTOBER

MARY'S VISIT TO HER COUSIN ELIZABETH

What gentleness and charm in this three months' visit made by Mary to her beloved cousin! Each of them is about to bear a child, but for the Virgin Mother this is the most sacred maternity that it is possible to imagine on earth. Their two songs mingle and respond in a sweet harmony: "Blessed are you among women" (Luke 1. 42) on the one hand, and on the other: "God my Saviour has regarded the low estate of his handmaiden: for behold, henceforth all generations will call me blessed" (Luke 1. 48).

What takes place here, at Ain-Karim on the hill of Hebron, sheds a light, both very human and divine, on the relations that bind Christian families, brought up in the ancient tradition of the holy rosary: the rosary recited every evening at home, in the family circle, the rosary recited not just in one or a hundred or a thousand families but by every family, by everyone, everywhere in the world, wherever there is one of us "suffering, fighting and praying" (A. Manzoni, *La Pentecoste*, v, 6) someone who has answered a call to the priesthood or to missionary service or to a dream which will turn out to be an apostolate; or wherever men are constrained by those legitimate if obligatory demands of labour or trade, military service, study, teaching or any other occupation.

There is a beautiful reunion, during the ten Hail Marys of the Mystery, of so many countless souls, linked together by blood or by domestic ties, in a relationship which hallows and thereby strengthens the love that binds our dearest ones together: parents and children, brothers and relations, people from the same locality, people of the same race. All this with the purpose and intention of sustaining, increasing and irradiating that universal charity, the exercise of which is the most profound joy and supreme honour of our lives.

19 OCTOBER

THE BIRTH OF JESUS
IN THE STABLE AT BETHLEHEM

At the hour appointed by the laws of the human nature he had assumed, the Word of God, now made man, issues from the holy shrine, the immaculate womb of Mary. He makes his first appearance in this world in a manger: the cattle are there, chewing their hay, and all around are silence, poverty, simplicity and innocence. Angels' voices are heard in the sky, announcing peace, that peace which the new baby has brought to us. His first worshippers are Mary his mother and Joseph, thought to be his father, and after these some humble shepherds who have come down from the hills, led by angels' voices. Later on comes a caravan of distinguished persons guided from far, far away by a star; they offer precious gifts, full of a mysterious meaning. Everything that night at Bethlehem spoke a language that the whole world could understand.

Pondering this mystery every knee will bow in adoration before the crib. Everyone will look into the eyes of the divine Infant which gaze far away, almost as if he could see one by one all the peoples of the earth, one after the other, as if he were reviewing them all as they pass before him, recognizing and identifying them all and greeting them with a smile: Jews, Romans, Greeks, Chinese, Indians, the peoples of Africa and of every region of the world, of every age of history, the most desolate, deserted lands, and the most remote, secret and unexplored; past, present and future ages.

The Holy Father, as the intention of these ten Hail Marys, wishes to commend to the new-born Jesus the infinite number of babies—and who could count them all ?—who in the last twenty-four hours, by night or day, have been born, some here, some there, all over the world. An infinite number indeed! And all, whether baptized or not, belong by right to Jesus, to this Child who is born in Bethlehem; they are his brothers, called to establish this rule of his which is the most sublime and the most gentle that can be found in man's heart or in the history of the world, the only rule worthy of God and man: a rule of light, a rule of peace, the "kingdom" for which we pray when we say the Our Father.

20 OCTOBER

THE PRESENTATION OF JESUS IN THE TEMPLE

Jesus, carried in his Mother's arms, is offered to the priest, to whom he holds out his arms: it is the meeting, the contact of the two Covenants. He is already the "light for revelation to the Gentiles" (Luke 2. 32), he, the splendour of the chosen people, the Son of Mary. St Joseph also is there to present him, an equal sharer in this rite of offerings according to the law.

This episode is continually repeated in the Church, indeed is perpetuated there in forms which vary but are similar in the substance of the offering. As we repeat the Hail Marys, how beautiful it is to contemplate the growing crops, the rising corn: "Lift up your eyes, and see how the fields are already white for the harvest." (John 4. 35). These are the joyful and rising hopes of the priesthood, and of those men and women who co-operate with the priests, so numerous in the kingdom of God and yet never enough: young people in the seminaries, in religious houses, in missionary training colleges, also—and why not? are they not Christians also, called likewise to be apostles?—in the Catholic universities. There are also all the other young shoots of the future and indispensable apostolate of the laity, this apostolate which, increasing in spite of difficulties and opposition, even within nations tormented by persecution, offers and will never cease to offer such a consoling spectacle as to compel expressions of admiration and joy.

This Child is the "light for revelation to the Gentile", and the glory of the chosen people.

21 OCTOBER

Jesus is now twelve years old. Mary and Joseph have
brought him with them to Jerusalem, for the ritual
prayers. Without warning he disappears from their
sight, although they are so watchful and so loving. Great
anxiety and a fruitless search for three days. Their
sorrow is followed by the joy of finding him again, there,
under the porches of the Temple. He is speaking with
the doctors of the Law. How significant is the account
given us by St Luke, with his careful precision! They
found him then, sitting in the midst of the doctors
"listening to them and asking them questions" (Luke
2. 46). In those days an encounter with the doctors was
very important and meant everything: learning, wisdom,
and the direction of practical life by the light of the Old
Testament.

Such, in every age, is the task of the human intelligence: to garner the wisdom of the ages, to hand down
the good doctrine and firmly and humbly to press ahead
with scientific investigation. We die, one after the other,
we go to God, but mankind moves towards the future.

Christ, in natural as in supernatural revelation, is
never absent; he is always in his place, in the midst:
"For you have one master, the Christ" (Matt. 23. 10).

This is the fifth decade of Hail Marys, the last of the
joyful mysteries. Let us keep it as a very special invocation for the benefit of those who are called by God, because of their natural gifts, or the circumstances of their
lives, or the wishes of their Superiors, to the service of
truth, in research and in teaching, in the imparting of
ancient learning or modern skills, by means of books or
wireless and television—for all these too are called to
follow Jesus. They are the intellectuals, the professional
classes and the journalists; the journalists especially,
who have the particular task of honouring the truth,
must transmit it with religious fidelity and great discretion, without fantastic distortions or inventions.

We pray for them all, priests and laity; we pray that
they may listen to the truth, and for this they need great
purity of heart; that they may understand it, and for this
they need profound humility of mind; that they may
defend it, and for this they need what made the strength

236

of Jesus and of his saints: obedience. Only obedience wins peace, which means victory.

22 OCTOBER

JESUS IN THE GARDEN OF GETHSEMANE

Our heart is moved as we continually return to the image of the Saviour, in the place and hour of his supreme anguish: " . . . and his sweat became like great drops of blood falling down upon the ground" (Luke 22. 44). Suffering of the innermost soul, extreme bitterness of loneliness, exhaustion of the broken body. His suffering can only be measured by the imminence of his Passion which now Jesus sees, no longer as far away, or even as near at hand, but as present in that hour.

The scene in the garden strengthens and encourages us to force all our will to an acceptance, a full acceptance, of suffering sent or permitted by God: "Not my will but thine be done" (Luke 22. 42). Words which tear the heart and heal it again, for they teach us what passionate fervour the Christian can and must feel if he is to suffer with Christ who suffers, and gives us the final certainty of the indescribable merits he obtained for us, the certainty of the divine life, a life which today is lived in grace and tomorrow in glory.

A special intention should be borne in mind as we dwell on this mystery: the "anxiety for all the Churches" (II Cor. 11. 28), an anxiety which torments us, as the wind tormented the lake of Gennesaret, "for the wind was against them" (Matt. 14. 24), the daily prayer of the Holy Father, the anxiety of the highest pastoral ministry in the most critical hours; the anxiety of the Church, scattered all over the earth, which suffers with him, and which he bears with the Church, present and suffering in him; anxiety for countless souls, whole sections of the flock of Christ, who are subjected to persecutions directed against liberty of belief, thought and life. "Who is in trouble, and I not in trouble with him?" (cf. II Cor. 11. 29).

To share in our brothers' pain, to suffer with those who suffer, to weep with those who weep (Romans 12. 15), will confer a blessing, a merit on the whole Church. Is this not what we mean by the "communion of saints", everyone of us sharing in common the blood of Jesus,

237

the love of the saints and of good people, and also, alas! our sins and failings? Do we ever think of this "communion" which is union, and almost, as Jesus said, unity: "That they may be one"? (John 17. 22 and cf. John 10. 30). The Lord's Cross not only raises us up but draws the souls of men, always: "And I, when I am lifted up, will draw all men to myself" (John 12. 32). All things, all men.

23 OCTOBER

THE SCOURGING

This mystery reminds us of the merciless torture of the many stripes inflicted on the pure and holy body of Jesus.

Man is made up of body and soul. The body is subjected to the most humiliating temptations: the will, which is even weaker, may easily be overcome. In this mystery then there is a call to practise penance, a salutary penance, since it is important for man's true health, which is health in the bodily sense and also health in the sense of spiritual salvation.

There is a great lesson here for us all. We may not be called to endure a cruel martyrdom, but we are called to the exercise of constant discipline and the daily mortification of our passions. This way, a real "Way of the Cross," our daily, unavoidable and indispensable duty, which at times becomes even heroic in its requirements, leads us step by step towards a more and more perfect resemblance with Jesus Christ, and a share in his merits and in the atonement through his innocent blood for every sin in us and in all people. We cannot do this in any other way, by facile enthusiasms, or by a fanaticism which, even if innocent, is always harmful.

His Mother, sorrowing, saw her Son scourged in this way: what pain she too must have felt! There are so many mothers who would like to have the joy of seeing their children grow up, initiated by them into the discipline of a good training and a healthy life, and who instead have to mourn the vanishing of so many hopes, and weep that so much care and anxiety have come to nothing.

So our Hail Marys of this Mystery must implore the Lord to give purity of morals to our families and to society, especially to our young people who are most exposed to the temptation of the senses. At the same time they will beg him to give them strength of character and fidelity at all costs to the teachings they have received and the resolutions they have made.

24 OCTOBER

THE CROWNING WITH THORNS

The contemplation of this Mystery is particularly indicated for those who bear grave responsibilities in the government of society: hence it is the Mystery for rulers, law-givers and magistrates. This King wears a crown of thorns. They too wear crowns, which have their own undeniable dignity and distinction, crowns representing an authority which comes from God and is divine; nevertheless they are so mixed with burdensome and hurtful elements that sometimes we are perplexed and almost disheartened by these pricking thorns and preoccupations, as well as by all the suffering caused by the misfortunes and sins of men; this suffering is the greater the more we love men, and it is our duty to represent to them their Father who is in heaven. Then love itself becomes, as it did for Jesus, a crown of thorns woven by cruel men for the head of one who loves them.

Another useful way of thinking about this mystery would be to consider the grave responsibilities of those who have received greater talents and are therefore bound to make them yield greater fruit, through the continual use of their faculties and intelligence. The ministry of the mind, that is the service required of those most richly endowed with intelligence, in order to be a light and guide to all others, must be undertaken with great patience, resisting all the temptations of pride, selfishness and the disintegration which is destructive.

25 OCTOBER

THE WAY OF THE CROSS

The life of men is a pilgrimage, continual, long and wearisome. Up and up along the steep and stony road, the road marked out for all upon that hill. In this Mystery Jesus represents the whole race of men. Every one of us must have his own cross to bear; otherwise, tempted by selfishness or cruelty, we should sooner or later fall by the roadside.

From the contemplation of Jesus climbing up to Calvary we learn, first with our hearts and then with our minds, to embrace and kiss the Cross, and bear it bravely and with joy, as we read in *The Imitation of Christ*: "In the Cross is our salvation, in the Cross is our life, in the Cross is our defence against our foes, and our heavenly sweetness" (Book II, XII, 2).

And how can we fail to include Mary in our prayers, Mary who followed Jesus sorrowing, sharing so intimately in his merits and his sufferings.

The Mystery should set before our eyes a vast vision of poor suffering souls: orphans, old people, the sick, the weak, prisoners and exiles. We pray for strength for all these, and the consolation which alone brings hope. We repeat with emotion and, we must admit, with secret tears, "Hail, O Cross, our only hope" (Roman Breviary, Vesper Hymn for Passion Sunday).

26 OCTOBER

THE DEATH OF JESUS

"... in strange and awful strife
Met together death and life."
(Roman Missal, Sequence from the Easter Mass)

Life and death are the two significant and decisive elements of Christ's sacrifice. From his smile at Bethlehem, the same smile which lights up the faces of all the children of men when first they appear on earth, to his last gasp and sob on the Cross, which gathered all our sufferings into one to hallow them, and wiped away all our sins by atoning for them, we have seen how Christ lived in this our earthly life. And Mary is still there, beside the Cross, as she was beside the Babe at Bethlehem. Let us pray to her, this Mother, pray to her so that she too may pray for us "now and at the hour of our death."

In this Mystery we might see foreshadowed the mystery of those who—what sadness in this thought!—will never know anything about the blood that was poured out for them too by the Son of God; and above all the mystery of obstinate sinners, of unbelievers, of those who have received, still do receive and then refuse the light of the Gospel! With this thought our prayer expands in a vast longing, in a sigh of heartfelt reparation, the longing to reach to the ends of the earth with our apostolate; and we earnestly pray that the Precious Blood, poured out for all mankind, may at long last bring to all, to all men everywhere, salvation and conversion, that the Blood of Christ may be to all the pledge and promise of eternal life.

27 OCTOBER

THE RESURRECTION OF OUR LORD

This is the mystery of death challenged and defeated. The Resurrection marks the greatest victory of Christ, and likewise the assurance of victory for the holy Catholic Church, beyond all the adversities and persecutions of past yesterdays and tomorrow's future. "Christ conquers, reigns and rules." We do well to remember that the first appearance of the risen Christ was to the pious women, who were near to him during his humble life, who had accompanied him in his sufferings as far as Calvary, and stayed with him there.

In the splendour of this Mystery we see with the eyes of faith, as living and united with the risen Jesus, the souls who were most dear to us, the souls of those who lived with us and whose sufferings we shared. How vividly the memory of our dead rises in our hearts in the light of the Resurrection of Christ! We remember and pray for them in the very sacrifice of our crucified and risen Lord, and they still share the best part of our life, which is prayer and Jesus.

The Eastern liturgy wisely concludes the funeral rite with the "Alleluia!" for all the dead. While we implore the light of eternal habitations for our dead, at the same time our thoughts turn to the resurrection which awaits our own mortal remains: *Et exspecto resurrectionem mortuorum*. Learning to wait, trusting always to the precious promise of which the Resurrection of Jesus gives us a sure pledge—this is a foretaste of heaven.

28 OCTOBER

THE ASCENSION OF JESUS INTO HEAVEN

In this picture we contemplate the "consummation", that is the final fulfilment of the promises of Jesus. It is his reply to our longing for paradise. His final return to the Father, from whom one day he came down among us in this world, is a surety for us all, to whom he has promised and prepared a place above: "I go to prepare a place for you" (John 14. 2).

Above all, this mystery brings light and guidance for those souls who are absorbed in the study of their own vocations. We see within it that spiritual longing, that yearning to soar upwards, which burns in the hearts of priests who are not hampered or distracted by the wealth of this world but intent only on opening the way, for themselves and others, to holiness and perfection, to that degree of grace which is to be attained, privately and in common, by priests, men and women in Religious Orders, men and women missionaries, lay people who love God and his Church, and numerous souls, those souls at least that are like "the aroma of Christ" (cf. 2 Cor. 2. 15), who make the presence of Jesus felt wherever they are, for indeed they are already living in constant communion with the life of heaven.

This decade of the rosary teaches and urges us not to let ourselves be hampered by things that burden and encumber us, but to abandon ourselves instead to the will of God which draws us heavenward. As Jesus ascends into heaven to return to his Father, his arms are open to bless his first apostles, to bless all those who in the footsteps of the apostles continue to believe in him, and his blessing is in their hearts a tranquil and serene assurance of their final reunion with him and with all the redeemed, in everlasting bliss.

29 OCTOBER

THE DESCENT OF THE HOLY SPIRIT

At the Last Supper the apostles received the promise of the Spirit; later, in that very room, in the absence of Jesus but in the presence of Mary, they received him as Christ's supreme gift. Indeed, what is his Spirit if not the

Consoler and Giver of life to men? The Holy Spirit is continually poured out on the Church and within it every day; all ages and all men belong to the Spirit, belong to the Church. The Church's triumphs are not always externally visible, but they are always there and always rich in surprises, often in miracles.

The Hail Marys of the present mystery have a special intention during this year of great enthusiasm when the whole Holy Church, a pilgrim on this earth, is preparing for the Ecumenical Council. The Council must succeed in being a new Pentecost of faith, of the apostolate, of extraordinary graces for the welfare of men, and the peace of the world. Mary the Mother of Jesus, always our own sweet Mother, was with the apostles in the upper room for the miracle of Pentecost. Let us keep closer to her in our rosary, all this year. Our prayers, united with hers, will renew the miracle of old. It will be like the rising of a new day, a radiant dawn for the Catholic Church, holy and growing ever more holy, catholic and growing ever more catholic, in these modern days.

30 OCTOBER

THE ASSUMPTION OF MARY INTO HEAVEN

The queenly figure of Mary is illuminated and glorified in the highest dignity which a creature may attain. What grace, sweetness and solemnity in the scene of Mary's "falling asleep", as the Christians of the East imagine it! She is lying in the serene sleep of death; Jesus stands beside her, and clasps her soul, as if it were a tiny child, to his heart, to indicate the miracle of her immediate resurrection and glorification.

The Christians of the West, raising their eyes and hearts to heaven, choose to portray Mary borne body and soul to the eternal kingdom. The greatest artists saw her thus, incomparable in her divine beauty. Oh let us too go with her, borne aloft by her escort of angels!

This is a source of consolation and faith, in days of grief or pain, for those privileged souls—such as we can all become, if only we respond to grace—whom God is silently preparing for the most beautiful victory of all, the attainment of holiness.

The mystery of the Assumption brings home to us the

thought of death, of our own death, and gives us a sense of serene confidence; it makes us understand and welcome the thought that the Lord will be, as we wish him to be, near us in our last agony, to gather into his own hands our immortal soul.

"May your grace be always with us, Immaculate Virgin."

31 OCTOBER

CORONATION OF MARY ABOVE ALL THE CHOIRS OF ANGELS AND SAINTS

The meaning of the whole rosary is summed up in this scene of joy and glory, with which it ends.

The great mission which began with the angel's announcement to Mary has passed like a stream of fire and light through all the Mysteries in turn: God's eternal plan for our salvation has been presented to us in one scene after another, accompanying us along our way, and now it brings us back to God in the splendour of heaven.

The glory of Mary, Mother of Jesus and our Mother too, is irradiated in the inaccessible light of the august Trinity and reflected in dazzling splendour in Holy Church, triumphant in heaven, suffering patiently in purgatory in the confident expectation of heaven, and militant on earth.

O Mary, you are praying for us, you are always praying for us. We know it, we feel it. Oh what joy and truth, what sublime glory, in this heavenly and human interchange of sentiments, words and actions, which the rosary always brings us: the tempering of our human afflictions, the foretaste of the peace that is not of this world, the hope of eternal life!

NOVEMBER

1 NOVEMBER

FEAST OF ALL SAINTS

One of the greatest joys, as well as one of the most solemn acts, of the pastoral office of the Bishop of Rome is that of raising the saints to the supreme honours of the altar and holding them up for the veneration of all Christians. And indeed the saints respond to the Pope's voice from every far horizon.

There are the joyful praises heard on earth in the voice of the supreme authority of the Church, which exalts her worthiest children with an outpouring of holy enthusiasm, and there are the everlasting songs of praise in heaven, which seem to throb with new and fuller harmonies.

It is in this mingling of earthly and heavenly music and as sharing in both, that the saints appear: "Let the faithful exult in glory; let them sing for joy on their couches!" (Psalm 149. 5).

Blessings upon our saints! At the very beginning of their public veneration there are naturally set forth the particular motives which link the glory of heaven with the needs of this world, links of nature and of grace, of history and of tradition, and also of external forms of the apostolate. For it is through these links that the Lord's light passes, raising some souls to the heights of sanctity and offering them as examples for all to imitate, thus making it easier for all to draw nearer to Christian perfection.

245

ALL SOULS' DAY

The devotions of Holy Church which flower around the altar of the Blessed Sacrament and the altars of the Virgin and the saints are all beautiful and precious. But this devotion to the memory of our dead "who are gone before us with the sign of faith" is particularly worthy. It is above all a meditation on eternal truths, enabling us to perceive what it is that passes away and what is destined to survive.

Today we have come to pay our respects to the memory of the dead, and a tribute of prayers to the Lord for their souls, in the hope that divine mercy may finally receive them in the glory of heaven. But the memory of those who have gone before us, to whom we are linked by bonds of fidelity and gratitude, must also accompany us in all the acts of our daily life.

For this is the memorial that they deserve: this redounds to their honour; this is the spirit of Christian prayer for the dead, which is inseparable from Christian life and practice.

While the melancholy but stirring Liturgy of the Dead rises in the air with the chant: "Deliver me, O Lord", we are as it were invited to raise our eyes from their graves and look elsewhere for those who were and are so dear and familiar to us; parents will seek their children, children their parents, the bridegroom his bride and the wife her husband—and all those who have benefited from the ministry of a soul consecrated to God will recall the image of him or of her who was a spiritual father or mother to them.

3 NOVEMBER

DEVOTION TO THE SAINTS

In Catholic tradition devotion to the saints is not merely a mark of respect or a brief prayer on certain occasions which seem to grow fewer as life proceeds, but a deeply felt spiritual communion, an attentive study of the precious examples and lessons which the saints give us to cheer and encourage us. "Thy saints, O Lord, will give thee glory."

The saints bless God and obtain God's blessing for us. But this blessing is intended as guidance for our spiritual progress, especially if we beg for this from those who are the noblest children of the Church and, by the grace of God, have done great work for him: the first apostles of the Gospel, those who defended and preached the heavenly doctrine, the glory of their own age and of the ages that followed.

4 NOVEMBER

THE LITANIES OF THE SAINTS

There are so many beautiful prayers, and new ones are constantly being offered for the Church's approval. But the best prayers—and those with which we must try to become ever more familiar—are those of Holy Church. Among the most ancient we find the Litanies of the Saints.

The Litanies of the Saints can be divided into three parts. In the first part are the prayers to the Mother of God, to the Apostles and Martyrs, Confessors and all the holy men and women now in heaven. In the second part are our petitions, in the ever present memory of the Mysteries of the Life, Passion, Death and Resurrection of our Lord Jesus Christ. In the third part are the prayers in which, after we have acknowledged our own failings, we implore the special graces of Holy Church for the Pope and for all the orders of the ecclesiastical hierarchy.

Here too we pray that the rulers of the peoples may by God's grace live in peace and true brotherhood, that our separated brethren may return to our loving embrace, and that those who are still far away, but ever present to Our Lord's heart, may receive the truth, the knowledge of him.

5 NOVEMBER

THE PURPOSE OF THE ECUMENICAL COUNCIL

What does the Council, about to begin its labours, propose to effect, if not the strengthening and diffusion of holiness in the Church? It is not therefore a question of themes that can be briefly dealt with. On the contrary, most important subjects are to be carefully examined and all of these are dedicated to the praise of Jesus Christ, the Redeemer of mankind, to the preaching of his law of love, justice and peace, and to the life of his grace in us and in all peoples.

This whole conception of generous intentions and lofty purpose proves that our century is not so bereft of good will as is frequently asserted by those who see all good things only in the past. No, today also, and with even greater eagerness, the heralds of the light feel impelled to move and act to increase the glory of their great Mother, the Church. It is true that this epoch, like all others, is not without its persecutions, frequently cruel and oppressive. But in reality these do but strengthen the resistance of the children of God and testify to the indomitable fidelity of the Christian people.

The witness of faith, hope and charity never fails. By means of these fundamental virtues we become more and more enabled to understand and put into practice our Saviour's teaching. We can almost foresee what those who follow us along the right road will say about us, and almost hear the blessings they will shower upon the present Council, a shining synthesis of the past, present and future, and of the holiness and heroism of all the saints, whether they be bishops, martyrs, confessors, members of the religious Orders, or ordinary faithful followers.

6 NOVEMBER

JESUS, OUR TRUE PEACE

Our true peace is the peace of Christ. God has in fact left man free will, even after his first sinning, so that all that he does may win him merit in heaven. To this gift of freedom, the exercise of which ennobles and exalts us, Jesus adds his own divine example, which shows the triumph of obedience. What lessons and what an admonition we find in Christ, who was obedient to death! What solemn meaning in St Paul's words: *"Therefore God has highly exalted him!"*

This obedience has been characteristic of the whole course of the history of the Church, and of all who did honour to her in the way of holiness and in the apostolate, at all times and in all parts of the world! So the peace of Christ means obedience to Christ: Christ reigning in the souls of men.

For the doctrine of the early Church listen to St Ignatius: "Respect the bishop as you respect the Lord's Christ," and the other clear command: "Let nothing be done without the bishop's authority". This is the discipline handed down for two thousand years, and still so vitally important that nothing is effectively accomplished in the history of the Church and of the Christian people, and nothing resists the corrosive effect of time, unless it is built upon this *foundation of the apostles and prophets in Christ Jesus.*

What we have said about the *peace of Christ* concerning the work of grace in individual souls is true also of every association of human and Christian energies employed for the progress and tranquillity of the public and social order.

7 NOVEMBER

THE JOY OF THE CROSS

"Let us approach with confidence the throne of grace." Human life abounds with crosses and sacrifices. Although it is impossible to avoid them, life becomes beautiful, dear and blessed when we accept our crosses in the light of the most Holy Trinity. During my thirty years as bishop I was given, or I acquired, several crosses of different metals. Among them all is a favourite one of gold, very simple and expressive: upon it is engraved an eloquent reminder of the mystery of the Holy Trinity.

I know well that you too are bearing your crosses. Remember that the Cross is the most beautiful symbol of the life of Jesus, and of our life in the Holy Trinity. Let us all bear our crosses with honour; then we shall become aware of their beauty and joy. Let us repeat together the exultant cry of heaven and earth: "Glory to the Father and to the Son and to the Holy Ghost".

8 NOVEMBER

PEACE FOUNDED ON A GOOD CONSCIENCE

Peace! The peace of the soul united with God is peace

founded on the faithful performance of our Christian duties, founded on the frequent reception of the sacraments and on the avoidance of sin and evil. It is founded upon the growth of virtue, the study of the truths of the faith, and upon zeal to extend the kingdom of God. And peace must be established also in our social relationships, in the sanctuary of our family life, and in the various forms of private and public activity . . .

So you must never let yourselves be led astray by any doctrine which is contrary to the Gospel. All that disturbs tranquillity and order, whether domestic, social or international, the order on which peace depends, is illusion and deceit. It would bring merely an illusion of happiness and well-being, never true wealth and progress.

9 NOVEMBER

THE CHURCH'S MISSION

The Church, continuing to bear witness to Jesus Christ, does not wish to divest man of any of his rights; she does not dispute his claim to his achievements or the merit of the efforts he has made. She wants to help him to rediscover himself and to recognize himself for what he is, to reach that fullness of knowledge and conviction which has at all times been desired by wise men, even by those who have not received divine revelation.

In this immense field of activity which opens before her the Church embraces all men with her motherly affection, and wishes to persuade them to accept the divine Christian message, which gives a sure direction to individual and social life.

This is the mission of the Church, catholic and apostolic, to re-unite men whom selfishness and disillusionment might keep apart, to show them how to pray, to bring them to contrition for their sins and to forgiveness, to feed them with the Eucharistic Bread, and to bind them together with the bonds of charity.

The Church does not claim to effect every day the miraculous transformation worked in the apostles and disciples at the first Pentecost. She does not claim this—but she works for it, and never ceases to pray to God for the repetition of this miracle.

She is not surprised to find that men do not immediately understand her language, that they are tempted to reduce to the small scale of their own lives and personal interests the perfect law of individual salvation and of social progress, and that sometimes they slacken their pace. She continues to exhort, to implore and to encourage.

The Church teaches that there can be no discontinuity or break between the religious practice of the individual and the laws that govern human society.

As she has inherited the truth she wishes to enter every field; she prays God to grant her the grace of sanctifying all things in the domestic, civic and international order.

10 NOVEMBER

Commemoration of the Dedication of the Archbasilica of S. Salvatore, the Cathedral of Rome, St John Lateran.

TRUTH, JUSTICE AND PEACE

The truth! We all know how many snares are set to discredit and destroy it. From our childhood on, we have been taught that every Christian must feel a horror for falsehood. Yet, today, one might think that the whole world had adopted a general practice of falsehood, deliberate and organized. One can rarely read or hear an expression of truth that is unimpaired, complete and sincere. Very frequently an attempt is made to cover with a semblance of truth what is in reality the contrary.

But, faced with the grave problems of life, death and the life after death, we must always honour the truth. The Lord is the Truth, and he is our Master.

And with truth justice! The fundamental rules governing human relations in the family and domestic circles and in the civic and social order must always be borne in mind, not only in so far as they concern our relations with God, with the Gospel and with the great doctrine that must always be a light to our path, but also in all that, in dependence on the providence of God, is material welfare.

And finally peace, holy peace! As we look around we see innumerable people who, during recent years, have witnessed the most painful situations and indescribable destructions, and who have found solace only in praying to God for the priceless gift of peace.

11 NOVEMBER

Feast of a great apostle of charity, St Martin of Tours.

THE SOCIAL OBLIGATIONS OF WEALTH

Our predecessors have constantly taught us that in the right to hold private property is intrinsically contained an obligation towards society.

In fact, in the scheme of creation the good things of the earth are pre-ordained primarily for the maintenance of decent living conditions for all human beings . . .

Today the State, and various public bodies also, have extended and continue to extend the scope of their authority and initiatives. But this does not mean, as some are inclined mistakenly to think, that there is no longer any social duty inherent in the possession of private property—for this duty springs from the very nature of the right to possess.

Moreover, there is always a vast range of painful situations and personal needs which are intimate and acutely felt, and with which the official organizations for public welfare have no means to cope, and so cannot remedy. So there is always a vast scope for human awareness of others' needs, and for the charity of individual Christians.

12 NOVEMBER

"WHAT WILL IT PROFIT A MAN?"

Because of our sense of fatherly responsibility, as universal Shepherd of Souls, we frequently beg our children to examine their consciences in order to keep alive and active the consciousness of the correct order of values, in their ordinary worldly activities and in the pursuit of their individual and immediate ends.

Certainly the Church has always taught, and always continues to teach, that scientific and technical progress and the resultant material improvements of our life are good things and mark an important step forward in human progress. But they must be valued for what they really are in their own nature, that is as instruments or means to be used for the effective furthering of a higher purpose, which is that of facilitating and per-

252

fecting the spiritual development of human beings in the natural as in the supernatural order.

Our divine Master's warning cry still rings in our ears: "What will it profit a man, if he gains the whole world and forfeits his life ? Or what shall a man give in return for his life ?" (Matt. 16. 26).

13 NOVEMBER

"PRAYER TO THE HOLY GHOST"

O Holy Ghost, Paraclete, perfect in us the work begun by Jesus: enable us to continue to pray fervently in the name of the whole world: hasten in every one of us the growth of a profound interior life; give vigour to our apostolate so that it may reach all men and all peoples, all redeemed by the Blood of Christ and all belonging to him. Mortify in us our natural pride, and raise us to the realms of holy humility, of the real fear of God, of generous courage. Let no earthly bond prevent us from honouring our vocation, no cowardly considerations disturb the claims of justice, no meanness confine the immensity of charity within the narrow bounds of petty selfishness. Let everything in us be on a grand scale: the search for truth and the devotion to it, and readiness for self-sacrifice, even to the cross and death; and may everything finally be according to the last prayer of the Son to his heavenly Father, and according to your Spirit, O Holy Spirit of love, which the Father and the Son desired to be poured out over the Church and its institutions, over the souls of men and over nations.

14 NOVEMBER

FEAST OF ST JOSAPHAT

Today is the Feast of St Josaphat, bishop and martyr. As he is not very well known, it is as well to remind ourselves that he was beatified by Urban VIII twenty years after his glorious death, and canonized by the Servant of God, Pius IX, in 1867, during the memorable celebrations for the eighteenth centenary of the martyrdom of the Prince of the Apostles.

St Josaphat was born and carried out his pastoral

mission, giving evidence of possessing the noblest virtues, in countries which do not today enjoy conditions favourable to all that concerns religious freedom. Nevertheless, his memory is still profoundly revered, particularly for his simplicity, fortitude and spirit of self-sacrifice.

We may say that as a monk of the Order of St Basil, and as priest and bishop, he wrought miracles of apostolic zeal and determination, in his efforts to spread everywhere the grace of the Gospel, the truth of Christ. Although, in the sight of the world, his end was violent and tragic, in the eyes of God it was another triumph of the faith, for "precious in the Lord's sight is the death of his saints".

Throughout the centuries of our history we frequently find the sublime figures of those saints who in various ways proved their indomitable loyalty to the precepts, the will and the purposes of God. So we find always and everywhere the splendour of holiness.

15 NOVEMBER

Feast of St Albert the Great, the Master of St Thomas Aquinas.

CHRISTIAN STUDIES

We must beware lest we lose sight of the Lord in our thinking, our studies and researches, and in our interpretation of the nature and meaning of the various sciences—because where Christ has been left out, ignorance abounds.

Obviously for the Christian, and above all for the Catholic, it is Christ who reveals and explains all that concerns the objects of profound research, even when these have nothing to do with asceticism or theology.

All teaching is good, when its substance and presentation are of this order, and not only when the object of study is the understanding of divine things: God himself, the Father, Son and Holy Spirit—but also when we are engaged in other branches of knowledge, for all study must bring its own enlightenment with it.

So the light of Christ must be shed over all applied science. Whether the field of research be old or new, truth is one and eternal, although it may inspire a multiplicity of forms, gleams of light, discoveries and other brilliant manifestations.

We are firmly assured, then, that everything must be done in the light of Christ, who is the way, the truth and the life. Let us maintain all our libraries and archives, and try to do them honour, but always under the guidance of the Master himself. He says little, but his words remain for ever.

16 NOVEMBER

WORKERS IN THE VINEYARD

We are the workers in the vineyard, as St Augustine so well reminds us . . .

Yes, we are all workers. We do our duty, as was agreed with our employer. We look forward to the end of the day, when "each shall receive his wages" (I Cor. 3. 8). He who has called us to this work and accepted our labour will not leave us to fall by the wayside. We are sure of our reward. He who has called us into the vineyard will reward his workers: "each shall receive his wages".

But at this point St Augustine looks into the far horizon. . . which widens and gleams in a more sublime light. Our employer is God himself, our Creator and Redeemer, who in our own age too continues to reward his workmen; but he rewards them by giving them food not only for their stomachs but also for their souls.

If it were not for this priesthood which I represent among you, if it were not for this pastoral ministry which provides for your souls the food they most need, I would not be speaking to you here. St Augustine proclaims aloud that this is my ministry, our ministry: "We preach not to your stomachs but to your minds".

17 NOVEMBER

THE READING OF THE SACRED BOOK

We beg you . . . to do as our fathers did, to read the Sacred Bible, the Old Testament, and the New Testament in which you will find something which is even more beautiful and substantial than anything you read about in the Old: the account of the life of Our Lord, from the Angel's announcement to the Holy Virgin to the birth of Christ, and his Resurrection and Ascension into heaven.

If our dear children would but read, each in his own language, the Psalms and many other pages in the Sacred Book, they would find great joy as well as great spiritual advantage in their attendance at the liturgical services.

Instead of reading here and there, in a desultory manner, things which at times offend your eyes and feelings, you must pay more attention to the Sacred Book which teaches and ennobles all who read it. I beg you to take it into your homes and to encourage others also to feel a love and veneration for this holiest and most beautiful of books, and to familiarize yourselves with those prayers which teach the doctrine of the Redeemer.

The earth and all that is contained therein belong to the Lord. The Successor to Peter must care for every part of the world, in which, alas! so many people are caught in the snares of the Prince of this world, who prowls around like a roaring lion, seeking souls to destroy them.

But wherever there is light there is the grace of Our Lord, who enlightens us and supports us in all dangers, our protection and our guide to salvation.

18 NOVEMBER

Commemoration of the Dedication of the Basilicas
of the Holy Apostles Peter and Paul.

UNITY OF THE CHURCH

For every well instructed Christian the concept of unity is essential, and is resplendent in Christ and in his Church. I can give you but a rapid summary of a great doctrine. When we speak of Christ as dwelling in his Church, we refer to Christ and his priesthood in the sacraments, especially in those of Baptism and the Eucharist. The unity of Christ and of his Church must be understood not only in its ontological reality but as union in the truth, in teaching, in faith and in the organic hierarchical government of the Church—all represented in the one original Head, the Roman Pontiff, at the summit of the Catholic hierarchy which comprises the bishops, priests, laity and all the faithful in union with Peter's successor, the Vicar of Christ.

The "source of revelation" of this sacred doctrine is found in the Scriptures, in the Old and New Testaments. The images used are many: the ark rescued from the Flood, the chosen people who alone were led into the desert and out of it again, the Lord's mountain overtopping all the other mountains, and the perfect bride, "My love, . . . my dove", the Church of Jesus. Yes, his Church founded by him and for him: the Shepherd and the fold, "one flock, one shepherd". Then again, one Spirit only and one Food; Jesus and his Church in one Body of which the Head is Christ, the Saviour of the whole Body.

19 NOVEMBER

MARRIED LOVE

Christian happiness starts from the cradle, with the parents gazing in wonder at their child. Then it is all smiles—but the tears come later on, as the child grows. If the soul, however, is constantly open to God's word and listens to it and obeys it, the joys also increase.

Two souls meet and go before the altar to offer their youth to the Giver of all grace and all light, in order to found a new family, through the Sacrament of Matrimony. Nothing can be nobler than this, which is the way followed by most men and women: nothing can be nobler, because it is co-operation with God, the author of all life. . .

No one can be unmindful of the fact that cares and crosses will be present our whole life long. At times they take the form of silent and concealed hostility, and at other times of disastrous calamities such as terrible wars, from which we beg the Lord to free the world for ever. But in all the painful circumstances of the trials which will inevitably confront us, those who have clear consciences, who do their duty faithfully and live according to a high and noble purpose, know that all things work together to lead them to the enjoyment of an eternal and incorruptible life, and that, beyond the end of time, there extends the divine purpose that has no end.

THE DIGNITY OF GOD'S CHILDREN

If the good Christian lives by the rules set out in the Catechism, which have prepared him to grow to manhood in the Church, if he lives in the light of Catholic doctrine and observes the usual practices of liturgical piety (and this sublime poetry is an education in itself), and if he studies the texts issued by the Church for the guidance of all the faithful, then he will never stray from the right path.

Before his eyes, veiled in mysterious light, will be the twofold truth of faith, as Jesus Christ revealed it to the world: God, One and Three, who pours into us his power and his love, and the Son of God made man to restore us to our dignity as adopted children of God. For we know that from this truth derive, as from their primary source, the devotions to the Name, the Heart and the Blood of Christ.

He is always resplendent, as we see him enthroned in majesty in the apses of our cathedrals: it is he who is known and loved, and made known and loved. His Name contains the mystery of his birth and death; his Heart proclaims the twofold commandment to love God and love our neighbour; his Blood is the supreme sign of his redeeming sacrifice, which is re-enacted actually and mystically in the Holy Mass, and gives meaning and direction to the Christian's life.

Everything is here: the outpouring of the Saviour's infinite love, announced in the Name, symbolized in the Heart, eloquent in the Blood.

The pure and precious doctrine teaches the Christian how to share ever more in the divine mysteries of the altar and, in accordance with this doctrine, to regulate his own conduct and his apostolate of personal witness and social service.

21 NOVEMBER

FEAST OF THE PRESENTATION OF THE BLESSED VIRGIN MARY

Every Christian heart is glad to recall the event celebrated today in the sacred liturgy: St Joachim and

St Ann going up to the temple of God with their child Mary, the purest of creatures, chosen by the Lord to receive the incomparable privilege of being the Mother of God.

Today reminds His Holiness of an incident in his childhood when he was taken by his mother to visit a small shrine dedicated to Mary, built on land belonging to his native village, where the Mother of God is honoured with special devotion on 21 November. The little sanctuary, called *"alle Caneve"*, is set among trees at the end of a country lane.

When the child Angelo Giuseppe arrived with his mother at the tiny chapel they could not go in because it was so full of people, and so the only way to see the revered statue of Our Lady was through one of the two windows, both high up and barred, on either side of the entrance door. So the loving mother lifted her child in her arms, saying to him: "Look, look at Our Lady! She is Our Lady of this Feast day, 21 November: Holy Mary presented at the temple."

This is the Pope's first clear and most vivid memory of his childhood and of his mother. What sweet and profound joy he feels in the thought that it is a memory of an act of piety, an act of devotion to our Heavenly Mother!

22 NOVEMBER

FEAST OF ST CECILIA

Cecilia, the virgin martyr! The liturgy has much to say about her, for she is an example of singular beauty, of heavenly light and sweetness, deeply conscious of the truths of the Christian faith and of her duty to God.

It was said of St Cecilia that wherever she went she bore witness to the Gospel. How blessed are all those who, following her example, do likewise, and above all how blessed are those who show us what a great honour it is for the follower of Christ to sacrifice everything, even life itself, when faced with the choice of denying justice, brotherhood, mutual love and peace or obeying the teaching of the Redeemer whom these precious ideals brought into our world to save us all.

Therefore the Pope's wish for all men is that they should live frankly and generously, in obedience to every precept of the Gospel. By so doing everyone will win supreme honour, the saints will be multiplied and the provident ministry of the Church of God will be established throughout the world.

23 NOVEMBER
Feast of the fourth Pope, St Clement I.

THE POPE AS UNIVERSAL SHEPHERD

In the New Testament God continues to communicate with man, not for the sake of one race but for all. Thus the mystery of the chosen people is finally revealed. The Lord, who on many occasions and in various ways had formerly spoken through Moses and the prophets, now sends his own Son, God made man, Jesus Christ, to speak with more power and majesty, to teach and to spread the universal and perfect Law, declaring himself to be the Light of the world, the Way, the Truth and the Life, and sealing with his Blood the great mystery of the intimate union of divine and human nature. The Law of Christ: the sacred code of regenerated mankind, the eternal Gospel which shall be announced to all present and future generations, to men of all races, nations and tongues!

Among the heirs of his Testament, Jesus had deliberately singled out one. He was called Simon, the son of John: Jesus wished him to be called Peter, to express more vividly through the very meaning of this symbolic name the eternal destiny he willed for the man he had chosen. What words these were! "You are Peter and on this rock I will build my Church, and the powers of death shall not prevail against it. . . I will give you the keys of the kingdom of heaven . . . feed my sheep and my lambs. Strengthen your brethren in the faith . . . I am with you always, to the close of the age" (cf. Matt. 16. 18-19; 28. 20; John 21. 16-17; Luke 22. 32).

Just as Moses, Aaron's brother in the Old Testament, was the trusted confidant of God, the law-giver and prophet, so in the New Testament, Peter, Andrew's brother, was made prince of the apostles, their teacher, pontiff, and universal pastor. The Pope, Bishop of Rome, is the continuation and perpetual survival of St Peter through the centuries. Where the Pope is, there is Peter, there is Christ.

24 NOVEMBER

Our life is pre-ordained according to a law common to all by Our Lord, the Son of God, the Divine Word and, as a man among men, the Son of Mary. He also followed this pattern, and all his earthly life is summed up in the Cross. Now human and Christian life is like a great procession of people, all going forward together under the sign of the Cross, the same which Jesus bore.

Bearing the Cross is very wearisome and entails sacrifice, and yet, if we want to go forward, we must consent to bear it.

The world likes to enjoy itself; at all times men are driven by this desire for pleasure. We must however remember that our road has as its end an eternity of everlasting joy, won for us by Christ with his passion and death.

The Cross symbolizes the greatest event in human history; it expresses in the most solemn manner the victory of the Redeemer, because he was crucified and humiliated, he died and was buried, but three days later behold the glory of the resurrection, the Easter morning, the songs of praise!

Our life is formed after the pattern of Christ's, and although we may permit ourselves legitimate enjoyment, we must never forget the "sign of the Holy Cross". Beginning at a tender age, all must learn moderation in food, temperance in all activity and self-denial, which strengthens the character and helps to spread joy, peace and charity.

25 NOVEMBER

BRINGING CHRIST INTO THE WORLD

The apostolate is a great boon for the world; for it means bringing to it the sense of Christ, it means being full of Christ. . .

We bring Christ where he is unknown, sometimes to souls who despise him, where there is a great confusion, where complex things must be simplified, where we can seldom expect immediate success. We sow Christ like a small seed which will not quicken at once but will one day bud and bear its own grace.

Sometimes Christ is like an arrow: an arrow that wounds a little bird, that continues to fly although this tiny wound will cause its death. And our action will be like a little wound, a tiny thing which has pierced a soul, and through this little wound something of Christ has entered; the soul has been as it were pierced and dies of this wound, but the result is not death but life.

At times we seem to be engaged in hunting souls in this way and when evening comes and we go over the different actions of the day to count our successes, we feel we have wasted our time and we are tempted to set our bow and arrow aside.

And yet we have had some success, for sometimes, years afterwards, we find that our arrow had reached and wounded a soul.

But, you see, in order to do this, we must all make Christianity attractive.

26 NOVEMBER

AN APOSTOLATE OF TRUTH AND LOVE

The words, the example, the love of Christ have become for you a rule of life and the inspiration for a generous apostolate. What a vast field lies open to your endeavours, upon which the bold confidence of youth confers a guarantee of success.

May yours be an apostolate of truth! Convinced of Christian principles, which you have learnt from studying the Catechism, you must spread the truth around you. This is the dearest wish of all young, honest and thoughtful souls, to learn the truth, to study it profoundly and to understand it. Seek out the truth in order to possess it and to sow it widely. The world, in spite of appearances to the contrary, respects Christians who are willing to serve great ideals and who are firmly anchored to something which, as we say, is valid for all times and all circumstances.

Only the truth of Christ can make us free (cf. John 8. 32); it gives the answer which everyone awaits but which at times— because of the great effort it demands—everyone is afraid to hear. Be then living witnesses of the truth, and by so doing your hearts will always be full of sincere and profound joy.

May yours be an apostolate of love! Youth seeks an

understanding heart, even more than a wise teacher. Multiply your efforts to cast fire upon the earth, that fire which Jesus brought with him: "I came to cast fire upon the earth, and would that it were already kindled" (Luke 12. 49).

27 NOVEMBER

WOMAN, THE APOSTLE OF LOVE

May your apostolate be one of action! But you must act with the grace of discretion, prudence and patience, and with the enthusiasm that springs from profound conviction and, above all, from a robust spiritual life. There are many different forms of the apostolate today, and they vary according to the circumstances of everyone of you, and according to age, and to the opportunities of time and place. But may you always endeavour to seize all the possibilities that come your way, "making the most of the time" (Eph. 5. 16), and bearing with you everywhere the fragrance of Christian witness.

This is what we expect of you, this is the noble mission entrusted to you by the humble Vicar of Christ. Let our own era see the gentle and generous fervour of the women apostles of the primitive Church, the faith of Cecilia, Agnes, Catherine, Agatha and Lucy.

Two thousand years ago, at the beginning of our Christian era, the world was almost wholly submerged in the darkness of a corrupt and corrupting paganism. Women sighed for their lost dignity. And by God's grace, with the prayers, example and sacrifices of those heroic women, social life began to change for the better. Today human society is gradually improving just because many Christians honour their baptismal vows with the faithful lives they lead and the winning example they set for others to follow.

28 NOVEMBER

THE SPIRIT OF CONTRADICTION

If we consider the general state of men's dealings one with another, within national communities and in international relations, we can see that we are still far from that divine teaching which shines in the Old Testament centuries and becomes radiant with heavenly light in the fullness of time, with the coming of the Divine Master. This teaching invites us all to seek peace, because we are told that peace-makers are blessed; but here on earth, underneath the fine phrases (that is, when at least the formalities are observed, for even these are frequently ignored) there is often a spirit of opposition to peace.

It is the pride of the powerful, wishing to dominate; it is the greed of those who amass wealth, closing their hearts to their brothers in need (cf. I John 3. 17); it is the hard-heartedness of those who make merry, shutting their ears to the deep sighs of suffering humanity; it is the egoism that thinks only of the self.

What is lacking is still the "goodness of Christ". This must first of all provide the antidote to the spirit of contradiction and hard-heartedness, and then it must teach us to consider everything in a more peaceful spirit.

29 NOVEMBER
OFFERING THE WHOLE SELF TO GOD

This is the joy of the religious vocation which we, with an eager and trustful heart, offer to the consideration of Christian families, for it is in their warm atmosphere of virtue, enlightened by divine grace, that there spring those hopes of future generations, those "olive shoots" (Psalm 127 (128), 3) of tomorrow's harvest, and we are thinking especially of those young men and women who are most aware of the need to extend the kingdom of God, and most eager to perfect their own spiritual life and save souls for Christ. We remind them: the voice of Christ still rings through the world, gently and firmly drawing to himself all those who wish to become, with prayer, apostolic labour and suffering, fishers of souls. Jesus calls them to follow him.

It means losing yourselves to find yourselves again; it means giving to God, who can repay "a hundredfold now in this time. . . and in the age to come with eternal life" (cf. Mark 10. 30) your energies of mind and body, your talents and your labours for the coming of his kingdom.

The innumerable families of Religious, scattered all over the world in their work of prayer and Christian witness, offer the young the fullness of an ideal worth living and dying for. In fact, the Church offers generous souls many and various forms of total consecration to God, from the ancient monastic and contemplative seclusion to the Orders and Congregations who lead an active life in the world, thus perpetuating in time a special aspect of the Lord's mission.

To answer that voice which calls you means to find your own life again when you dedicate it to Christ and to his Gospel (Mark 8. 35).

30 NOVEMBER

FEAST OF ST ANDREW THE APOSTLE

Every Christian knows . . . that St Andrew is the apostle of the Cross. It seems that to this dear disciple, whom he loved so much, Jesus entrusted the mission of preaching the love of the Cross, while he bestowed upon Peter the special gift of robust faith and upon John the tenderness of love.

Faith, love and the Cross together make a worthy priest. The Holy Roman Church, mother and mistress of all churches, can think of no more expressive way of praising the apostle of the Cross than by reciting in his honour the most moving passages of the Acts of the Apostles, all imbued with the poetry that this noble subject inspires.

What words are these! Sometimes the ordinary and innocent occupations of our daily life, the enjoyment of various expressions of thought, even the different dispensations of charity according to different circumstances, may distract us from fidelity to the principle duties of the apostolate.

The voice of Jesus reaches the group of his most faithful disciples, saying: "Come, follow me. I will make you fishers of men." And that moment has arrived when grace is most deeply felt and most compelling. The blessed Andrew abandons his nets . . . to run after Christ, who was to ask him to make other and greater sacrifices.

St Andrew, the "good teacher and friend of God", at the last, as if this were the long desired and joyful crowning of his whole life, allowed himself to be led to the Cross, and when it was brought towards him greeted it with great joy: "Hail, most precious Cross! receive the follower of him who hung on thee, my Master, Christ!"

Andrew is a name that speaks of meekness, joy and peace.

DECEMBER

1 DECEMBER

OBEDIENCE TO GOD'S LAW

"In the beginning God created the heavens and the earth . . ." How often we have heard and read these words! Sometimes we hear them recited, or recite them ourselves, merely as a matter of habit. But if we ponder a little over them, if we think of all that these simple words reveal and teach, none of us can refuse to see the wonderful doctrine which they express.

We are, by divine grace, followers of our Lord Jesus Christ. But we cannot understand the mystery of the Incarnation of the Son of God, and the Redemption he wrought, unless we know what had happened before he came into this world.

Beginning with the first parents of mankind, Adam and Eve, there is a vast and crowded sequence of historical events which form the preparation for the coming of One who was to offer himself in sacrifice to make amends for the first sin and for all others, and so to open to every man the way to salvation.

But God wants us to co-operate with him, that is, to obey his law. From the first commandment given in Eden to the Decalogue of Moses, and then to the Gospel, we have been clearly told what we must, and what we must not, do. If you respect and obey this holy law you receive a blessing; if you fail to do so, you will have to suffer in expiation.

2 DECEMBER

In 1925 Angelo Roncalli was appointed Apostolic Visitor in Bulgaria, and was made bishop. Ten years later, when he left Bulgaria, he spoke a few simple words of farewell . . .

THE LOVE OF POVERTY

Here in your presence and before the holy altar of God I am glad to acknowledge that the Bulgarian people, from its highest representatives to the humblest classes of the people, have always shown me respect, consideration and affection. Our relations have always been happy, and I shall testify to this wherever I go, and in whatever company.

What little good I have been able to do in the carrying out of my apostolic mission is recorded in the Book of Life. May God grant that in my last days it may be for me a reason for eternal joy. As for my failings, my faults and my limited capacities, if I have been negligent, or involuntarily offended anyone, please forgive me as good brothers do. I too am a man like you. But I can say that although during these ten years my hands were the means of distributing much material assistance, sent by the Holy Father to satisfy public or private needs, to build churches to God, and to be used in other useful and honourable ways for the salvation of souls, none of these sums has been used for my own convenience.

I go away a poor man, poor but contented, for I have given all away, and I leave it all here. The Lord will provide for my future needs. He will provide for me as he will provide for you too, my dear brothers. Boundless trust in divine Providence is our greatest consolation.

3 DECEMBER

Feast of St Francis Xavier, Universal Patron of Missions.

A PRAYER FOR MISSIONARIES

O Lord, remember your missionaries, priests, nuns and lay people, who give up all they have to testify to your Gospel and your love. Be for every one of them a powerful protector, a stronghold, a shelter in all danger, a refuge in the noonday heat, their support lest they falter, their succour when they fall! Strengthen them in moments of difficulty, fortify them, console them, crown their labour with the victories of the spirit. They do not seek success in this world, or its fleeting joys, but only your triumph and the salvation of souls.

May the sacred crucifix which accompanies them throughout their lives speak to them of heroism, of self-denial, of love and of peace. May it be their comfort and guide, their light and strength, in order that through their endeavours your blessed Name may be made known throughout the world, and that, surrounded by the ever growing numbers of your children, they may raise to you the hymn of thankfulness, redemption and glory. Amen.

4 DECEMBER

ADVENT

All the liturgical seasons of the year have their own charm for the good Christian, but Advent makes a special appeal because it tells us that Christmas is at hand, and teaches us how we must prepare our souls for so great a Feast.

Particularly for us who are Christians, there is nothing in the whole history of mankind more sublime and joyful than the vision of the Immaculate Virgin who presents to us her child Jesus, while her motherly eyes fill with unutterable tenderness and kindness at the sight of all the souls, all the peoples, who are to be redeemed by her divine Son.

This wonderful mystery contains all the poetry of Christmas, which will live for ever, through all future times.

At Christmas we think especially of small children, of these new lives and hopes of the future, for whom we must all do whatever we can, caring for them generously and lovingly and making an effort to set them good example. And let us always pray for these little ones—it is well known that every day the Pope recites the third Joyful Mystery of his rosary for all the babies born during those twenty-four hours.

Now there returns to our hearts and lips the prayer

that was the sublime hope of the Old Testament, and which the apostle St John expressed in these simple words of his Revelation: "Come, Lord Jesus!" With the Lord always with us, Emmanuel, who guides our steps and upholds us on the road of this life, we are sure that we shall live in righteousness and in the peace of God.

5 DECEMBER

The Apostolic Visitor in Bulgaria speaks of his apostolate.

THE UNION OF ALL THE FAITHFUL

If I were sure not to be misunderstood, I would like to address a word also to all our separated brothers. The difference in religious convictions with regard to one of the fundamental points of the teaching of Jesus recorded by the Gospel, that is, the union of all the faithful of the Church of Christ with the successor of the Prince of the Apostles, compelled me to observe a certain caution in my relations and my personal contacts with them. This was quite natural, and I think perfectly understood by them too. The respect which I have always sought to show, in public and private, for all and every one of them, my unbreakable silence which hurt no one, and the fact that I never stooped to pick up the stone that was hurled at me from one or the other side of the street, leave me with the frank assurance that I showed them all that I love them too in the Lord, with that brotherly, sincere and heartfelt charity that we learn from the Gospel.

Let us give serious thought to the salvation of our souls. That day will surely come when there will be one flock and one shepherd, because this is the will of Jesus Christ. Let us hasten with our prayers the coming of that blessed day. "Way of love, way of truth."

6 DECEMBER

Feast of St Nicholas.

FRIENDLINESS—A GREAT VIRTUE

"Do good, that is, be good, and you will always be surrounded with cheerful faces." These words shed their light over our whole life.

Doing good means bearing a worthy witness to Jesus,

the Son of God and Son of Mary, the universal Teacher and Saviour of the world.

There is no learning or wealth, there is no human power that is more effective than a good nature, a heart that is gentle, friendly and patient. The good-hearted man may suffer mortifications and opposition, but he always wins through in the end because his goodness is love, and love is all-conquering.

All through life, and especially at its end, the happiest tribute of praise is always the same: "he was so good, he had such a kind heart". And his name brings joy and blessing.

It is a mistake to think that kindness, that is, true friendliness, is but a minor virtue. It is a great virtue because it means self-control and a disinterested intention, with a fervent love of justice. It is the expression and the splendour of brotherly love, in the grace of Jesus. It is the way to attain human and divine perfection.

7 DECEMBER

Feast of St Ambrose.

THE TRIUMPH OF SIMPLICITY

A few days before his self-sacrifice, which was to cover him with ignominy in the eyes of the world, Christ prepared a triumphal entrance into his city. The crowds proclaimed him a worker of miracles, and wanted to make him their king; good and honest folk hailed him as the Messiah; his closest followers worshipped him as the Christ, Son of the living God: what further honours were reserved for him? Who was worthier than he of a royal reception, with the pealing of trumpets and the clattering of horses' hooves, amidst splendidly attired crowds of admirers singing hymns of worldly glory and godless joy? But nothing like this was to happen.

St Ambrose tells us that Jesus arranged for his triumph to be prepared by his own humble folk—those who were nearest and dearest to him. In fact, he said to two of his disciples: "Go into the village opposite you, and immediately you will find an ass tied, and a colt with her. Untie them and bring it to me" (Matt. 21. 2).

And so it was done. St Ambrose, commenting on St Luke's account of the same episode, writes: "The colt could not be untied without the Lord's command. It was the hand of an apostle that freed it."

So the triumph of Jesus is to be prepared by the hands of his apostles, but it is a triumph of simplicity, meekness and innocence, not of violence, cunning or arrogance such as is often the result of the passions, the claims and the ambitions of worldly life.

8 DECEMBER

FEAST OF THE IMMACULATE CONCEPTION

The Catholic doctrine of the Immaculate Conception of Mary, which exalts her glory, is familiar to every good Christian, and is the joy and delight of the noblest souls.

We find this doctrine in the liturgy, and in the writings of the Fathers of the Church, and it is felt in the eager longing of all those hearts that wish to honour Mary by offering to her the fragrance of their purity and the fervour of their apostolate for the reform of private and public morality.

Indeed, the neglect of purity and the perversion of morality now everywhere praised and boastfully exhibited, in so many forms of seduction and corruption, are reasons for dismay . . .

But our hearts are profoundly touched when we remember the innumerable brides and mothers, and humble housewives, whose charity and prudence are the true strength and nobility of families, and when we remember also those consecrated virgins who co-operate with the ministry of the priests. All their quiet labours are inspired by the light of the divine law, and express the human and Christian virtues, adorned by the dignity and purity of their conduct.

O Mary Immaculate, O Morning Star that scatters the shadows of the dark night! We turn to you with confident hearts. Give us purity of life, prepare a safe way for us to follow. Remove from our path the many seductions of the worldly enjoyment of this life; strengthen us, not only in our youth, but in every age, for all ages are equally exposed to the temptations of the Evil One.

9 DECEMBER

We must solemnly proclaim that human life is transmitted through the family, which is founded on marriage, one and indissoluble, raised for all Christians to the dignity of a sacrament. The transmission of human life is entrusted by nature to a personal and conscious act and, as such, is subject to the supremely wise laws of God: inviolable and unchangeable laws that must be acknowledged and obeyed. Therefore it is not permissible to use means and methods that may be allowed in the transmission of the life of plants and animals.

Human life is sacred. From its very beginning it is the direct result of the creative action of God. When men disobey these laws they offend his Divine Majesty, degrade themselves and their common humanity and sap the strength of the community to which they belong.

It is of the utmost importance that the new generations shall receive an adequate cultural and religious education, and it is the duty and right of parents to see to this. They must also be trained to have a profound sense of responsibility in all the activities of their lives, and therefore in all that concerns the creation of a family and the rearing and training of children. Children must be taught to live by faith and with profound trust in divine Providence, so that they may be ready to accept toil and sacrifice in the fulfilment of a mission so noble, and frequently so arduous, as that of collaborating with God in the transmission of human life and in the rearing of children.

10 DECEMBER

The birth of Jesus is announced in the sublime glory of the heavens, and in the ever recurring joy of human brotherhood shared by all who have been created and all who will in their turn be created and dwell upon this earth.

In fact, what happiness the Christian heart finds in the angelic radiance which every year at Christmas streams over the shepherds watching by night in the fields, and shines again in that holy night which marks the divine meeting point between heaven and earth! How our hearts are stirred by that announcement from heaven declaring "the great joy which will come to all the people", and then by that chorus of the heavenly choirs, praising God and saying "Glory to God in the highest, and on earth peace among men with whom he is pleased" (Luke 2. 11-14).

Venerable brothers and beloved children, permit us this Christmas to have the joy of lingering on these words from the liturgy of the Feast. We have here already two themes of the great Festivals which are approaching:

1.   The glory of the Lord declared by the angels' song.

2.   The coming of peace on earth, and its enjoyment by all, to satisfy the longing in the hearts of all the peoples.

11 DECEMBER

UNFALTERING FAITH

Here we have . . . the vision of Bethlehem, the light of the Incarnate Word, the grace and truth of Jesus who wishes to draw everyone to himself.

The silence of the holy night, and the contemplation of this peaceful scene, are full of eloquent meaning. Let us turn to Bethlehem with pure eyes and eager hearts.

And it is in the presence of the Word of God, made man for us, in the "goodness and loving kindness of God our Saviour" (Titus 3. 4), that with great respect and affection we wish to make a special appeal to the highest representatives of public authority throughout the whole world, and to those responsible for the education of the young generations, and for the coming of public opinion—exhorting all to acquire a more mature sense of their respective duties and responsibilities, and to do what is incumbent upon them with sincerity and courage.

We place our trust in God and in the light which comes from him. And we trust in all men of good will, content that our words arouse in all honest hearts a spirit of manly generosity.

WITNESSES OF THE BIRTH OF CHRIST

Oh what a miracle we see before us! From the royal throne of his divinity Jesus, the Son of God, has deigned to come down to this earth and be born in a wretched hut. Leaving his high estate, where he was begotten before time began and received the worship of the angels, he becomes man among us and, like us, poor, wearied and wretched.

His name tells of his supreme grandeur: "the government is upon his shoulder". He is acclaimed in heaven as "Wonderful, the strong God, the Prince of Peace, the Father of the world to come".

If he had not been foretold by the prophets, if the angels had not warned the shepherds that they would find a baby, wrapped in poor clothes, laid in a wretched manger, who could have recognized him? No one, no one at all. Here he lies between the ox and the ass. "The ox knows its owner, and the ass its master's crib." Alas! his own people would not have recognized him if a band of winged angels of the heavenly host had not once more filled the air with their chant: "Glory to God in the highest, and on earth peace among men with whom he is pleased!"

And it is to this testimony of the prophets, the angels, the shepherds, and later on of the Magi, that the Catholic faith has pronounced its assent, because these testimonies are true; they were revealed to the world because the future was already sure: they were revealed because they had already come to pass.

GOD MADE FLESH

Everything in the world had been created and ordained by God the Lord and Father, in beauty and perfect harmony. At the summit of the divine creation was placed man, rightly called the eternal priest of the created world, with the special mission assigned to him of causing the endless chant of gratitude, worship and love to rise to the source of all truth and goodness.

If man had only understood, and right from the beginning, this task assigned to him! But he did not understand. The good things of heaven and earth were all at his disposal and at his service. A sacred law regulated their use and their enjoyment. He could not, would not understand or respect it. He was ungrateful to his Lord and benefactor. When he had to endure inevitable punishment he lost the sense of his own nature, of his dignity and of the nobility that was still his; he set his heart on things that were hostile to God and indulged in material and godless pleasures, until he was subdued to the will of a "petulant female"—in the words of St Lawrence—to the desire of an importunate and greedy woman.

And yet God still loved ungrateful man . . . and because he did not wish to leave the masterpiece of his creation to perish, behold the Incarnation: behold the birth of Our Lord! He who had been offended, the Heavenly Father, the Almighty, the Lord and Creator of heaven and earth, chose the intercessor for his reconciliation with man the sinner. His only-begotten Son, the Eternal Wisdom through whom all was made that was made, took on our human nature; the Word of God made Man came to seek man who was lost in the wilderness of his own solitude, and who became his brother through the Incarnation.

14 DECEMBER

THE GOOD NEWS OF CHRISTMAS AND OF BETHLEHEM

"In the beginning was the Word, and the Word was with God, and the Word was God . . . All things were made through him . . . In him was life, and the life was the light of men. The light shines in the darkness, and the darkness has not overcome it" (John 1. 3-5). There was a man called John, chosen to bear witness to the light; he was not that light, but only a witness who tried to make the world ready to receive it. The Word of God, with an act of divine condescension, assumed a human nature and lived on earth, familiarly conversing with men.

All those who recognized him, and welcomed in him the Word of God made man, calling on his sacred and blessed name: Jesus Christ, Son of God and Son of Mary, were admitted to the same filial relationship with

God; he gave them the "power to become children of God".

It is with this simple and fundamental reminder of our doctrine and history that the good news of Christmas and of Bethlehem is announced to us. These are sacred words, which run like music through our lives, spreading sweetness and beauty, and rising to full harmony in the threefold poem of the Creation, the Redemption through Christ's Blood, and the Church, one, holy, catholic and apostolic. All this divine teaching is offered to all who can receive it, for the perfection here below of the souls of individuals and of nations.

15 DECEMBER

PRINCE OF PEACE

Jesus, the Redeemer of all mankind, is born in Bethlehem. Pointing him out to the crowds who were thirsting for light and spiritual joy, John the Baptist said of him: "Behold, he who takes away the sins of the world". This is the first, the great blessing of Christmas: every man purifies himself, sees more clearly what lies before him, and prepares to shoulder his responsibilities more faithfully, inspired and strengthened by no other ideal than this, of service to the Redeemer.

All our glory lies here, in Jesus the new-born child. "The Lord will give strength to his people," ... without him human life is a long lamentation of individuals and of peoples, the complaints of all who seek in vain to build something that will last, in their individual domestic or social life.

As it was yesterday, so it will be in the future. Those who build on other foundations than that of Jesus, who do not accept his teaching and example and the redemption he brought us, or even reject it, are all destined to see their work crumble and crack at the first puff of wind, which will be followed by a hurricane.

The new-born Jesus is truly "our Peace". He is the "Strong God, the Ruler, the Prince of Peace". The mighty see only the frail child in a lonely cave, but the humble are called and led to him by faith: they recognize his great power and worship him. His peaceful rule requires the most watchful and willing co-operation of all men, with self-control, discipline of mind and body, dignity of life and firmness of intention.

Think well of this, my children. Everthing we need is here: Jesus who redeems us, Jesus who gives us glory in heaven, Jesus who grants us peace.

16 DECEMBER

THE ROAD TO BETHLEHEM

With infinite tenderness our thoughts accompany the holy people who are travelling towards Bethlehem: Jesus, hidden in the immaculate womb of Mary, Our Lady, exposed to so many hardships while she is performing her duty to God and men, and Joseph, her humble and silent husband, strong and faithful. The shepherds and the Magi kings also follow the same road, which will lead them to worship in the cave. The procession is on the move . . .

We are all invited to join this happy band of souls who go to present their gifts to the Son of God, and to find strength, light and courage for their daily duties, because only in him, through him and with him, does our work become a means of glorifying the Lord, of benefiting our neighbour and of attaining indestructible peace in our own hearts.

May the Word of the Father, whose "goodness and loving kindness" we shall contemplate a few days from now, and who appeared in this world to save mankind, grant to you all the fullness of his grace!

"Rejoice in the Lord, O you righteous! Praise befits the upright" (Psalm 32 (33) 1).

In fact, the message of our Saviour Jesus was indeed a joyful announcement: it was the "good news". And it would be a great mistake to imagine, as many thinkers and poets of past times have done, that Christianity is something dismal and lugubrious. No, Christianity is joy, joy in order and peace, with God, with ourselves, and with our fellow men.

17 DECEMBER

THE SUN OF JUSTICE

From the beginning of Advent we hear Christmas foretold in the strong voices of the prophets, and we already see the light of his coming in the radiance of the Mother of Jesus on the Feast of the Immaculate Conception.

From Mary is born this "Sun of Justice", who truly came down from heaven to reconcile heaven and earth, God and man.

The dramatic events of the first Christmas took place in a cave, with great simplicity, poverty and humility—and all were contained in the mystery of the Mother who showed herself to the new race of believers, the shepherds and the Wise Men, holding the Child in her arms.

The author of the *Imitation of Christ* understood very well one of the underlying principles of the divine scheme: "Humility and simplicity", he writes, "are the two wings which raise aloft all that is truly great in the eyes of the Most High, and all that is destined to bring real benefit to mankind."

Every year the circumstances of Bethlehem are re-enacted, and fill us with joy and hope.

O sweet Child of Bethlehem, grant that we may share with all our hearts in this profound mystery of Christmas. Put into the hearts of men this peace for which they sometimes seek so desperately, and which you alone can give them. Help them to know one another better, and to live as brothers, children of the same Father. Reveal to them also your beauty, holiness and purity. Awaken in their hearts love and gratitude for your infinite goodness. Join them all together in your love. And grant us your heavenly peace. Amen.

18 DECEMBER

OBEDIENCE TO THE TEACHING OF CHRIST

The Child that murmurs in the cradle of Bethlehem, lit by the flaming countenances of the angels, is not merely the Son of a highly favoured woman: he is the Son of God. It is he who "enlightens every man" (John 1. 9), the Sun of Justice, before whose beams the shadows of human errors are dispersed: he is to reveal the mysteries hidden for countless ages in God; he is the Redeemer of the world, the Giver of eternal life. For us Christmas means willing acceptance of the truth of his doctrine, and the exercise of charity so that "we, upon whom is poured the new light of thy Word made flesh, may show forth in our actions that which by faith shineth in our minds".

This is an occasion for joy. On this night the angel announced: "Behold, I bring good news of a great joy which will come to all the people: for to you is born this day . . . a Saviour who is Christ the Lord" (Luke 2. 10-11). Here lies the secret of true happiness, which we do not find in the noisy rejoicing of the world, the happiness which nothing, not even tribulation, can extinguish, for it is the joy of knowing that we are redeemed, that Jesus is our kind and loving brother, that in him we have been made "partakers of the divine nature" (II Pet. 1. 4), raised to a close union of life with God. My beloved children, may the joy of this day, mingled with profound gratitude to the Lord, remain with you throughout the coming year and never leave you again.

And finally, it is an occasion of peace. Peace is a gift from heaven, which is offered on earth to all sincere and right-minded people. It is the immortal theme of the heavenly messengers' song this holy night.

19 DECEMBER

THE LORD IS NEAR

"The Lord is near!" What can the whole year offer us more precious, lovely and joyful? Christmas is the shining Feast of nature and of life, full of grace and charm. Everything comes to us from that Child whom his Mother gives to every one of us and presents to the whole world.

After two thousand years the beloved image is still the same, wonderful, vivid, full of fascination and appeal ...

Christmas is the joy of our homes, bringing happiness even where there are tears, where there are anxieties and sadness. This vision is enough to soothe the most anguished hearts, and to arouse tenderness, compassion, and impulses of kindness and generosity.

Now more eagerly than ever the redeemed of the Saviour join with his representative on earth to come into the presence of Jesus, Mary and Joseph, and to draw from this sublime reality new inspirations for doing good and for bringing about the true brotherly union of the sons of God.

We all belong to our Lord Jesus Christ, our brother;

we all share in the Redemption he wrought. It is true that there are still some who have not received this gift of faith, for reasons extraneous to themselves for which they are not responsible. But there is the great family, not only of Christians, but of the whole universe, for all is the work of God, and dependent upon him.

20 DECEMBER

THE WORD, MESSENGER OF TRUTH

St Augustine gives a name to the divine Word which appeared at Bethlehem: he calls him the Truth, because he is the Only-begotten of the Father, shining in all the glory of his divine nature to enlighten the whole created world, visible and invisible, material and spiritual, human and superhuman.

The two Testaments contain the revelation of a doctrine which is from eternity, the essence and splendour of truth, shining through all the ages and revealed to man, because he is considered the masterpiece and high priest of the visible world. It is truly the living substantial doctrine of the development of both the natural and supernatural orders.

In fact the first words of the Old Testament describe the origin of the world; the last words of the New Testament: "Come, Lord Jesus", are the summary of the whole history of law and of grace.

It is natural that the souls created by God and destined for eternal life should seek to discover the truth, the primary object of the human mind's activity. Why must we speak the truth? Because truth comes from God, and between man and the truth there is no merely accidental relationship but one which is necessary and essential.

21 DECEMBER

WHAT WE LEARN FROM CHRISTMAS

A few days before Christmas we have the Feast of the Apostle St Thomas, of whom the Gospel speaks in the last chapter of the earthly life of the Son of God. But the special lesson we learn from him is the exaltation of the most intense faith.

Faith accompanies us from Bethlehem to the Last

Supper, to Calvary, to the Resurrection and the Ascension.

During the years of his preaching the divine Master chose his apostles, to send them out to extend his kingdom in the world. They have always dedicated themselves to this undertaking, even at the cost of their lives. They have always been inspired by the most sublime faith.

Every one of us is called by the Lord: the important thing is to know how to answer his call. We must learn how to devote ourselves to Jesus, to learn from him, and follow him as closely as we can, in his teaching and example; we must learn to rejoice in his company, like the disciples of Emmaus on the day of his Resurrection, like Mary and Joseph at the dawn of that life of miracles and saving grace.

Holy Christmas is approaching. Everything in the grotto of Bethlehem is a living lesson for all who wish to live by our faith, and be faithful to it.

If the Christian succeeds in preserving this spirit of Christmas he will be greatly strengthened to overcome the dangers and obstacles of daily life; he will know how to repel the assaults of materialism, and be more and more convinced of the truth that we come from God and must return to him.

22 DECEMBER

CHRISTMAS IS FOR THE WHOLE WORLD

How eagerly and lovingly we read the pages of the Sacred Book which describe the birth of Jesus!

A stable, out in the open country, in the darkness of night. Perhaps the gleam of a small lantern. Here is St Joseph, the just man, chosen by God, here is the Mother of the new-born child, radiant with joy at this surpassing miracle, and here is the divine Babe in the arms of the purest of creatures. He has been so long awaited, through untold ages. But he has come in the hour appointed by God himself. He is tiny, and already subject to the harshest privations, and to suffering: but he is the Word of the Father, the Saviour of the World. The greater the poverty and simplicity, the greater the fascination and appeal of this Child.

Around him the world is stirring: the just have become aware that the great promise is about to be fulfilled. So the day of our redemption dawns, the day of reparation for what is past, of happiness for the eternal future . . .

The shepherds draw near: they see and feel that peace, joy and love flow out from that tiny Child.

The history of twenty centuries begins in this stable, for the Child is in very truth the source of all things. Through him, in fact, everything is renewed, death is overcome, sin is forgiven and Paradise restored.

We feel new fervour of love when we pause in prayer before the Crib.

Mankind also is a great, an immense family . . . This is proved by what we feel in our hearts at Christmas. The divine Child smiles at everyone; his beloved eyes shine in grace and splendour. Hard hearts are softened, anxieties soothed, suffering relieved.

Calm follows the storm, and sadness ends in joy.

23 DECEMBER

PEACE, THE GREATEST GOOD

With the "Glory to God" in high heaven, the mystery of the birth of Christ and its recurring memory come to us, who are pilgrims here below, as a good augury of peace for the whole world. "Peace among men with whom he is pleased!"

The word "heaven" frequently occurs in both Testaments, but far more frequently is found the word "earth". Now the most precious possession on earth, and the one most worthy of our attention, is peace. "Peace on earth", we sing with the angels of Bethlehem, peace on earth to all men of good will.

Among all the good things of our lives and of our history, enjoyed by individuals, families and peoples, peace is truly the most important and the most precious. The presence of peace, and the endeavour to achieve it, are the guarantee of tranquillity in this world. But peace is conditioned by the good will of one and all, peace to men of good will, because wherever this good will is lacking it is useless to hope for joy and blessings.

So we must seek peace at all times: we must try to create it in our own circle, so that it may spread throughout the world, and we must defend it from all dangers and in all trials, making sure never to offend or compromise it.

Oh what a great task this is for every Pope, now and always! During these four years of our humble service—service as we understand it and shall continue to understand it—our constant endeavour is to be a true Servant of the Servants of the Lord, who is truly the "Lord and Prince of Peace".

24 DECEMBER

Christmas Eve.

THE RESPONSIBILITY OF BELIEVERS

There are . . . circumstances and situations which at the time of this great Feast offer a most painful contrast with the joy of Christmas. In reminding you of this we do not mean to underestimate the service we all try to render to truth and justice, or to forget the immense good achieved by righteous people who have chosen to honour the divine law and the holy Gospel; we wish to encourage further valiant efforts to right wrongs and re-kindle in the world the fervour of the religious feeling and pious traditions of our forefathers, in order to honour the serene happiness of Christmas.

Beloved children, beside the cradle of the new-born Child, the Son of God made man, every one who lives and moves here below must reflect with a frank and open mind that at the end of life he will be asked to give a strict account of the gift of life he has received, and that, according to this account, he will be rewarded with eternal merit or punishment, with glory or shame.

And it is this point of view, that is, the awareness of this responsibility, that determines the share of Christians, the share of all men, in the great mystery we commemorate this night; hence our wish that from the radiance of the Word of God human civilizations may receive the spark to kindle them to greater splendour, for the good of all peoples.

Around the cradle of Jesus his angels sang of peace. And all who believed the heavenly message and did honour to him were given glory and great joy. So it was, and so it will be for ever.

The story of Jesus has no end. Blessed are those who understand it and draw from it grace, strength and blessing.

THE BIRTH OF JESUS OUR SAVIOUR

No philosophical studies and no great effort at modernization of techniques will be of any avail unless our hearts are opened wide to receive light and grace from heaven.

The truth of the Beatitudes proclaimed on the Mount is felt with particular poignancy at Christmas, demanding the attention of all.

The Child born at Bethlehem is humble and lowly of heart, poor and innocent; he has come to bring peace, and in this cause he is already preparing for the supreme sacrifice.

This is the way marked out for us by Jesus Christ; this is the lesson for every man who accepts the divine message with willing obedience, at whatever cost of effort and personal sacrifice.

At Bethlehem, beloved children, the course of history took a new turn, for the greater glory of all civilizations, but this new course of history is entrusted to the responsibility of every one of us.

In fact, because of the natural law of human brotherhood, and because of the Christian doctrine of the Mystical Body, human dignity, freedom and justice depend on us all, individually and collectively.

Bethlehem teaches us to apply its lessons to the problems of our social life: to the defeat of selfishness, the intelligent awareness of the needs of others, and to the wider observation of the law of forgiveness, the *law of forgiveness*, the triumph of perfect brotherhood.

"Come, ye nations, and adore the Lord, for this day a great light hath descended upon the earth. Alleluia!"

26 DECEMBER

FEAST OF ST STEPHEN, THE FIRST MARTYR

What glory and what power of prayer we see in the sacrifice of the first martyr, St Stephen!

It must not be forgotten that he was full of the Holy Spirit, and therefore "full of grace and fortitude", wholly inspired by faith, love and courage. From this beginning—for every one of us, through baptism and the other sacraments, has received the gifts of grace and strength—spring the three fundamental virtues of every

Christian: faith, hope and charity. To these are added, particularly in the case of those who wish to follow a way of special perfection, the other principal virtues: prudence, justice, fortitude and temperance.

All this helps to keep us mindful of the great truth that to be followers of Christ means being prepared to make sacrifices. Our obedience, purity, generous self-denial and renunciation sometimes draw blood, but they enable us to approach more closely to Jesus and to his Mother.

Accompanied and assisted by Mary we shall even be able—when the moment comes—to climb the hill of Calvary. From the practice of the Christian virtues, as we know, come confidence, victory and eternal peace and joy.

27 DECEMBER

FEAST OF ST JOHN THE EVANGELIST

We know that John the Evangelist was the "disciple whom the Lord loved" for the singular innocence of his life. We know that he received marks of divine favour, that he died at a great age at Ephesus, and that until the end of his earthly life he never tired of repeating the divine commandment of loving kindness: my little children, love one another.

Indeed, if this twofold commandment (loving God and loving one's neighbour) were obeyed, every kind of prosperity would flourish on this earth; even material problems and the relations between peoples would find positive and peaceful solutions.

The spirit of Christmas is the sure pledge of peace. The peace of the heart welcomes and cherishes love. Brotherly love dispels hatred, rivalries and misunderstandings, and makes it possible for all men to give willing obedience to God and to his law.

28 DECEMBER

FEAST OF THE HOLY INNOCENTS

It is fitting that . . . in these days there should be songs and celebrations of universal joy.

But the "great joy" announced by the angel, the great joy for the event which brought eternal salvation to mankind, cannot be disassociated from the thought that the work of redemption has begun, and that it necessitates another element, which we must accept as a means of acquiring merit and virtue. This is sacrifice, it may be of our blood.

The echoes of the angelic choirs celebrating the birth of Christ had hardly faded when innocent creatures were struck down by the cruel hand of a tyrant. All the children of Bethlehem under the age of two years were slain by his order. This was the first great grief, the first dreadful sacrifice; these were the first martyrs that mankind offered to the Saviour.

And more suffering was to come. Mary's Child himself had to endure hardships in the flight to Egypt, and later on in the poverty of their home at Nazareth, and in manual labour. After he had preached for three years the day came when his own Mother accompanied him to Calvary and stood at the foot of the Cross. Her Son was crucified; he gave his life for all men. Mary did not give way to her terrible and incomparable grief. She knew that now his real triumph was to begin, and so with motherly love, she obeyed the last request of her dying Son when he entrusted us all, in the person of the apostle John, to her care. So, through the sacrifice of Christ and around his Cross we have all become sons by adoption of his most holy Mother, and we may call ourselves brothers of Jesus.

Therefore we must remember that through this wonderful adoption we have also inherited our share of suffering.

29 DECEMBER

FLOWERS OF BETHLEHEM

Men were in a wretched state; their Creator decided to rescue them by sending to this earth his only-begotten Son, the Word of God made man; and Jesus met with unbelievable difficulties and opposition. The episodes of the shepherds and the Wise Men were but a short parenthesis: afterwards the Holy Family had to flee. They were forced to seek safety by leaving their own land. The Son of God who had come among men to save them had to flee from men, and from the man who represented power and might: Herod.

We know what happened later. His discussion at the age of twelve, with the Doctors of the Temple, not about temporal and material questions but about the prerogatives, the wishes and the law of the heavenly Father; his laborious life at Nazareth; his public preaching with all its accompanying hardships, and finally his Passion and his Death on the Cross.

At Bethlehem we find, as it were, a foretaste and a summary of what was to happen later on. We too must make ourselves familiar with the "flowers of Bethlehem", our daily sufferings or privations, difficulties and poverty. When all this sum of adversity is patiently endured for love's sake, for the love of Jesus, and the reasons for Christian joy are thus made known, when, for example, a sick man who has been helpless for ten years can accept his suffering and, offering it to God, exclaim: If the Lord so wishes, I welcome ten more years of pain; when other men can forgive the inevitable unkindness of their neighbours and can recognize their own weaknesses and many diverse forms of selfishness and all the other sins, then we can be sure that we know well the flowers of Bethlehem and the language which they speak.

30 DECEMBER

As we approach the end of the year we find this place for Pope John's farewell message to us:

THOUGHTS ON APPROACHING DEATH

This bed is an altar; the altar requires a victim: I am ready. I offer my life for the Church, for the good progress of the Ecumenical Council, for the peace of the world and for the union of all Christians.

The secret of my priesthood is to be found in the crucifix I placed before my bed. He looks at me and I speak to him. In our long and frequent conversations at night the thought of the redemption of the world has seemed to me more urgent than ever before "I have other sheep that are not of this fold" (John 10. 16).

His outstretched arms show us that he died for all, *for all*; no one is denied his love and his forgiveness.

But it was to his Church that Christ gave his special mandate: "that they may be one". The sanctification of the clergy and people, the union of all Christians, the conversion of the world, form the special task of the Pope and the bishops.

I was granted the supreme grace of being born into a Christian family, poor and humble but God-fearing, and of being called to the priesthood. From my childhood onwards I never thought of anything else, or desired anything else.

Along my way I have met with saintly priests, exemplary Superiors. Ah, Monsignor Radini! Cardinal Ferrari! All have helped me and loved me, and from all I have received encouragement. For my own part, I do not think I have offended anyone, but if I have I ask for forgiveness, and I beg you, if you know of any colleague or other person who found my conduct unedifying, to ask him to have compassion on me and forgive.

In this final hour I feel tranquil, and I am sure that the Lord in his mercy will not reject me. Unworthy as I am, I have wished to serve him, and I have tried only to honour truth, justice and charity and to be "meek and lowly of heart" after the Gospel pattern.

My earthly day is drawing to its close. But Christ lives, and the Church continues on her way. Oh the souls, the souls of men—"may they be one! May they be one!"

31 DECEMBER

From his Spiritual Testament. "These pages written by me are valid as proof of my final dispositions, in the case of my sudden death."   Venice, 17 September 1957.

POPE JOHN'S SPIRITUAL TESTAMENT

... The sense of my littleness and worthlessness has always kept me good company, making me humble and tranquil, and permitting me the joy of putting my best efforts into a continual exercise of obedience and love for souls and for the interests of the kingdom of Jesus, my Lord and my all. To him be all the glory: for me and for my own merits, only his mercy. "God's mercy is my only merit." "Lord, you know all things: you know that I love you!" This is enough for me.

I ask forgiveness from those whom I have unknowingly offended, and those whom I have not influenced for good. I feel that for my own part I have nothing to forgive anyone, because in all those who knew me and had dealings with me—even if they have offended or despised me or, no doubt justly, had little regard for me, or given me cause to suffer—I recognize only brothers and benefactors, to whom I am grateful and for whom I pray and will pray always.

... In the hour of farewell or, better, of leave-taking, I repeat once more that what matters most in this life is: our blessed Jesus Christ, his holy Church, his Gospel, and in the Gospel above all else the Our Father according to the mind and heart of Jesus, and the truth and goodness of his Gospel, goodness which must be meek and kind, hardworking and patient, unconquerable and victorious.

My children, my brothers, I take leave of you. In the name of the Father, the Son and the Holy Ghost. In the name of Jesus our love; of Mary, his sweet Mother and ours; of St Joseph, my first and most beloved protector. In the name of St Peter, of St John the Baptist, and of St Mark; of St Lawrence Giustiniani and St Pius X. Amen.

APPENDIX

Passages for the Movable Feasts
of the Liturgical Calendar

1. ASH WEDNESDAY

Lent is a particularly useful time for all who wish to live according to the Gospel, to correct their faults and purify their souls. How often we acknowledge our sins: "through my fault, through my most grievous fault", before heaven and earth, and the apostles Peter and Paul who will be our judges!

It is easy to understand why we need to do penance. Even if our eyes are constantly looking towards heaven the dust of this world may settle more or less thickly on our shoes and clothes. There may be failings even in our endeavours to do good, and to perfect ourselves. In any case, where there is sin there must be penance.

The ten commandments remain in all their original authority, deeply engraved on all men's hearts. Moreover we have the commandment of charity, taught us by our Lord Jesus Christ, and we must imitate him in patient acceptance of suffering. He, the Just Man, the God-Man, the Sinless One, took upon himself to suffer, and by so doing to atone for all the sins of the world; and he invites us too to endure with patience all adversities and hardships, as reparation for our sins and for those of others.

2. PASSION SUNDAY

The thought of suffering is naturally ever present with us during this Passion week which will culminate, next Sunday, in the Feast of Palms, reminding us of the triumph of Jesus, the Son of God, amidst his people, while innocent children paid their own tribute to his divine Majesty, hailing him with Hosannas and singing: "Blessed is he that comes in the name of the Lord!" It was but a brief and passing triumph, but enough to symbolize the sure and final victory of the Son of God through all ages.

A few days later we have the great tragedy of suffering and death. From the treacherous kiss of Judas, the cowardice and flight of the disciples, to the unbelievable insults and blows, the condemnation, the scourging and the crucifixion.

The scene of Calvary is re-enacted before our eyes: but

it is followed by the miracle worked by the Redeemer of the world himself, when he removed the stone from the sepulchre and emerged triumphant.

So it is just as necessary for us to accompany him during this week of his Passion, as it is to celebrate with him the joyful Feasts of Christmas, Easter and Pentecost.

3. PALM SUNDAY

The solemn liturgical celebration of the next few days and, later on, the joyful Alleluias of Easter teach us to remain united, as we have been during this penitential season, and to follow in Our Lord's footsteps, so that in brotherly union we may see on this earth manifestations of human and Christian kindness, simple and appealing. This Feast is made more beautiful by the presence of children. They provide the escort for Jesus who is riding upon an ass's colt, and they stir our hearts with their Hosannas to the Son of David.

We know by experience that without suffering and self-denial there is no hope of true spiritual tranquillity, either domestic or civic, nor any hope of winning merit in heaven for that hour when we pass into a life that has no end.

What begins as a triumphal procession to the gates of Jerusalem ends on the fatal hill of Calvary; the Hosannas end in the cries of "Crucify him!"

Beloved children, this is a summary of our life here below. All who accept it in loving obedience will enjoy a spiritual happiness which flourishes in peace and serenity; others, who accept life grudgingly, are subject to the most disquieting vicissitudes and a bitterness of soul which is seen in the hardening of character and conduct.

On our different ways of receiving the call to live a Christian life and to follow Jesus, riding humbly upon an ass's colt, depends the tranquillity and order of our life, in our families, in our communities and in our relations with our fellow men.

4. HOLY WEEK—MONDAY

A few weeks before the death of Jesus, while the divine

Master was speaking with Moses and Elijah on Mount Tabor, his glory was revealed, so bright and splendid that Peter exclaimed: "Lord, it is well that we are here!"

A few days later came the incident at Bethany with the two sisters Martha and Mary mourning for their brother Lazarus, who had died four days previously and been entombed. Jesus wept with them. But from the tears of the divine Friend of Lazarus sprang the victorious first announcement of the Easter mystery.

Oh what wonderful words passed between Jesus and Martha, expressing the certain hope of resurrection and of the life guaranteed to all mankind redeemed by the power of Christ's Blood!

"I am the resurrection and the life; he who believes in me, though he die, yet shall he live, and whoever lives and believes in me shall never die" (John 11. 25-26.)

Indeed, the reality of Easter—already foretold at Bethlehem—is all here, in the eternally renewed celebration of the mystery of Christ; of Christ the glorious and immortal King of all men and all ages, the strength and inspiration of all mankind redeemed by him and destined for a triumphal eternity, and destined also to achieve the peaceful victories of human brotherhood and of orderly prosperity on earth.

5. HOLY WEEK—TUESDAY

Holy Week sets before us the vision of all the sufferings of mankind, of Christ suffering in union with us all.

The application of certain recent liturgical reforms has throughout the world enabled the faithful to play a more lively and personal part in the ceremonies of Holy Week. This new awareness is one of the psychological realities which the doctrine of the Mystical Body illuminates and inspires. We are enabled to hear the groans of Christ amid the imploring cries of all mankind in this age when, in some vast regions of the world. . . human liberties are smothered, destroyed, or at least continually threatened with suppression.

Following the noble and impressive thought of St Leo the Great, we begin to understand "the Passion of Christ, which is summed up in the Cross, for us a sacrament and an example" (Sermo 72).

It is a sacrament that contains and transmits to our souls the power of divine grace; an example which encourages us to bear all suffering with patience, that patience of which Christ is the supreme Master.

How fine is this observation of St Leo the Great! Human learning is so proud of its errors that once it has attached itself to a teacher it follows his opinions and imitates his example blindly. What sort of a communion have we with Christ if we do not learn to be inseparably united with him who has declared himself to be the "Way, the Truth and the Life"? (John 14. 6). The way of holy union with him, the truth of divine doctrine, the life of eternal happiness.

6. HOLY WEEK—WEDNESDAY
Priests.

When, from the eminence of this papal office which Providence has conferred on us we consider the immense aspirations of mankind, the grave problems of the evangelization of so many lands, and the religious needs of Christian peoples, everywhere and at all times, it is the thought of our priests that comes to our mind. Without them, without their daily labours, what would become of our initiatives, even those most needed in this present hour? And what would even the most generous lay apostles be able to do? To these beloved priests, on whom rest so many hopes for the progress of the Church, we dare to appeal, in the name of Jesus Christ, begging them to preserve a whole-hearted loyalty to the spiritual requirements of their priestly vocation. . .

And we beg all the faithful to pray for priests and, as far as lies in their power, to help them to sanctify themselves. Today eager Christians expect much from the priest. They wish to see in him—in a world which shows the triumph of the power of money, the seduction of the senses, the exaggerated prestige of technical power—a man bearing witness to the invisible God, a man of faith, forgetful of himself and full of charity. We tell these Christians that they can do much to encourage their priests to be faithful to this ideal, by their religious respect for their priestly office, by a more perfect understanding of their pastoral tasks, and of their difficulties, and a more active collaboration in their apostolate.

7. HOLY THURSDAY
(Institution of the Eucharist)

We cannot think of this great sacrament, and of the mystery which it contains and glorifies, without remembering the words of the prophet Isaiah (cf. 7. 14), when he announced the coming of Emmanuel, "God with us", which the evangelist St Matthew so aptly recalls in his first chapter: "and his name shall be called Emmanuel, which means God with us" (Matt. 1. 23).

The Lord is with us! With us his creatures, the objects of his love, the work of his hands. At the summit of creation is man, made in the likeness of God and destined, as God's masterpiece, to give a name and a meaning to all creatures. But, since man turned faithless and defaced the image impressed on him by the Almighty, God chose to re-create him in another and more perfect way, through Redemption: "God with us" a second time.

In this work of Christ made Man is seen the great mystery of charity, willed by the Son of God who came among us. He reveals it at Bethlehem, as a humble child, and again in his atoning sacrifice on the Cross. And it is still revealed from age to age, in the conquest of the whole world at his command: "Go therefore and make disciples of all nations" (Matt. 28. 19).

And even this is not enough. The Redemption is to be made perfect by another supreme manifestation of love. Before he left this world, in the sacred hour of his last will and testament, he worked the greatest miracle of all. "Take and eat: this is my Body; take and drink: this is my Blood!" and St Luke remembered to add: "Do this in remembrance of me".

This is the Blessed Sacrament! It may be said to contain all the splendour of the Creation, Incarnation and Redemption, the whole life of Jesus, and to present it all to the faithful as their daily nourishment of love, prayer and contemplation.

8. GOOD FRIDAY

The image of the Crucified, ... the sign and the companion of your mission, will remind you of the road you must follow in order to ensure full success for your labours. Christ nailed to the Cross, put to death by painful torture, holds out his hands as if to embrace all men. He will teach you what it costs to save the world. He is the model and example for you to follow. St Leo says: "You can only reach him by imitating his patience and his humility. On this road you will have to face fatigue and exhaustion, the clouds of sadness and the storms of fear.

"You will meet with the snares set by the evil-minded, the cruelties inflicted by unbelievers, the threats of the powerful, the insults of the proud: all things which the Lord of all power and King of glory has suffered in our frail human form, in order that we may not seek to shun the perils of this present life by taking to flight, but seek rather to endure them with patience" (Sermo 67, 6; PL 54, 371-2).

Do not place your trust in any other expedient or in any human assistance.

9. HOLY SATURDAY

The blessing of the Easter candle is one of the most moving ceremonies of the night of Holy Saturday, and it is still more moving to see the blessed candle borne into the church, and to hear the words of the white-robed deacon who bears it aloft. He raises his voice as he hails it three times: "Light of Christ: light of Christ: light of Christ!", and the people rise from their knees to reply "Thanks be to God!"

The risen Christ is presented to us as a shining light which came into the world to enlighten every man. It was thus that the evangelist St John described him, adding that in this light was life, and that by this light everything was made. This identification of the Son of God with light and life, the light that shines in the darkness which the darkness could not overcome, expresses in sublime terms the whole history of the world.

For one day this light which is life, this divine Word,

by whom all that exists was made, deigned for man's sake to become man, and without in any way diminishing his divine nature he came to place himself at the service of all men, sinful and wounded to death, in order to ransom them and set them once more on the paths of righteousness and immortality.

What a great mystery St John expresses in his prologue: "And the Word became flesh and dwelt among us", and completes: "and we have beheld his glory!" We too have beheld the glory of God who became flesh and came down to dwell with us, full of grace and truth.

10. EASTER SUNDAY

O Prince of Peace, O risen Jesus, look graciously on all mankind. To you alone we turn for help, and healing for our wounds. As in the days of your life on earth, you still seek out the poor, the humble and the suffering; you still go in search of sinners. May everyone pray to you, everyone find you, and in you the Way, the Truth and the Life! Preserve us in your peace, O Lamb slain for our salvation! "Lamb of God who takes away the sins of the world, grant us peace".

This, O Jesus, is our prayer.

Remove from the hearts of men all that can endanger peace, and strengthen them in the truth, in justice and in brotherly love. Enlighten the rulers of the peoples so that, with due care for their brothers' welfare, they may guarantee and defend the great treasure of peace; kindle the wills of all men, so that they may overcome the barriers that divide them, restore the bonds of mutual charity, and be ready to understand, to pity and to forgive one another so that in your name all the peoples may be united, and peace, your peace, may triumph in all hearts, and in all families, and throughout the world.

11. MONDAY WITHIN THE OCTAVE OF EASTER

By drawing our attention to the sufferings of the Lord who for our sake was willing to become "despised and rejected by men, a man of sorrows and acquainted with grief" (Is. 53. 3), the Easter celebrations invite us to die to sin, to "cleanse out the old leaven. . . the leaven of malice and evil" (I Cor. 5. 7-8), in order to become new creatures.

If he who is of his own nature the Son of God became "obedient unto death, even death on the Cross" (Phil. 2. 8) we, whom he has made sons of God by his grace, are bound to follow him and imitate his deeds. As Christians we have been made to share in this mystery of spiritual death with Christ. We wish to repeat to you the Apostle's exhortation: "Do you not know that all of us who have been baptized into Christ Jesus were baptized into his death? We were buried therefore with him by baptism into death, so that as Christ was raised from the dead by the glory of the Father, we too might walk in newness of life. . . Let not sin therefore reign in your mortal bodies" (Rom. 6. 3-4, 12).

So our Easter is for us all a dying to sin, to passion, to hatred and enmity and all that brings about disorder, spiritual and material, bitterness and anguish. This death is indeed only the first step towards a higher goal—for our Easter is also a mystery of new life.

12. TUESDAY WITHIN THE OCTAVE OF EASTER

Easter is for Holy Church the meeting, the marriage of the Bride with her Bridegroom. The Bridegroom comes forth from his tent which was a tomb, but which he has transformed into a pavilion of victory; and his Bride, Holy Church, sings with heart and voice the hymns of joy and exultation: "This is the day that the Lord has made, let us rejoice and be glad!" We rejoice because he has risen again, and because in him we too shall rise.

May the risen Christ remain always with us! Cheered by our hope of ensuring our future resurrection, let us begin once more our race to win the prize of victory, with our gaze fixed on the "pioneer and perfecter of our faith" (Heb. 12. 2) who for our sake fought with death to give us life. He who rose in triumph, the firstborn of the dead, the Prince of the rulers of the earth, has won and bestowed upon all predestined souls the grace and glory of resurrection.

Let us sing hymns and psalms of joy to the Bride-groom of the Church, the blessed King of all ages. Amen.

13. WEDNESDAY IN THE OCTAVE OF EASTER

"Christ, our hope, has risen again—there is salvation in no one else" (cf. Acts 4. 12). We are with the risen Jesus; let us remain with him. This firm certainty, which springs from the mystery of the Redemption, gives us great reason for encouragement.

Today the Christian peoples announce to one another the same joyful news which has been for almost two thousand years a principle of faith, a gift of heavenly grace, a spur to faithful endeavour.

Christ is risen: everyone and everything must shine in his light; men and families, laws and customs, and the various forms of social life among the nations. For as Christ has conquered sin and death, establishing a new relationship between man and God, nothing can now be considered as exempt from his divine rule which ordains that "as Christ was raised from the dead by the glory of the Father, we too might walk in newness of life" (Rom. 6. 4).

Christ has risen, alleluia! The greeting denotes the hope of a glorious future: not death but life, not enmity but peace; not selfishness but charity; not falsehood but truth; not what demeans and debases us but the triumph of light, with mutual service, which does the Christian honour. Let this be your testimony, now and always, my beloved children.

14. THURSDAY IN THE OCTAVE OF EASTER

The gift of peace will make everyone aware of his responsibilities and duties, so that he may give to his fellows what they require, and what they have a right to expect. So it will be less difficult for us all resolutely to confront the complex problems and relationships of humanity, so that we may extend the "Peace of

Christ" which sets everything in a right order and eliminates the sources of domestic and civil discord.

This is the meaning of the Lord's Easter: the paschal sacrifice, the good news, and the new conquest of the world. How truly the Catholic liturgy sings: "Christ, our paschal lamb, has been sacrificed" (I Cor. 5. 7).

This means that with the coming of Jesus to this earth everything has changed. He became man, he preached and worked miracles, he died and rose again. So we do not win eternal life and glory, or real success, which consists in the good of all, except through sacrifice. The impressive liturgical rites of these days have once more touched our hearts. The Lamb that was slain never opened his mouth before his persecutors (cf. Is. 53.7), and so in his manner of dying taught us the secret of true success.

Let this be a convincing example for all who are responsible for the new generation: parents, teachers and all who, invested with authority, must consider themselves in the service of their fellows. May it be an encouragement to all those who long to spread the light of the Gospel in the world, the message of Christ's resurrection, in tranquil obedience and brotherly discipline and solidarity.

15. FRIDAY IN THE OCTAVE OF EASTER

Easter reminds us of these fundamental requirements of the Christian life: the practice of piety and the exercise of patience. Through piety we live detached from human frailties, in purity of mind and body, in close union with Christ. Through patience we succeed in strengthening our character and controlling our temper so as to become not only more pleasing to the Lord for our own sake, but an example and encouragement to others, to our fellow men, in the various contingencies of social life.

The Resurrection of the Lord truly represents—and for this reason it is celebrated every year—the renewed resurrection of every one of us to the true Christian life, the perfect Christian life which we must all try to live.

"The Resurrection of Christ is the sacrament of new life".

My beloved brothers and children! First of all let us look closely at our pattern, Jesus Christ. You see that everything in his life was in preparation for his resurrection. As St Augustine says: "In Christ everything was working for his resurrection".

Born as a man, he appeared as a man for but a short time. Born of mortal flesh, he experienced all the vicissitudes of mortality. We see him in his infancy, his boyhood, and his vigorous maturity, in which he died. He could not have risen again if he had not died; he could not have died if he had not been born; he was born and he died so that he might rise again.

This is what St Augustine tells us in simple, sublime words.

16. SATURDAY IN THE OCTAVE OF EASTER

We are still in the light of the risen and glorified Christ, presented to us for our wonder and as our example on the day of his triumph.

He points out the way to be followed by all who call themselves Christians. This "light of Christ" is a doctrine of pure and heavenly truth, and a source of grace for individual souls who can find in it a great store of most precious spiritual power for their daily task of self-sanctification.

For the Church, the Mystical Body of her Founder, the light of Christ is also a mysterious power which gives life to this sacred structure, still substantially intact after centuries of warfare and dangerous wear and tear. Today she is still rightly admired and greeted as "Mother of Saints", the image of the heavenly Jerusalem.

And finally the light of Christ is necessary for the social order which has found in the Gospel and in Holy Church the fullness of those immortal principles which promote the welfare of all, with progress, prosperity and peace. What does Christian civilization mean if not the splendour of Christ and of the Church's doctrine, applied to the life of families, nations and peoples?

17. THE OCTAVE OF EASTER
Sunday "in Albis".

O Jesus, you are no mock king, although Herod, the Tetrarch of Galilee, tried to present you as such to the people. We have full confidence in your promises. We shall always pray to you for justice, liberty and peace.

O Jesus, conqueror of death, we beg you before all else to give us peace . . . In all ages there have been grave threats to peace. Even now, in our day, there are some light, evanescent clouds, questions and problems which appear, disappear and reappear, and could become dangerous for the harmony and good understanding of the peoples.

Above the glorious sepulchre, we wish to express the hope that in the light of Christ, the source of all life, the conqueror of death, the good efforts of all who are responsible for the destinies of nations may find, in a spirit of justice and collaboration, the harmonious solution of all disputes, in the superior interests of the whole world.

In this hope and prayer for life let us, Father and children, exchange a mystical embrace and set out once more on our long pilgrimage, reasserting in our hymns our Catholic faith in the risen Christ who triumphed over sin and death, and who brings with him joy, justice and peace.

18. THE ASCENSION

This is the fortieth day that Jesus spent on earth after he had risen again, no longer in mortal flesh but in a glorified body.

To the twelve who met together, first on Mount Sion for the Last Supper and then on the Hill of Olives, he spoke his last farewell, repeating his promise of the imminent coming of the Holy Spirit who was to perfect in them the work he had begun and prepare them to conquer the whole world, until the end of time, which means for ever. And there on the Mount he smiled at them for the last time, and his look was like a last ray of his loving kindness, before he was gently lifted up into heaven, and a little cloud hid him from their enraptured gaze (cf. Acts 1. 9).

The holy liturgy presents to us, in the light of Easter, this figure of the Crucified Christ who rose from death, and now it shows us his ascension into heaven on the fortieth day, under the symbolism of the great candle that was blessed and carried in triumph on the night of Holy Saturday, and which now after the singing of today's Gospel, will be extinguished, to return to us for other, far away Easters . . .

We bless you, O Easter candle, the shining column which for forty days has gladdened our hearts with its bright and sacred flame.

We bid you farewell. God grant that we may see you again a year hence in the blessed recurrence of these liturgical celebrations which follow each other regularly through the seasons. This is the Christian life: to follow the events of the mortal life of Jesus, trying to make our spirit one with his, in his joys and griefs, his sacrifices and his victory.

19. PENTECOST

(Fifty days after Easter)

At the Feast of Pentecost I take the sacred Book in my hands and turn eagerly to the first page of the Old Testament, and then to the first page of the New.

The first page of the Old Testament describes the creation of the world, saying that "the Spirit of God was moving on the waters". This refers to the whole universe, the seas and land masses, the animal, vegetable and mineral kingdoms: a triple realm, a manifold order; and it refers also to the governments of men, of races, peoples and tribes, inspired and moved by energies common to all mankind, and to the history of humanity slowly evolving through the centuries according to a divine plan.

All nature, then, belongs to the temporal order, but always in the sight of God and subject to his power.

And now we turn to the first page of the Gospel, the New Testament, which begins with the sound of an angel's voice: "Do not be afraid, Mary, for you have found favour with God . . . You will bear a son, and you shall call his name Jesus."

With this announcement to Mary there begins the

epic of Redemption, which has Christ for its all-radiant Sun, the source of divine life and sanctifying grace.

20. TRINITY SUNDAY

(Octave of Pentecost)

God is One and Three! Jesus, the Son of God, always referred to his Father and, for the future guidance of his Church, he foretold the coming of the Holy Spirit. It is not necessary to expound this further. Wiseacres may find some explanations to offer to the humble faithful, but no explanation is adequate, especially if it is tinged with pretentiousness. The pious soul will understand.

Frequently the Catholic's devotion is limited to the Mother of Jesus—which is always good, but not enough, or to the saints, particularly to certain saints—and this is mistaken and dangerous. We must once more clearly state: the three Divine Persons must be considered as having equal rights to our worship. It is very natural that they should be most clearly perceived in the central figure Jesus Christ, because in him the divine nature is mingled with the human, our own nature which he came to save and to sublimate; but the worship of the Church—as we see in the liturgy—is directed equally to the Father, the Son and the Holy Spirit. In the liturgy everything begins, develops and is brought to a conclusion "in the name of the Father and of the Son and of the Holy Spirit."

There are so many beautiful and useful devotions, but the principal, the most sublime and the most divinely inspired, is the devotion to the Holy Trinity.

21. CORPUS CHRISTI

(Thursday after the Feast of the Most Holy Trinity)

God is with us. The Lord of the universe has poured out his spirit over all creation, and has made man his masterpiece, in his own divine image.

This is a grand thing, my beloved children, the likeness of God impressed upon the whole of creation and made most resplendent in the human form. The Lord, the Beginning of all things, the Word, the Divine Word, loved man so much that he wished to dwell in his company on earth, as a brother among brothers. "The Word was made flesh and dwelt among us."

And since our human nature was wounded and humiliated he ransomed it at the cost of his own blood—he bestowed upon us all the merits of his sacrifice and associated us with it, while respecting every man's freedom to accept or refuse the benefit and the honour.

Now the supreme manifestation of "God with us" is the sacrament of the Body and Blood of Christ . . .

The Feast of Corpus Christi not only reminds us of the Son of God, our Creator, Redeemer and Brother, but it speaks of Jesus who, by the power of the great eucharistic sacrifice, has become the most precious spiritual food of human life.

Our great Doctor and mystic Thomas Aquinas cries most joyfully: "Behold the bread of angels, made the food of wayfaring man; this is the children's bread".

Devotion to the Eucharist fills our hearts with sweetness, but what matters most to the good Christian community, and what may be taken as the measure of true spiritual fervour, is the love of Jesus in his Sacrament, the faithful attendance at his Tabernacle, the companionship willingly offered to console the mysterious solitude which has such power to bless!

22. FEAST OF THE SACRED HEART

(Friday after the second Sunday after Pentecost)

Margaret Mary Alacoque was a humble nun, without any ambitions or pretensions but with a sincere heart eager to receive divine grace. The Lord was pleased with her angelic purity, enchanting simplicity, and absolute indifference to worldly interests. So one day, while the faithful saint was in the convent garden, busy about her duties—in themselves trifling and of little importance but full of merit, due to obedience—she received the gift of extraordinary revelations, some of them relating to that sublime apostolate which the Master was about to ask her to initiate: the devotion to the

Sacred Heart and the glorification of its mysteries of love.

The reply to the divine request came at once: there was a general and immediate acceptance of the new way of honouring Jesus although, as always happens in this world, there was some opposition from men who sought to make their own private judgment prevail. At the end, however, it was a triumph of charity, of loving souls. The devotion to the Sacred Heart has been of incalculable benefit to the Church and to mankind. This can be said even more truly of our own times which have the advantage of a deeper understanding and more enthusiastic response than were possible in the age of St Margaret Mary.

This does not mean that we need no longer fear the temptations of our old Adversary, or that the lure of the world is less insidious. On the contrary. Nevertheless, the faithful are familiar with the ways of grace, the never failing help given them by the Redeemer, and the beauty and sweetness of constant recourse to the powerful intercession of Mary our Mother, whose arms are always ready to welcome us, who comforts and consoles us and obtains for us all, from her divine Son, the most valid and precious gifts.

23. FEAST OF CHRIST THE KING
(The last Sunday in October)

Today is the Feast of Christ the King. In the Epistle of the Mass, as in the pages of the Breviary, the faithful see the sublime and majestic figure of the King of Peace.

This royal majesty is the divine Saviour's by right, because he is of the same substance as the Father, who has given him supreme and absolute dominion over all created things, and because of the wonderful and adorable union of the human and divine, which makes him the Head of the human body, and because of his redeeming sacrifice which has reconciled the whole human family to the Father . . .

As the Church sings his praises she prays that all the families of peoples who have been scattered by the invasion of sin, may submit to his gentle rule. If we wish to attain real peace and to bring about a just distribution of wealth and lasting concord, God's rights must be respected by all. By violating them man degrades himself and loses his dignity. Therefore all forms of social, economic and political life must be raised and transfigured in the light of Jesus our Saviour, who alone can perfect them and give them supernatural value. This is the meaning of today's Feast: this is the ardent wish expressed in the Breviary hymn:

"May the rulers of the peoples exalt you with public tributes of honour; may scholars and magistrates worship you, may our laws and achievements sing your praises!" O how beautiful is the vision of peace, a foretaste on earth of the serene joys of Paradise!

24. THE HOLY NAME OF JESUS

(Sunday between New Year's Day and the Epiphany)

The name of Jesus occurs most frequently in the letters of St Paul. Our everlasting tribute of worship and love is offered to Jesus as the "power", the "cornerstone" and the "name".

What strength we find in the almighty power of the Son of God! What confidence we feel, knowing that Jesus is with us whenever our hearts are truly eager for his love! Indeed, he is so infinitely merciful that he patiently awaits our return when we pursue what induces us to disobey his Law. In his power lies the sublime strength of his grace.

So we understand why Jesus Christ is called the cornerstone, for he truly unites and supports the most divergent forces. In him is the foundation for the union of the whole world; he is the only rock upon which it is safe to build.

And finally his Name! Peter always pronounces it with the most profound reverence and love. Without that Name nothing can be begun or continued in this world. All life and all things will have strength, vigour and prosperity only when they are considered and undertaken in the Name of Jesus.

These are simple notions that do not require scientific or theological explanations, and yet they are grand truths. Let us all therefore remember our childhood when our mothers taught us to invoke and greet the name of Jesus, when our minds were first beginning to understand the Gospel and the sweetness of the doctrine which this name signifies and illuminates. Then every one of us may expect, in every moment of life, the comfort which, when our last hour comes, we shall receive from that Name, as the dearest word of hope and heavenly longing that we know.

25. FEAST OF THE HOLY FAMILY

(First Sunday after Epiphany)

Today is the festival of the family, which means the exaltation of our human affections which are not only most dear to us, but most holy and sacred.

We like to think of all the Christian families moving along the road in the company of the Three Wise Men of the East, following the track of light marked on the earth by the Star of Bethlehem. And we like to think of Jesus welcoming them all, comforting and sustaining them, showing them with infinite graciousness that all must learn from his love, and from the shining example of his Holy Family.

O my beloved children, here we have the sublime example of family life; here the love of God shines as if in its own fiery source; here burns the flame of mutual love. Do you know what those lights are that make the night of Christmas, and the night of the visit of the Wise Men such a festival of light? All these lights have names: gentleness and obedience, simplicity and humility, resignation and sacrifice, a radiance which sheds its glow on all Christian families.

O may peace and tranquillity reign, may prayer and obedience to God's law, and obedience which is prompt and loving, be honoured by all! Without God, my children, there is nothing but unhappiness and anxiety. May parents be generous and set their children good example, so that they may receive their willing obedience. As Jesus lived at Nazareth, so may he live in every Christian family; may he keep our families united in his love, in an everlasting bond, for every hour of time and for eternity. So Jesus will guard that domestic peace which alone can soothe the bitter sorrows of life.

SOURCES

JANUARY

1. Discorsi IV, p. 780.—2. Cantagalli, 1963, I-II, p. 270.—3. Discorsi II, p. 86.—4. Discorsi II, p. 87.—5. Discorsi I, p. 101.—6. Discorsi III, p. 626.—7. Scritti e Discorsi III, p. 145.—8. Discorsi V, p. 150.—9. Discorsi II, p. 85.—10. Discorsi V, p. 389.—11. Discorsi V, p. 391.—12. Discorsi IV, p. 110.—13. Discorsi V, p. 147.—14. Discorsi I, p. 413.—15. Discorsi II, p. 32.—16. Discorsi IV, p. 106.—17. Scritti e Discorsi III, p. 422.—18. Scritti e Discorsi II, p. 14.—19. Discorsi V, p. 140.—20. Souvenirs, p. 54.—21. Scritti e Discorsi III, p. 239.—22. Scritti e Discorsi II, p. 170.—23. Discorsi V, p. 48.—24. Discorsi V, p. 473.—25. Discorsi V, p. 92.—26. Discorsi V, p. 94.—27. Scritti e Discorsi II, p. 394.—28. Discorsi II, p. 687.—29. Scritti e Discorsi II, p. 317.—30. Discorsi II, p. 714.—31. Scritti e Discorsi I, p. 99.

FEBRUARY

1. Discorsi III, p. 631.—2. Scritti e Discorsi III, p. 33.—3. Scritti e Discorsi I, p. 74.—4. Discorsi III, p. 62.—5. "Il Cardinale Cesare Baronio", Angelo Roncalli, an address given 4 December 1907 in the Seminary of Bergamo: Ed. Storia e Letteratura, Rome, 1961, p. 33.—6. Discorsi V, p. 463.—7. Discorsi III, p. 86.—8. Scritti e Discorsi IV, p. 32.—9. Scritti e Discorsi IV, p. 54.—10. Scritti e Discorsi IV, p. 160.—11. Scritti e Discorsi III, p. 516.—12. Discorsi III, p. 87.—13. Discorsi III, p. 88.—14. Scritti e Discorsi I, p. 93.—15. Discorsi I, p. 510.—16. Discorsi I, p. 506.—17. Discorsi I, p. 506.—18. Discorsi I, p. 507.—19. Discorsi I, p. 507.—20. Discorsi I, p. 508.—21. Discorsi I, p. 509.—22. Discorsi IV,

p. 162.—23. Discorsi III, p. 93.—24. Scritti e Discorsi II, p. 152.—
25. Discorsi III, p. 412.—26. Discorsi III, p. 41.—27. Discorsi V,
p. 73.—28. Discorsi II, p. 623.

MARCH

1. Discorsi II, p. 718.—2. Discorsi V, p. 162.—3. Discorsi V,
p. 164.—4. Discorsi I, p. 113.—5. Discorsi V, p. 428.—6. Discorsi
I, p. 295.—7. Discorsi I, p. 429.—8. Scritti e Discorsi II, p. 34.—
9. Discorsi III, p. 602.—10. Discorsi II, p. 603.—11. Discorsi I,
p. 202.—12. Discorsi III, p. 637.—13. Discorsi III, p. 535.—14.
Discorsi V, p. 145.—15. Discorsi V, p. 146.—16. Discorsi V,
p. 409.—17. Discorsi III, p. 172.—18. Discorsi IV, p. 732.—19.
Discorsi III, p. 184.—20. Scritti e Discorsi II, p. 34.—21. Souvenirs p. 70.—22. Discorsi I, p. 258.—23. Scritti e Discorsi III, p. 500.
—24. Scritti e Discorsi IV, p. 61.—25. Discorsi IV, p. 558.—26.
Discorsi I, p. 231.—27. Cantagalli, 1961, V-VI, p. 67.—28. Discorsi II, p. 688.—29. Discorsi III, p. 60.—30. Discorsi III, p. 382.—
31. Discorsi III, p. 773.

APRIL

1. Discorsi I, p. 433.—2. Discorsi I, p. 434.—3. Discorsi I, p. 435.—
4. Discorsi II p. 591.—5. Discorsi II, p. 592.—6. Discorsi II,
p. 595.—7. Discorsi I, p. 41.—8. Scritti e Discorsi I, p. 81.—9. Discorsi IV, p. 395.—10. Daily Bulletins of the Ufficio stampa Vaticana, 24 Jan. 1959.—11. Discorsi I, p. 737.—12. Scritti e Discorsi I,
p. 77.—13. Scritti e Discorsi I, p. 78.—14. L'Osservatore Romano,
20 Sept. 1959, p. 3.—15. Ibid.—16. Ibid.—17. Cantagalli 1961, IV,
p. 95.—18. Scritti e Discorsi III, p. 662.—19. Scritti e Discorsi III,
p. 660.—20. Scritti e Discorsi III, p. 663.—21. Discorsi III, p. 90.—
22. Discorsi III, p. 190.—23. Discorsi V, p. 477.—24. Scritti e
Discorsi III, p. 526.—25. Scritti e Discorsi I, p. 23.—26. Scritti e
Discorsi III, p. 527.—27. Discorsi I, p. 210.—28. Scritti e Discorsi
III, p. 525.—29. Scritti e Discorsi III, p. 85.—30. Scritti e Discorsi
I, p. 199.

MAY

1. Discorsi V, p. 232.—2. Discorsi III, p. 356.—3. Discorsi V,
p. 482.—4. Discorsi I, p. 172.—5. Discorsi II, p. 51.—6. Discorsi II,
p. 52.—7. Ibid.—8. Discorsi II, p. 53.—9. Discorsi V, p. 231.—
10. Scritti e Discorsi IV, p. 59.—11. Souvenirs, p. 79.—12. L'Osservatore Romano, 20 Sept. 1959, p. 3.—13. Discorsi IV, p. 850.—
14. Scritti e Discorsi III, p. 618.—15. Discorsi V, p. 486.—16. Discorsi III, p. 639.—17. L'Osservatore Romano, 20 Sept. 1959, p. 3.—
18. Ibid.—19. Souvenirs, p. 99.—20. Discorsi III, p. 91.—21. Discorsi V, p. 304.—22. Discorsi V, p. 446.—23. Scritti e Discorsi II,
p. 166.—24. Scritti e Discorsi III, p. 518.—25. Souvenirs, p. 98.—
26. Souvenirs, p. 56.—27. L'Osservatore Romano, 20 Sept. 1959,
p. 3.—28. Discorsi I, p. 31.—29. Discorsi III, p. 585.—30. Scritti e
Discorsi II, p. 169.—31. Discorsi V, p. 487.

JUNE

1. Scritti e Discorsi III, p. 215.—2. Discorsi IV, p. 84.—3. Discorsi IV, p. 86.—4. Scritti e Discorsi II, p. 519.—5. Discorsi I, p. 219.—6. Discorsi V, p. 185.—7. Scritti e Discorsi III, p. 88.—8. Discorsi II, p. 622.—9. Discorsi IV, p. 5.—10. Discorsi IV, p. 24.—11. Scritti e Discorsi IV, p. 159.—12. Scritti e Discorsi II, p. 301.—13. Discorsi IV, p. 332.—14. Discorsi V, p. 410.—15. Scritti e Discorsi II, p. 289.—16. Scritti e Discorsi II, p. 285.—17. Discorsi I, p. 232.—18. Discorsi II, p. 193.—19. Scritti e Discorsi II, p. 164.—20. Discorsi IV, p. 80.—21. Daily Bulletins of the Ufficio stampa Vaticana, 5 June 1959.—22. Scritti e Discorsi II, p. 33.— 23. Scritti e Discorsi I, p. 98.—24. Souvenirs, p. 68.—25. Scritti e Discorsi I, p. 45.—26. Discorsi IV, p. 897.—27. Discorsi V, p. 474.—28. Discorsi V, p. 471.—29. Discorsi I, p. 399.—30. Scritti e Discorsi II, p. 36.

JULY

1. Discorsi II, p. 579.—2. Discorsi I, p. 64.—3. Discorsi III, p. 383. —4. "Mons. Giacomo Maria Radini Tedeschi, Vescovo di Bergamo," Angelo Roncalli, Ed. Storia e Letteratura, Roma, 1963 (3rd Ed.), p. 306.—5. Discorsi I, p. 279.—6. Discorsi I, p. 280.—7. Cantagalli, 1959, IV, p. 14.—8. Discorsi IV, p. 491.—9. Discorsi I, p. 63.—10. Discorsi V, p. 452.—11. Discorsi V, p. 130.—12. Discorsi II, p. 622.—13. Discorsi IV, p. 898.—14. Discorsi III, p. 85.— 15. Cantagalli, 1963, I-II, p. 285.—16. Discorsi IV, p. 343.—17. Scritti e Discorsi III, p. 168.—18. Discorsi I, p. 203.—19. Cantagalli, 1963, I-II, p. 278.—20. Scritti e Discorsi III, p. 157.— 21. Scritti e Discorsi III, p. 159.—22. Discorsi III, p. 650.—23. Scritti e Discorsi II, p. 29.—24. Scritti e Discorsi III, p. 170.—25. Discorsi IV, p. 339.—26. Discorsi III, p. 653.—27. Scritti e Discorsi III, p. 178.—28. Discorsi V, p. 460.—29. Discorsi III, p. 189.—30. Discorsi IV, p. 108.—31. Scritti e Discorsi IV, p. 93.

AUGUST

1. Discorsi I, p. 739.—2. Scritti e Discorsi III, p. 108.—3. Discorsi V, p. 138.—4. Scritti e Discorsi II, p. 207.—5. L'Osservatore Romano, 20 Sept. 1959, p. 3.—6. Discorsi IV, p. 666.—7. Discorsi IV, p. 896.—8. Cantagalli, 1959, IV, p. 44.—9. Discorsi IV, p. 136.—10. Cantagalli, 1959, IV. p. 91.—11. Discorsi V, p. 139.—12. Scritti e Discorsi I, p. 46.—13. Scritti e Discorsi II, p. 180.—14. Discorsi V p. 288.—15. Scritti e Discorsi I, p. 261.—16. Discorsi III, p. 67. 17. Discorsi V, p. 290.—18. Discorsi V, p. 401.—19. Scritti e Discorsi III, p. 106.—20. Discorsi II, p. 562.—21. Cantagalli, 1961, IV, p. 60.—22. Cantagalli, 1961, IV, p. 107.—23. Discorsi II, p. 534.—24. L'Osservatore Romano, 23 Jan. 1963.—25. AAS 51, 1951, p. 489.—26. Scritti e Discorsi III, p. 39.—27. Scritti e Discorsi III, p. 345.—28. L'Osservatore Romano, 16 March 1959.—29. Cantagalli, 1959, IV, p. 119.—30. Cantagalli, 1961, IV, p. 81.—31. Scritti e Discorsi III, p. 575.

SEPTEMBER

1. Discorsi III, p. 214.—2. Discorsi III, p. 259.—3. Scritti e Discorsi I, p. 259.—4. Discorsi III, p. 543.—5. Discorsi I, p. 481.—6. Discorsi IV, p. 560.—7. Scritti e Discorsi I, p. 203.—8. Discorsi II, p. 749.—9. Discorsi IV, p. 483.—10. Discorsi II, p. 751.—11. Scritti e Discorsi III, p. 593.—12. Discorsi I, p. 786.—13. Cantagalli, 1961, IV, p. 80.—14. Discorsi II, p. 753.—15. Discorsi III, p. 670.—16. Discorsi IV, p. 137.—17. Discorsi IV, p. 543.—18. Scritti e Discorsi II, p. 332.—19. Scritti e Discorsi II, p. 333.—20. Ibid.—21. Discorsi II, p. 758.—22. Discorsi IV, p. 835.—23. Discorsi IV, p. 63.—24. Discorsi III, p. 47.—25. Discorsi III, p. 68.—26. Cantagalli, 1961, IV, p. 69.—27. Cantagalli, 1961, IV, p. 74.—28. Discorsi IV, p. 137.—29. Discorsi IV, p. 897.—30. Discorsi I, p. 38.

OCTOBER

1. Discorsi III, p. 756.—2. Discorsi II, p. 762.—3. Scritti e Discorsi I, p. 318.—4. Discorsi III, p. 678.—5. Discorsi III, p. 760.—6. Cantagalli, 1961, IV, p. 83.—7. Scritti e Discorsi II, p. 210.—8. Scritti e Discorsi II, p. 207.—9. Scritti e Discorsi II, p. 208.—10. Scritti e Discorsi II, p. 209.—11. Discorsi III, p. 394.—12. Discorsi IV, pp. 470-1.—13. Scritti e Discorsi II, p. 427.—14. Cantagalli, 1963, I-II, p. 309.—15. Cantagalli, 1963, I-II, p. 316.—16. Cantagalli, 1963, I-II, p. 317.—17. Discorsi III, p. 762.—18. Discorsi III, p. 763.—19. Ibid.—20. Discorsi III, p. 764.—21. Discorsi III, p. 765.—22. Discorsi III, p. 766.—23. Discorsi III, p. 767.—24. Ibid.—25. Discorsi III, p. 768.—26. Ibid.—27. Discorsi III, p. 769. —28. Discorsi III, p. 770.—29. Ibid.—30. Discorsi III, p. 771.— 31. Ibid.

NOVEMBER

1. Discorsi V, p. 83.—2. Scritti e Discorsi III, p. 269.—3. Discorsi III, p. 339.—4. Discorsi II, p. 538.—5. Discorsi V, p. 442.—6. Scritti e Discorsi IV, p. 157.—7. Scritti e Discorsi II, p. 9.—8. L'Osservatore Romano, 22 Dec. 1958.—9. Discorsi IV, p. 344.— 10. Discorsi IV, p. 724.—11. Cantagalli, 1961, IV, p. 41.—12. Cantagalli, 1961, IV, p. 79.—13. Discorsi IV, p. 350.—14. Discorsi V, p. 441.—15. Discorsi II, p. 555.—16. Scritti e Discorsi III, p. 528.— 17. Cantagalli, 1959, IV, p. 33.—18. Scritti e Discorsi III, p. 236.— 19. Cantagalli, 1961, II, p. 66.—20. Discorsi IV, p. 325.—21. Discorsi V, p. 444.—22. Discorsi IV, p. 773.—23. Souvenirs, p. 85.— 24. Discorsi IV, p. 793.—25. Souvenirs, p. 58.—26. Discorsi IV, p. 320.—27. Discorsi IV, p. 321.—28. Discorsi IV, p. 106.—29. Discorsi IV, p. 90.—30. Discorsi I, p. 65.

DECEMBER

1. Discorsi V, p. 465.—2. L'Osservatore Romano, 22 Dec. 1958.— 3. AAS 52, 1960, p. 420.—4. Discorsi IV, p. 774.—5. L'Osservatore Romano, 22 Dec. 1958.—6. Scritti e Discorsi II, p. 499.—7.

Discorsi I, p. 216.—8. Discorsi III, p. 73.—9. Cantagalli, 1961, IV, p. 65.—10. Discorsi V, p. 42.—11. Discorsi III, p. 92.—12. Scritti e Discorsi II, p. 274.—13. Scritti e Discorsi II, p. 272.—14. Discorsi III, p. 82.—15. Discorsi IV, p. 124.—16. Discorsi I, pp. 93-4.— 17. Scritti e Discorsi III, p. 389 & Cantagalli, 1960, VI, p. 159.— 18. Discorsi II, p. 98.—19. Discorsi V, p. 448.—20. Discorsi III, p. 84.—21. Discorsi III, p. 622.—22. Discorsi V, p. 324.—23. Discorsi V, p. 44.—24. Discorsi V, p. 64.—25. Discorsi V, p. 67.— 26. Discorsi V, p. 328.—27. Discorsi IV, p. 779.—28. Discorsi V, p. 326.—29. Discorsi II, p. 552.—30. Discorsi V, p. 618.—31. Discorsi V, p. 610.

APPENDIX

1. Discorsi II, p. 599.—2. Discorsi III, p. 634.—3. Discorsi III, p. 182.—4. Discorsi III, p. 188.—5. Discorsi I, p. 218.—6. Cantagalli, 1959, IV, p. 72.—7. Discorsi II, p. 590.—8. Discorsi I, p. 458. —9. Scritti e Discorsi III, p. 560 —10. Discorsi V, p. 210.—11. Discorsi I, p. 210.—12. Scritti e Discorsi II, p. 384.—13. Discorsi V, p. 212.—14. Discorsi V, p. 208.—15. Scritti e Discorsi III, p. 524.—16. Scritti e Discorsi III, p. 561.—17. Discorsi I, p. 220.— 18. Scritti e Discorsi III, p. 560.—19. Scritti e Discorsi III, p. 571.— 20. Scritti e Discorsi IV, p. 69.—21. Discorsi I, p. 349.—22. Discorsi IV, p. 762.—23. Discorsi I, p. 494.—24. Discorsi V, p. 338.— 25. Discorsi IV, p. 140.